STRATEGIC
DENIAL
AND
DECEPTION

STRATEGIC DENIAL AND DECEPTION

The Twenty-First Century Challenge

editors

Roy Godson & James J. Wirtz

Transaction Publishers
New Brunswick (U.S.A.) and London (U.K.)

Sixth paperback printing 2008

Library of Congress Catalog Number: 2001044348
ISBN: 0-7658-0113-2 (cloth); 0-7658-0898-6 (paper)
Printed in the United States of America

Library of Congress Cataloging-in-Publication Data

Strategic denial and deception : the twenty-first century challenge / Roy Godson and James W. [i.e. J.] Wirtz, editors.
    p. cm.
  Includes bibliographical references and index.
  ISBN 978-0-7658-0898-1 (paper : alk. paper)
      1. Deception (Military science) 2. Military intelligence—United States. 3. Strategy. 4. Military art and science. 5. United States—Politics and government—1945-1989. 6. United States—Politics and government-1989- I. Godson, Roy, 1942- II. Wirtz, James J., 1958-

U167.5.D37 S77 2001
327.1'4—dc21   2001044348

Contents

1

Strategic Denial and Deception

Roy Godson and *James J. Wirtz*

A concern about the threat of high-level denial and deception has waxed and waned among Americans since the end of World War II. Sometimes they fear that denial and deception has shaped threat assessments: witness the 1976 "A Team/B Team experiment" in a competitive intelligence analysis undertaken by the Gerald R. Ford White House.[1] At other times, the threat of denial and deception—here the euphoria accompanying the end of the Cold War comes to mind—seems to fade into insignificance. As the United States reigns as the only superpower and the world experiences a communication revolution, how much of a threat does denial and deception pose to American interests today? Do globalization, proliferating communication technologies, and the dissemination of vast amounts of information make effective foreign denial and deception more or less likely? Will more information and data sources make policymakers better informed or will the proliferation of information simply create confusion?[2]

Strategic Denial and Deception Defined

Denial and deception (D&D) is a term often used to describe a combination of information operations that a nation undertakes to achieve its objectives. *Denial* refers to the attempt to block information that could be used by an opponent to learn some truth. *Decep-*

Originally published in the *International Journal of Intelligence and CounterIntelligence*, 13:424-437, 2000. Copyright © Taylor & Francis. Reprinted by permission.

tion, by contrast, refers to a nation's effort to cause an adversary to believe something that is not true.

Although they are distinct activities, denial and deception are intertwined in practice and are used as a single concept here. To deceive an opponent about the true intentions or goals of the deceiver, accurate information (e.g., about a military development program, a policy, a course of action, etc.) must be concealed or "denied" to the target. Deception, the effort to cause an adversary to believe something that is not true, can be undertaken together with denial operations. This involves using "leaks," planted information, or decoys to create the impression that the truth is other than it actually is, thereby creating an "alternative reality" for the target. When denial and deception works, the deceiver leads the target to believe a "cover story" rather than the truth. The target will then react in a way that serves the deceiver's interests.

The term "strategic," more difficult to define, is used here to denote a high level of importance. D & D is strategic if it directly affects the national fortune and interests. Strategic denial and deception is related to the "big picture." It concerns the major policies of a government, rather than the details of policy implementation. Strategic deception is thus aimed at the highest levels of a government or of the military chain of command (e.g., chiefs of state, cabinet members, or senior military commanders). The subject of the deception effort must be something that a high-level official would deal with personally. Similarly, strategic denial would be the effort to withhold information of the sort that is handled primarily by senior officials.

Foreign denial and deception occurs when state or nonstate actors (e.g., terrorist groups, criminal organizations, or separatist movements) use denial and deception to achieve their objectives against U.S. targets, interests, or policies. D&D also can be used by foreign adversaries as a strategic instrument in the sense that it becomes a primary means for disadvantaging the United States—politically or militarily. For terrorist or criminal organizations, D&D is a strategic instrument, much in the same way as the navy or nuclear weapons are strategic instruments for the United States. Criminals and terrorists use D&D as a strategic instrument to shape the environment so that they can better achieve their objects.

Various "channels" of communication are used by D&D practitioners. Sometimes intelligence sources and methods channel "corrupt" information to policymakers. Often, however, less clandestine methods of communication are used: media (television, radio, Internet) outlets, diplomatic interactions, academic exchanges and international travel and tourism. D&D does not require "dedicated" communication channels to be effective. In fact, D&D is often facilitated when the transfer of information appears to be incidental to the ostensible purpose of an event or contact. Diplomats, academics, and business travelers offer convincing conduits for the information they discover by "accident" during the regular course of their professional activities.

Successful Denial and Deception

Based on historical experience and deductive logic, a successful denial and deception campaign[3] requires several components. First, the campaign benefits from strategic coherence. The deceiver nation must have an overall plan in mind for the achievement of its objectives; it must determine in advance how the target should behave and how deception will contribute to that outcome. The deceiver also must predict how the target will react in the wake of both successful and unsuccessful deception. This is no small task. Those contemplating deception may engage in wishful thinking when predicting the consequences of their deception campaign.[4] Additionally, the deceiver must integrate its actions with (a) efforts to deny an opponent accurate information and (b) deceptive cover stories. Again, this is no small task. D&D campaigns require coherent, if not coordinated, action from many departments, agencies, or ministries. Public statements, press articles, and Internet communications must be shaped to support the goals of the nation intent on deception. As this corrupt information is disseminated, steps must be taken to prevent accurate information from reaching the target.

Second, deception is enhanced when the strategic culture of the adversary is understood. To be successful, the deceiver must recognize the target's perceptual context[5] to know what (false) pictures of the world will appear plausible. History, culture, bureaucratic preferences, and the general economic and political milieu all influence the target's perceptions.[6] False information should conform to the idiosyncrasies of strategic and even popular culture. Mistakes are easily detected and often appear comical to the target audience.[7] Thus, deception requires creative planning: experience shows that successful deception planners manage to escape the routine and culture of large bureaucracies. In sum, deception planners "need to know a great deal about the worldview of those they are trying to manipulate, and recognize the human proclivity for self-deception."[8]

Third, deception requires information channels to reach the adversary. Supplying the target with corrupt information in creative ways can also increase its credibility in the eyes of the target. Deception planners thus require the authority and imagination to exploit traditional channels and develop new ones on an ad hoc basis.

Fourth, a successful D&D campaign benefits from feedback mechanisms to collect data about the target's behavior. Discovering the way the target has interpreted received data is especially important. A deception campaign is a dynamic enterprise: cover stories, communication channels, and specific initiatives require fine-tuning to take advantage of unforeseen opportunities or problems. Knowing that a deception campaign is succeeding also can be crucial to the achievement of grand strategic objectives. To pursue a course of action that relied on deception if the target failed to "take the bait" would be foolhardy. Alternatively, if an initial deception plan failed, the feedback mechanism could activate backup D&D campaigns.[9]

Practitioners of Denial and Deception

Deceivers can be divided into four categories: democracies; authoritarian regimes; regimes in transition (changing from authoritarian to democratic or vice versa); and nonstate actors (criminal organizations, terrorist groups, separatist organizations). At one time or another all types of actors launch (and suffer from) successful deception campaigns.

Democracies

Democracies employ D&D mostly in wartime. But democracies are quite capable of deceiving even in peacetime. From the Revolutionary War campaign at Yorktown, to the D-day landings in World War II, to the "feint" of a Marine amphibious assault during the Gulf War, United States history is replete with instances in which deception was used to U.S. military advantage. Throughout the twentieth century, Great Britain and other democracies also occasionally showed themselves to be effective at D&D in war and peace. For example, Israel's and, more recently, India's programs to develop nuclear weapons benefited from sophisticated D&D campaigns. But Americans are often unaware of the successful D&D campaigns of other democracies, especially in peacetime.

Authoritarian Regimes

In contrast to democracies, authoritarian and especially totalitarian regimes use denial and deception as a regular instrument of governance.[10] This increases their reliance on similar tactics in foreign policy and defense matters. Especially disturbing is the tendency of authoritarian and totalitarian regimes to use D&D to support the initiation of hostilities. For example, Operation BARBAROSSA (the 1941 Nazi invasion of the Soviet Union) and Japan's attack on the United States and Great Britain in December 1941 were accompanied by sophisticated D&D campaigns. Authoritarian regimes also are adept at other uses of D&D: witness Iraq's continuing efforts to elude international inspection and destruction of its weapons of mass destruction.[11]

Nonstate Actors

The way nonstate actors employ D&D poses a rising threat to U.S. interests and those of other democracies. Transnational businesses, criminal syndicates, revolutionary organizations, terrorists, and religious groups pursuing illicit objectives, all must seek cover to operate effectively. For criminals, rebels, and terrorists, denial becomes their *raison d'être*. The shadowy world of the terrorist or the criminal is an alternative reality, not a temporary expedient to achieve limited objectives. The criminal flourishes in the hidden world created by denial while the gunman uses denial and deception to enter the world of legitimate power. The clandestine underground is a way of life and a strategic instrument for highly illicit organizations.

For clandestine groups, denial creates a parallel world that exhilarates, offers a safe haven, and enhances the life of the committed. Evidence of this type of behavior can be observed both in the Sicilian Mafia, which seeks respect, power, and money, and in terrorist organizations that seek to change the direction of history through violent action. A cult may be perceived as benign by outsiders—witness how a group of Islamic extremists were generally ignored prior to their 1993 attack on New York's World Trade Center or how the *Aum Shinrikiyo* operated in Japan, Russia, and the United States with little interference from the authorities—until it uses violence to fulfill objectives that are hidden from even its own rank and file.

By contrast, sustained and coordinated deception campaigns often exceed the resources of nonstate actors.[12] These clandestine groups rarely can afford the time and resources needed for an effective deception campaign. But as the activities of Columbia's Cali Cartel, the Irish Republican Army, and the Sicilian and U.S. Cosa Nostra demonstrate, they have on occasion deliberately deceived as well as denied.

When used by nonstate actors, D&D poses an immediate threat. Scarce foreign aid and intelligence resources are often squandered against fake or insignificant issues. When criminals use D&D, police time is spent "chasing after shadows." Investigative efforts are diluted to the point where they no longer yield significant results. Criminals and political terrorists often use D&D to eliminate their competition or to misdirect law enforcement investigators. For example, U.S. analysts and policymakers are alarmed about "starving sentries" at Soviet-built weapons plants and storage facilities. But once out of the spotlight, are senior Russian officials also conspiring to sell the inventories and infrastructures to the highest bidder?

Regimes in Transition

Some regimes are in transition from an authoritarian to democratic form of government. Some seek to reverse the process, while others may seek to increase their foreign capabilities to alter the international status quo. When increasing their military capabilities some powers are attracted to denial and deception as a means of protecting developing weapons and military infrastructures from outside interference or treaty commitments.

The history of how transitional powers have exploited D&D offers insights into such contemporary problems as the 1998 collapse of the monitoring efforts of the United Nations Special Commission for the Disarmament of Iraq (UNSCOM).

Decades earlier, during the interwar arms control and disarmament regime directed at the Weimar Republic, Germans had obfuscated, if not actually hidden, their rearmament efforts from international inspectors. Sometimes individuals, most interested in their own pecuniary interests, hid existing stocks of weapons or manufacturing equipment on their own initiative. At other times, officials engaged in coordinated actions to hide activity forbidden by treaty. "Advertising Squadrons," whose ostensible purpose was to provide skywriting and advertising services, actually served in the late 1920s as the first operational units of the reborn German air force.

The Inter-Allied Control Commission (1920-26), charged with verifying German compliance with the Treaty of Versailles, became aware of these German violations. But because the inspectors failed to uncover convincing evidence of systematic German violation of the treaty, the Allies accepted the mundane explanations provided when evidence of wrongdoing was uncovered. As the Control Commission concluded its work in 1926, for example, Commander Fanshawe, a British naval inspector, told his German counterpart: "You should not feel that we believed what you told us. Not one word you uttered was true, but you delivered information in such a clever way that we were in a position to believe you. I want to thank you for this."[13]

Parallels exist between German rearmament and the recent UNSCOM experience in Iraq since the 1991 Gulf War. Over time, plausible, if unlikely, explanations offered by Iraqis for apparent arms violations eroded international interest and commitment in pursuing evidence of weapons violations. No one seems to believe that Iraq is in compliance with U.N. mandates, but most governments are reluctant to act against murky evidence of arms violations.

Thus, transition regimes are advantaged because targeted nations "take the easy way out" by believing palatable lies and half-truths rather than confront disturbing information.[14] This may also apply to other forms of denial and deception.

Anticipating Threats

The United States, for several reasons, is likely to be a target of denial and deception by a variety of state and nonstate actors. First, D&D can be viewed as a form of asymmetric warfare. Likely opponents lack the military capability needed to effectively challenge U.S. forces on the battlefield. For the most part, officers and policymakers in the United States are preoccupied by asymmetric threats in the form of new technology or weapons (e.g., using advanced sensors and microprocessors to upgrade the performance of primitive mines).

But asymmetric warfare does not have to be based on exotic technology or be intended to exploit technical weaknesses in U.S. weapons systems. Denial and deception, for example, allows adversaries to compensate for U.S. superiority by delaying U.S. military action or by confronting policymakers with a fait accompli. In other words, opponents might hope to avoid confronting U.S. forces directly by increasing the costs of U.S. intervention. D&D also might prevent U.S. forces from creating the synergy in maneuver and firepower needed to overcome numerically superior opponents on the battlefield. Because U.S. forces increasingly depend on superior command, control, communication, and intelligence (C4I) to beat an adversary to the punch, opponents can expect to reap disproportionate benefits from a D&D attack on American C4I.

Second, the proliferation of weapons of mass destruction (WMD) is facilitated by D&D. Dual-use technologies or contraband materials and equipment are needed for the manufacturing of chemical, biological or nuclear weapons. Most states and manufacturers are unlikely to supply well-known proliferators with sensitive equipment. But D&D can be used to avoid the international condemnation and sanctions that would follow clear evidence that a nation was seeking to develop an arsenal of unconventional weapons. As Israel's June 1981 preventive attack on the Iraqi nuclear complex at Osirak demonstrates, a WMD infrastructure that is detected before weapons are readied faces the prospect of direct military action. D&D helps proliferators hide their activities and avoid international sanctions or military strikes intended to deny them their deadly arsenals.

Third, the United States is party to a record number of multilateral and bilateral arms control, human rights, and trade agreements. Because many of these treaties involve complex verification and compliance procedures, states seeking to violate these treaties will be tempted to use D&D. Multilateral treaties are especially vulnerable to this type of threat. The international community would be unlikely to abandon an international arms control regime (e.g., the chemical weapons convention) because suspicions are aroused that a state is failing to abide by its terms. The history of the interwar Inter-Allied Control Commission would suggest that political will is at a premium when it comes to sanctioning violators of multilateral regimes.

Fourth, the electronic media, especially all-news television networks and Internet coverage, provide new channels for D&D. Although these new media allow Americans to stay informed about global developments in real time, they provide adversaries with a way to communicate directly with U.S. citizens and elites. This access can provide adversaries with an advantage over efforts of the U.S. government to communicate its policy positions to a U.S. or a global audience. The public, especially under authoritarian regimes, rarely has access to new communication technology. In many respects, American government officials and the public are now part of a national village that often shares the same "virtual" experience, especially when it comes to extraordinary events.

To the extent that these images can be manipulated by foreign agents, new forms of media provide new opportunities for D&D. If Vietnam was the first television war and the Gulf Conflict was the first war with real time global coverage, then the 1999 war in Kosovo was the first "interactive war." Although not very sophisticated, supporters of Serbia used the Internet to contact individual Americans directly while Serbian officials debated various talk show hosts on national television. These techniques are likely to become more sophisticated in the future.

Fifth, the dissemination of knowledge about U.S. intelligence technology and an increased technological sophistication among U.S. opponents aided in part by the intimate and powerful experience of having done battle with U.S. armed forces, is increasing foreign awareness of U.S. intelligence sources and methods. In addition, the publication of heretofore-classified information supplied by officials and unofficial "leaks" can be and has been used by diligent adversaries to understand U.S. intelligence capabilities and biases. Intelligence sources and methods have been further compromised by espionage incidents and diplomatic demarches. This information has made it possible for adversaries to target the U.S. intelligence community for denial and deception.

Sixth, globalization, the breakdown of the traditional barriers to national sovereignty—increases the information and economic channels that can be used to conduct D&D. Tourism, business travel, legal and illegal migration, legal and illegal international trade, and increasingly interactive global financial markets and instruments offer subtle and credible ways to communicate corrupt information. Simultaneously, global financial markets and commerce form a new and profitable venture for D&D operations. The successful manipulation of financial markets and commerce not only undermines confidence in economic institutions, but also can adversely affect the quality of life of many Americans, including their investments and pension plans.

Minimizing Threats

Although the threat of D&D cannot be eliminated, there are ways to minimize its adverse impact: (1) develop a program to increase awareness in U.S. government circles of the use and methods of D&D efforts; (2) increase public and media awareness of D&D; (3) increase awareness of the trade-offs entailed in revealing current U.S. collection and analytic methods; (4) train intelligence collectors, analysts, and managers; and (5) synthesize available knowledge and prepare for the future. These initiatives require only modest expenditures of resources and effort, but they may yield significant dividends.

Increase Government Awareness

Policymakers would be advantaged by recognizing that they may be either the target or channel for D&D. This simple recommendation, however, is difficult to put into practice. Elected and senior officials pride themselves on their interpersonal skills. Like many people, they tend to rely on their own ability to accurately perceive their surroundings and to sense when they are being manipulated. Moreover, senior officials tend to place more stock in their own personal observations than in a mountain of contradictory information. There may be more than a little truth to the proposition that the more "savvy" the politician, the less likely he/she will be concerned about being targeted by a denial and deception campaign.

Increasing awareness among elected officials and other policymakers of D&D use and methods may be facilitated by case studies. By providing examples of past and current D&D activities, they could serve as a powerful reminder of their potential damage to U.S. interests especially when targeted against elected and appointed officials.

To further help prevent policymakers from falling victim to D&D, U.S. intelligence can provide policymakers with additional, up-to-date background information on their personal contacts and sources of information so as to place them in a more complete context.

Public and Media Awareness

The American public and especially the mass media can be made aware that they are being targeted by D&D efforts, whether to be used as a channel of communication to reach elected officials, or to shape broad political trends and opinion in the United States. Foreign officials planning deception will naturally have an interest in capturing public and media opinion in a democracy. But to exaggerate the threat posed by D&D would be counterproductive. Instead, accurate and consistent explanation that adversaries are interested in shaping public and media opinion to serve their own interests can sensitize individuals to the possibility that they are being manipulated. Awareness of how past, current, and possibly future D&D has targeted the media and other nongovernmental sectors will help minimize the effectiveness of strategic foreign deception efforts.

Awareness of Revealing Information on Intelligence Methods

Government officials are often placed in situations where there is an advantage in revealing information, either to the public or to other governments, that provides information about U.S. intelligence collection and analytic methods and capabilities. While decisions on whether or not to reveal certain information must be made on a case-by-case basis, officials need to be aware of the trade-offs involved. In particular, providing other governments, international bodies, or nonstate actors with indications concerning intelligence methods may facilitate the conduct of D&D against the United States. Those in a position to make such decisions, as well as other officials and the public, can and should be made aware of how their actions could affect U.S. intelligence sources and methods and the ability of the United States to detect future D&D operations. In addition, adequate records concerning such releases of information must be maintained to help determine what foreign governments or nonstate actors are likely to know about U.S. intelligence methods and capabilities that could help them plan their D&D operations.

Training Intelligence Collectors, Analysts, and Managers

Intelligence collectors, analysts, and managers must become more aware of the possibility of their being targets and channels for D&D. Education, briefings, and training programs could include case studies of successful D&D, especially those involving the extensive use of technical intelligence channels. Specific elements of a training program might involve:

- enhancing awareness of the extent to which technical intelligence sources and methods may be compromised (i.e., to what extent does the intelligence target and potential deceiver understand the operation of a given intelligence channel?);
- developing and implementing a rating system for technical intelligence collection comparable to that which exists for human source collection (e.g., whether collection is "expected" or "unexpected," degree of compromise of the channel, etc.);
- examining possible "feedback" channels a potential deceiver might use, including analysis of open source information (e.g., what information could a potential deceiver glean from official statements and actions?).

Increased Study of D&D History and Theory

The study of historical, theoretical, and foreign D&D should be fostered within the Intelligence Community. A great deal of intellectual capital was accumulated during the Cold War on how to assess and counter D&D. Many of these lessons can be used to anticipate current and future challenges. But the generation that developed counterdenial and deception practices and awareness in the aftermath of World War II is passing from the scene.

The few specialists remaining active are available, and usually willing, to work with a new generation of counter-D&D practitioners and researchers, in and outside the intelligence community, to pass on their knowledge and foster new studies of effective practices and indicators of D&D activity. A network of these specialists could be maintained and provided with an opportunity to help mentor scholars, research corporation analysts, and intelligence managers and trainers. In addition, the synthesizing and publishing of studies and the holding of conferences on D&D in other countries are likely to provide insights not only on past practices, but also on anticipated threats.

Minimizing the Threat

Foreign denial and deception affects the quality of life in the United States by causing policymakers to waste scarce public resources and to fail to anticipate strategic threats. Foreign D&D assists state and nonstate actors abroad, and even facilitates illegal activity in the Western hemisphere and U.S. border regions. The Intelligence Community, the Department of Defense, and other government agencies, as well as elected officials, the media, and the public need to be aware of efforts to influence policy debates and priorities within the United States. D&D cannot be eliminated, but its impact can be minimized.

Notes

1. The fear that American intelligence professionals and policymakers had been deceived about the Soviet military buildup led, in part, to the competitive estimates in the Ford years and later to White House interest during the Reagan administration.

2. For more on how the proliferation of sources and data can impede intelligence analysis, see Abram Shulsky and Gary Schmitt, "Intelligence Reform: Beyond the Ames Case," in Roy Godson, Ernest R. May, and Gary Schmitt (eds.), *U.S. Intelligence at the Crossroads: Agendas for Reform* (Washington, DC: Brassey's, 1995), pp. 46-59. For evidence that increased data and transparency can impede accurate perception, see Bernard I. Finel and Kristin M. Lord, "The Surprising Logic of Transparency," *International Studies Quarterly*, Vol. 43, No. 2, June 1999, pp. 315-339.

3. Since perception is in the mind of the beholder, denial and deception is not necessary or sufficient to misperceive the intentions of another. Common cognitive biases, bureaucratic politics, or intelligence pathologies (e.g., excessive compartmentalization) can produce misperception and intelligence failure. See Robert Jervis, *Perception and Misperception in International Politics* (Princeton, NJ: Princeton University Press, 1976); and James J. Wirtz, "The Intelligence Paradigm," *Intelligence and National Security*, Vol. 4, No. 3 (October 1989), pp. 829-837.

4. For example, Soviet leaders in fall 1962 failed to assess correctly the consequences of their denial and deception campaign to hide their deployment of missiles to Cuba from U.S. intelligence and defense officials. See James J. Wirtz, "Organizing for Crisis Intelligence: Lessons from the Cuban Missile Crisis," in James G. Blight and David Welch (eds.) *Intelligence and the Cuban Missile Crisis* (London, UK: Frank Cass, 1998).

5. Colin Gray interprets the notion of strategic culture in this manner. See Colin S. Gray, *Modern Strategy* (New York: Oxford University Press, 1999).

6. Strategic culture's role in shaping defense policies, doctrines, and priorities recently has generated much scholarly interest. See Alastair Ian Johnston, *Cultural Realism: Strategic Culture and Grand Strategy in Chinese History* (Princeton, NJ: Princeton University Press, 1995); Stephen Peter Rosen, *Societies and Military Power* (Ithaca, NY: Cornell University Press, 1996); Peer Lavoy, Scott Sagan, and James J. Wirtz (eds.), *Planning the Unthinkable: New Powers and Their Doctrines for Using*

Nuclear, Chemical and Biological Weapons (Ithaca, NY: Cornell University Press, Forthcoming); and Elizabeth Kier, *Imaging War: French and British Military Doctrine Between the Wars* (Princeton, NJ: Princeton University Press, 1997).

7.   During the Gulf War, for instance, Iraqi propagandists warned U.S. forces that while they were fighting in the Gulf their girlfriends were home with "Bart Simpson."

8.   Roy Godson, *Dirty Tricks or Trump Cards* (New Brunswick, NJ: Transaction Publishers, 2001) p. 236.

9.   Barton Whaley maintains, however, that only two out of two hundred and thirty deception campaigns he surveyed contained a "plan within a plan." He suggests that an explanation for the apparent absence of a backup plan might be that the high success rate of deception campaigns (83 percent) precluded the need to devise deceptions within deceptions. See Barton Whaley, "Conditions Making for Success and Failure of D&D: Nonstate and Illicit Actors," in Roy Godson and James J. Wirtz (eds.), *Strategic Denial and Deception: The Twenty-First Century Challenge* (New Brunswick, NJ: Transaction Publishers, 2002); and Barton Whaley, *Stratagem: Deception and Surprise in War* (Cambridge, MA: MIT Center for International Studies, 1969).

10.   Roy Godson (ed.), *Comparing Foreign Intelligence* (Washington, DC: Pergamon-Brassey's, 1988).

11.   David Kay, "Denial and Deception: The Lessons of Iraq," in Godson, May and Schmitt, op. cit., pp. 109-127; and Scott Ritter, *Endgame* (New York: Simon and Schuster, 1999).

12.   But as Bowyer Bell notes, the World Trade Center bombers, the Irish Republican Army, and the Sicilian Mafia surmounted various hurdles in conducting successful denial and deception campaigns. See J. Bowyer Bell, "Conditions Making for Success and Failure of D&D: Nonstate and Illicit Actors," in Roy Godson and James J. Wirtz (eds.), *Strategic Denial and Deception: The Twenty-First Century Challenge.*

13.   Fanshawe quoted in Barton Whaley, "Conditions Making for Success and Failure of D&D: Authoritarian and Totalitarian Regimes," in Roy Godson and James J. Wirtz (eds.), *Strategic Denial and Deception: The Twenty-First Century Challenge.*

14.   While Weimar Germany used denial and deception to hide its military buildup, Adolf Hitler used similar techniques to exaggerate the Nazis' military achievements in order to intimidate their opponents. Denial and deception is extraordinarily important for transition states. It helps them when they are most vulnerable—during power transitions when stronger states might move preemptively against them. In fact, denial and deception may explain the general absence of preventive war in power transition situations. See Richard Ned Lebow, "Windows of Vulnerability: Do States Jump Through Them?" *International Security,* Vol. 9, No. 1 (Summer 1984), pp. 147-186.

2

Elements of Strategic Denial and Deception

Abram Shulsky

Definitions

"Denial" refers to the attempt to block all information channels by which an adversary could learn some truth (e.g., about a military development program, a policy, a course of action, etc.), thus preventing him from reacting in a timely manner. "Denial" would thus refer to all the methods used to safeguard "classified" information, i.e., it would include security programs generally. This chapter, however, is concerned with the denial of information of particular importance (the term "strategic" is defined and discussed below), and focuses on special steps taken to deny particularly important pieces of information to an adversary.

"Deception" by contrast refers to the effort to cause an adversary to believe something that is not true, to believe a "cover story" rather than the truth, with the goal of leading him to react in a way that serves one's own interests, rather than his. This involves creating the impression (via "leaks," planted information, decoys, etc.) that the truth is other than it actually is, that is, creating an "alternate reality" in which the target is induced to believe.

Deception depends, ultimately, on implanting in the target's mind a view of reality that is at odds with the truth. This typically means presenting the target with false "information," but the occasional truth may be mixed in as well, as long as the overall effect is to help create the desired (false) picture in the target's mind. The function of this truth may be not only to enhance the credibility of the "channel" through which false "information" reaches the target; it may, paradoxically, be useful in building up the false picture itself.[1] For example, in the classic "good cop-bad cop" interrogation scenario, it may well be the case that the "good cop," compared to his colleague, is a friendlier fellow, more ready to understand the suspect's motives and sympathize with his plight. One imagines that the technique probably works better when this is the case. Nevertheless, the purpose of conveying this (true) information to the suspect is fundamentally deceptive, to convince him that it is in his own interest to be more open with the "good cop" than, in fact, it is prudent for him to be.

While "denial" and "deception" are separate terms that can be distinguished conceptually, they are closely intertwined in practice. Almost by definition, deception must include denial: in order to induce an adversary to accept a cover story, information that would reveal the true state of affairs must be denied him. Conversely, a strategic denial effort may well include some element of deception. In order to deny the adversary knowledge of the truth, it may be advisable to develop and provide him with a "cover story" to help explain any information about the actual state of affairs that might get through to him. If one is trying to deny information about a new weapon system that is being developed, for example, one must not only block the channels by which information about that system might reach the adversary, one should probably also develop a cover story (e.g., that the activity in question is related to the improvement of an already-existing weapon system), and provide faked "evidence" to that effect. Thus, if, despite one's denial measures, some information pertaining to the development program reaches the adversary (for example, he notices that high-level officials are making frequent visits to an out-of-the-way facility), there is the chance that he will misinterpret this accurate information in light of all the faked evidence he has received.

Thus, as a practical matter, the two notions are likely to go together. It is almost impossible to imagine a deception effort that does not involve denial (unless perhaps the goal is to deceive an adversary into believing that something is going on when, in fact, absolutely nothing is—a pure "Potemkin village" operation, as it were.) By contrast, it is easier to imagine a denial effort that does not involve a "cover story" (and hence does not involve an effort at deception); however, such a denial effort is likely to be more vulnerable to failure, since, if information about the activity slips out, the adversary will not have an "innocent" context in which to interpret it.

What is Meant by "Strategic?"

"Strategic" is a notably slippery word, but it is used here to denote a high level of importance. With respect to wartime activity, strategic denial and deception efforts deal with the "strategic" or "operational" levels of warfare (the entire war, or a theater of the war), rather than the tactical level (a single battle or engagement). More generally, "strategic" denial or deception deals with major policies of a government rather than details of implementation.

The best way to define "strategic" might well be in terms of the intended target of the deception: a "strategic" deception is one aimed at the highest levels of government or of the military chain of command (chiefs of state or government, ministers or cabinet members, the chairman of the JCS or head of the general staff, commanders-in-chief of theaters of war, and others). In other words, the subject of the deception effort must be something of sufficient importance that a high-level official of this type would typically deal with personally. The same standard would be applied to denial: "strategic" denial would be the effort to withhold information of the sort that a high-level official would typically deal with directly, were it available.

Thus, "strategic" deception would not include deception aimed at a lower-level officer, such as commander of a division or below, nor at the operational level of an intelligence agency. The use of decoys on the battlefield, or a feint intended to divert attention from the main axis of attack, would not constitute strategic deception. Similarly an operation intended to deceive an intelligence agency into accepting the *bona fides* of a potential double agent would not constitute strategic deception, although once the double agent's *bona fides* were established, he or she could be used as part of a strategic deception effort.

The value of this definition of "strategic" is twofold. First, it provides a relatively easy way of indicating which policies, military decisions, and so on are to be regarded as strategic and which are not. Second, and perhaps more important, it highlights the potential importance of certain types of deception methods (such as the employment of "agents-of-influence"), which are typically targeted on high-level officials.

When considering denial and deception operations conducted by nonstate actors (such as insurgents or organized criminal groups), the term "strategic" may be even more difficult to define. However, the main idea remains the same: "strategic" denial or deception involves information about the overall objectives or activities of the organization, rather than a specific operation. Thus, the Sicilian Mafia's steps to convince the public and law enforcement that it wasn't involved in drug dealing would count as "strategic" in nature.

The Relationship between Propaganda and Deception

In principle, we would want to distinguish between "deception" and "propaganda." The aim of deception is to induce a target to do something that is in the deceiver's interest but not necessarily the target's. Propaganda attempts to influence a target's beliefs more generally. Propaganda also targets the populace at large, rather than the nation's leadership. The ability of propaganda to deceive also should depend on the degree of suspiciousness with which the target audience regards the propaganda source.

Propaganda may be characterized by the extent to which the target audience is intended to be aware of the source of the propaganda message. Where the source of propaganda is openly revealed, it is termed "white" propaganda. International radio services such as Radio Moscow or Radio Free Europe both are examples of white propaganda. In "black" propaganda, by contrast, the source is concealed. For example, an article that an intelligence agency succeeds in planting in a foreign newspaper is black. Anonymous leaks to the press could be regarded as a form of domestic black propaganda on the part of the leaker. In between these two types of activities is "gray" propaganda. The source is neither proclaimed nor effectively hidden. The output of known front groups such as the various international organizations run by the Soviet Union would fall into this category.

Black propaganda could presumably deceive even a very suspicious audience, since most people would be unaware of its true source. By contrast, white propaganda's ability to deceive would *seem* to depend on the target regarding the source as friendly, or at least not particularly hostile; after all, why would one believe anything coming from a source whose interests are contrary to one's own? In practice, however, people can be persuaded by information they recognize as being presented by unfriendly sources. The entire advertising industry, after all, rests on the apparently well-founded belief that people can be persuaded by a message, even when the self-interested character of the source of the message is obvious. For this reason, it is important to pay attention to propaganda as a possible tool for use in the conduct of deception operations.

It is difficult to assess to what extent one should expect the leadership of a country to be vulnerable to persuasion by propaganda when it is aware that the source is not necessarily friendly. However, it seems clear that messages transmitted via propaganda, even "white" propaganda, can influence political leaders. For this reason, we will pay attention to propaganda as a possible tool for use in the conduct of deception operations.

Denial and Deception Methods and Channels

The notion of information or intelligence "channels" is important in order to analyze denial and deception methods. The term channel identifies the specific ways in which information about a given subject reaches an audience. A discrete piece of information that travels along such a channel may be referred to as a "signal."

These channels can be what are typically called intelligence sources and methods, but they also can be other, less clandestine, communication means, such as open sources (press or broadcast reports), diplomatic interchanges, other human sources (conversations with travelers, businessmen or others), or direct observation. In the case of intelligence sources and methods, the channels exist solely for the sake of obtaining information; in other cases, such as diplomatic or business activity, the passage of information is a byproduct of the main purpose for which the activity is undertaken.

Wartime typically blocks many communication channels between contending parties. "Closed" societies (or "denied areas") also attempt to regulate as many of these channels as possible, although various aspects of the globalization of commerce have made this an increasingly difficult task, at least for those countries unwilling to endure a North Korean-type existence. At the other end of the spectrum, industrial democracies are becoming increasingly open in terms of cross-border travel and communications systems. Similarly, nonstate actors have been able to take advantage of globalizing trends to act more easily across state boundaries.

In terms of channels, denial involves blocking (in principle) all channels by which signals revealing the true situation might be transmitted. Deception involves the manufacturing of false signals that can be fed into those channels; when those false signals are received by the intended targets of the deception, the latter must play their part in the process by putting the signals together to form the intended (false) picture.[2] If the false signals are transmitted, but the intended targets do not receive them, or, if they receive them but do not interpret them in the desired manner, then the deception is not successful.

Looking at the problem in terms of channels, another close connection between the realms of denial and deception becomes apparent. The more successful one is at denying an adversary information, the more reliant he will become on those few channels still open to him. Also, as denial increases, an adversary will become more eager to make use of any channels that remain available (i.e., potential human agents who are "dangled" as sources of information, or the relatively few objects that are left in places where they can be observed.) Thus, as denial operations succeed, the more likely it is that false signals can be passed on the few channels that remain.

The notion of channels also suggests a basic counterdeception technique: the use and comparison of signals from as many channels as possible. The greater the reliance that is placed on a small number of channels (or, at worst, a single one), the greater the vulnerability to deception. By comparing data obtained from a large number of channels, one complicates the potential deceiver's problem by forcing him to provide false messages in many different channels in a consistent manner.

Intelligence Channels

When we think about deception, the use of intelligence channels (human agents or technical intelligence collection systems) to pass false signals comes first to mind. Double agents are, of course, one of the most obvious methods of doing this. Similarly, a loyal agent who, unwittingly, collects false information strewn in his path serves the same purpose. With respect to technical intelligence collection, deceivers can use decoys and fake radio transmissions to pass incorrect information on to opponents.

Using technical intelligence channels to pass false signals can be easier in some respects, but in others, harder, than using human intelligence channels. It is easier in that the adversary's technical intelligence channels may be known with great specificity; for example, it may be possible to calculate the orbits of photo reconnaissance satellites, thereby learning what sites are within range at what times. The spread of knowledge about U.S. space systems—due to successful espionage by the Soviet Union and the efforts of amateurs—suggests an important vulnerability. Providing fake signals, however, may involve the actual construction of a decoy, which must resemble the real thing closely enough to deceive the target. This is likely to be a complicated and expensive matter. Conversely, providing a fake document or false information for a double agent to pass back is relatively simple; however, the identification of the channel (i.e., identifying an agent that is trusted by the opponent) may be a difficult task.

The more difficult it is for an adversary to recruit real agents among the target's officialdom and population, the easier it should be to get the target to accept double agents in the form of "dangles," "walk-ins," or defectors. Similarly, if stringent security practices are in place for technical intelligence collection, then those items which the adversary is "allowed" to see will assume a greater importance as an opponent tries to build up a total picture of activities.

Diplomatic Channels

The sardonic definition of a diplomat as "an honest man sent abroad to lie for his country" strongly suggests that diplomatic channels can be used for deception. Of course, since a foreign diplomat is assumed to be loyal to his government, an official of the target country ought to be aware that anything he says could be meant to deceive, and hence should be taken with a grain of salt. This, in turn, would seem to make diplomats an unpromising channel for deception; however, this is often not the way things work out for three reasons. First, unless two countries are outright enemies, they have to be able to do at least a minimal amount of business with each other. Hence, a certain amount of diplomatic activity is necessary, and this cannot be carried on without a measure of trust. In particular, personal relationships are likely to develop that facilitate routine diplomatic activity. An official is likely to come to believe that a given diplomat, while he represents an adversary country, is, nevertheless, not such a bad fellow. The diplomat might be perceived as someone who might fudge the truth, but not as a person who would tell an outright lie (if only because that will make life harder for both parties as they try to conduct routine business in the future.) This creates the possibility, at least, of passing false signals that will, nevertheless, be believed: the mere transaction of diplomatic business implies a certain willingness to believe what a foreign diplomat says, even if the fundamental hostility of his government is obvious.

Second, the mere fact that diplomatic activity is occurring conveys a message that the parties involved are interested in seeking a negotiated solution to their differences. This expectation, however, can be exploited for purposes of deception. In late 1941, for example, Japanese diplomats in Washington were continuing to negotiate even as the rest of their government prepared to launch an attack on U.S. forces at Pearl Harbor. This served a deceptive purpose, since it suggested that Japan had not yet taken the decision to go to war against the United States. That Tokyo had not taken its diplomats into its confidence (and that the diplomats themselves probably did not favor Tokyo's course of action) probably enhanced their ability to suggest that a peaceful outcome was still possible. Even if diplomats are aware of the true intentions of their government, they still might (falsely) insinuate that they are not entirely in accord with their government's policy, because they regard it as unnecessarily confrontational, poorly thought-out, or hobbled by a short-term perspective. The diplomat may gain a degree of credibility with his hosts despite the fact that he is nominally loyal to an adversary government.

Third, the target may simply underestimate the degree to which the diplomat's government regards its interests as diverging from those of the target's own government, and hence may not understand that the diplomat has a motive to engage in deception. In other words, if the deceiver is trying to present himself as better disposed toward the target than is in fact the case, diplomatic channels may be very useful means of deception.

The fact that diplomatic (and other non-intelligence) channels can be used for deception has important implications for the theory and practice of counterdeception. Detecting deception requires being able to compare the signals being transmitted in as many channels as possible. The signals transmitted in the diplomatic channel, however, may go directly to officials at the highest level of government. For legitimate reasons, high-ranking officials may wish to restrict tightly the circulation within the government of information relating to their diplomatic contacts. Hence, those involved in detecting deception efforts may find it hard to compare such sources with the signals received in other channels. Even more important, the high official receiving the signal may be induced, by the value he places on his "personal" relationship with the foreign diplomat, to rely too much on it. Thus, senior officials can come to rely on a single channel for information, which increases the risk of being deceived. To counteract the tendency of officials to be overly trusting of personal contacts, analysts seeking to engage in counterdeception will have to have access to sensitive non-intelligence information to do their job; alternatively, other parts of the government will have to develop their own counterdeception capabilities.

Propaganda Channels

Propaganda can serve the purposes of strategic deception. White propaganda, that propaganda whose source is not hidden, provokes some of the same considerations that apply to diplomacy. Propaganda may gain more credibility than would seem reasonable, given its known origin in an adversary government. Propaganda also can have a wide variety of sources, including various nonstate actors and groups whose relationships to a state are unclear. The various international "front" groups sponsored by the former Soviet Union were intended to work in this way, but their "cover" as independent organizations soon became threadbare. Soviet front groups might have been more effective, but Stalinist paranoia made impossible the operational autonomy needed to succeed. To the extent that future practitioners of this type of propaganda have learned lessons from the Soviet experience, we may expect that the nonstate groups will be controlled in a more sophisticated manner and that their ties to a given state will be less obvious.

New methods of spreading propaganda (such as via Internet web sites of non-governmental organizations [NGOs], or specialized email lists) allow a deceiver to reach target audiences via multiple channels. Many of these channels may remain relatively invisible to the public at large; thus, it may be harder to refute propaganda spread via the Internet to target audiences already receptive to it than it would be to refute propaganda spread by more traditional means. As has been noted in the literature about the information revolution, new technologies have allowed the formation of virtual communities of similarly minded people throughout the world, held together by Internet-based communications. Such virtual communities offer new methods of spreading misinformation in support of a propaganda or a deception campaign.

Front organizations and virtual communities gain additional significance if they are able to establish links with the more traditional news media, which can then spread their views (including misinformation or deceptive representations of the facts) to a larger public. In assessing the likelihood that the media will amplify messages supplied by information channels of relatively unknown credibility, one must consider the nature of the news media. Despite the media's self-image of hardheaded cynicism,[3] it is relatively vulnerable to this type of manipulation. Sophisticated leakers within governments are readily able to use the news media to propagate their own "spin" on events. Several factors explain the reporters' attention. The media find it difficult to report first-hand on events in out-of-the-way places, such as Zapatista activity in remote villages in southern Mexico. This is especially true in an era in which the main media organizations' international coverage is being cut back, and budgets for such reporting are being reduced. Individuals and organizations who can provide information from such locales become valued sources for the media. Indeed, without extensive local expertise, reporters may find it difficult to gain any understanding of what is going on. They may find themselves dependent on sources with local expertise that are able to interpret unfolding events. The organizations involved also may be able to play on the political sympathies of the (often young) reporters who are assigned to cover these events. In an atmosphere where meeting a deadline is necessary to succeed, it is not surprising that nonstate organizations are able to have a major influence on news coverage of certain events.

Agents-of-Influence

Among the other types of overt information channels, perhaps the most important is the "agent-of-influence," someone who is able to get close to important government officials and influence their views and actions with respect to major issues. Ordinarily, the target would have to be unaware of the loyalty of the agent-of-influence; in the best case, the target would view the agent as a friend who has his (the target's) best interests at heart, whereas the agent is loyal to an adversary. But such a complete misreading of the agent's real loyalties may not be absolutely necessary for him to operate successfully as an agent-of-influence. An agent also might be able to gain the confidence of the target even though the agent was openly loyal to the target's adversary. Such a case might be similar to the use of diplomatic channels for deception. The agent might, for example, claim to speak for a more moderate or reasonable faction of the adversary's leadership that wishes to take a course of action more favorable to the target, but is facing obstacles from its own hard-liners.

The most likely situation involving agents-of-influence, however, falls somewhere between the poles of total awareness and ignorance of the agent-of-influence's loyalties. For example, an agent-of-influence might be known to have some sympathy for a foreign government or its ideology, but the degree of sympathy might be underestimated and it might not be understood that the agent was under the foreign government's control. This seemed to be the case with Arne Treholt, a well-known pro-Soviet agent-of-influence in Norway; his left-wing views were known, but not the extent of his loyalty to the Soviet Union. Such agents-of-influence pose problems for counterdeception similar to those in diplomatic channels. Agents-of-influence may be in touch with high officials of the target government who might not be in a good position to compare the signals they are getting via this channel with signals received in other, more routine, channels.

Other Overt Channels

An agent-of-influence is usually thought of as someone under the control of an adversary, whose task it is to influence a target by various means, including deceptive information. There may be many other types of people who fulfill a similar function even though they are not under actual control. For example, if an adversary government can manipulate the views of a traveler, businessman, or relief worker that person can be a useful deception channel when he returns home and reports on what he has "learned."

Much of our putative information about the severity of the North Korean famine comes from international aid groups that work with the North Korean government to distribute food and other supplies. It is hard to assess whether or not the North Koreans are influencing those groups' reports by controlling their travel within the country, their access to ordinary North Koreans, and other sources of information. While few places on earth are as closed as North Korea in terms of ordinary interchange, it remains the case that travelers and other "instant experts" of various kinds can often be deceived about the actual conditions of the place they visit. When they return home, their views are endowed with a measure of credibility simply by virtue of having been in some denied area. "In the country of the blind, the one-eyed man is king."

Aside from these sophisticated methods of influencing opinion, there are others such as planting news stories, both at home and abroad. At the most basic level, for example, stories about dismissing reserve forces, or granting leave to active forces can be planted in domestic media outlets to deceive the adversary about plans for a surprise attack. A deception effort also could be implemented using stories planted in the media of other countries.

Feints and Other Actions

Finally, actions may speak louder than words. Actions can be taken for the sake of misleading an adversary about one's own real intentions. This is typical of military deception, but may have a role in political and economic matters, too.

Objectives of Strategic Denial and Deception

Strategic denial and deception involve much effort and imply that the highest levels of the deceiver state (or nonstate organization) are involved in planning the deception initiative. Only major objectives would be likely to be sought by such means.

In wartime, the objectives of a strategic denial and deception effort would be something on which the success of an entire campaign rested. For example, the elaborate deception efforts used by the Allies to confuse the Germans about the location of the Normandy D-day landings were critical to the success of the invasion itself. It is hard to see how the invasion could have succeeded had Germany been able to concentrate its forces on the Normandy beaches before the landings. Of course, even without deception, mere denial of information about the landing zones would have required the Germans to disperse their forces; however, the crucial nature of the deception operation was made clear by the fact that, even after the initial landings took place, Hitler still insisted on retaining major forces to deal with the expected "real" landing near Calais.

In a peacetime context, "strategic" deception would deal with major national decisions concerning fundamental issues of foreign policy, major decisions concerning military procurement, and assessments of the threats a nation faces. Again, the distinction between strategic and non-strategic may be difficult to draw. The level of the decision-maker who is targeted may be a better indicator than the substance of the deception.

In general, it is more difficult to describe the kinds of objectives that a state might pursue in peacetime, as opposed to wartime. In the latter case, it is easy to imagine the kinds of objectives for which strategic deception would be useful: in essence, one wishes to attack an enemy who is not prepared because he misestimated when, where, or how an attack would occur. Similarly, in wartime one wants to conceal from the enemy the development of new weapons, and, if possible, to deceive him about how new weapons work. During World War II, for instance, the British deceived the Germans about the operation of a new radar system that could detect submarines traveling on the surface; instead, the Germans believed that the British were using an infrared detector, and wasted a great deal of effort on coatings that would reduce their submarines' heat signature.

In peacetime, however, the objective of a strategic deception is not so obvious and the deception may be practiced in a variety of ways. For example, if an adversary believed that his opponents were stronger than was in fact the case, he might be induced to make concessions that he otherwise would not. A false appearance of strength might keep an adversary from exploiting an opportunity to attack or from exerting political or military pressure to achieve concessions. Alternatively, conveying a false appearance of weakness or threat might dissuade an adversary from building up his own military forces or adopting a more watchful and suspicious policy. In some cases, a country might even wish to convince an adversary that the regime was threatened by domestic opponents who stood a good chance of toppling it; this could persuade the adversary not to attempt to weaken the regime on the grounds that it was on its last legs anyway or, in any case, was too weak to cause any trouble. Similarly, if an adversary believed a third party were considered the main threat and the principal target of hostility, he might then relax his guard.

Following both strategies at the same time—appearing both stronger and weaker than one is—seems impossible. If the target government contains both "hawks" and "doves," however, then, ideally, the deceiver might want to appear strong to the hawks, to deter them from hostile action, and weak to the doves, to convince them it is safe to follow conciliatory policies. A deceiver might try various efforts directed at both results, hoping to be able to target its actions sufficiently well to avoid confusing the two messages. Whether or not this is other than a theoretical possibility is an interesting question.

A particularly interesting set of deception cases would deal with efforts designed to cover up the violation of an arms control treaty or other international agreement or norm. The purpose might be either to benefit from an adversary's continued adherence to the agreement without behaving in a reciprocal manner, or to avoid international criticism and pressure. This could provide a very structured objective for a strategic denial and deception program. There are many examples of this type of behavior by Germany in the 1920s and early 1930s.

Alternatively, the intense focus that accompanies the arms control verification effort may facilitate a country's attempt to appear stronger than it is—in essence, to appear to have obtained weapons in violation of an agreement when that is not the case. North Korea, for example, might be following such a policy to scare the United States and South Korea into believing that it might possess nuclear weapons. U.S. and South Korean fears of nuclear proliferation are one of North Korea's best bargaining chips.

Similarly, a nonstate actor (such as an insurgency or organized criminal group) might wish to appear less threatening than it is to reduce government efforts to combat it. Or, it may wish to deceive with respect to certain tactics or methods to avoid obloquy and the enhanced repression it could entail. The Sicilian Mafia may have had such a motive when it set out to convince law enforcement and the public that, whatever other crimes it might have committed, the Mafia would not, as a matter of principle, engage in drug dealing.

Requirements for the Conduct of Strategic Denial and Deception

What are the main requirements for successful deception? A few preliminary observations are made here to suggest some topics that should be kept in mind as the individual instances of strategic denial and deception are presented by the contributors to this volume.

Strategic Coherence

The deceiver must have some coherent strategic plan in mind to achieve his own objectives; otherwise, he cannot determine how he wishes the target to act. In peacetime, there must be an element of longevity to the plan, since implementing strategic deception takes time and the deceiver cannot change policy from week to week. In wartime, by contrast, events may move more quickly; a deception attempt may become moot once the actual attack has been made. The deceiving government or group must have the ability to forge a coherent policy that all departments, ministries or agencies within it can be required to follow. In addition, it may be necessary for other public statements or press articles to be consonant with official actions. This may constrain the ability of democracies to conduct most large-scale deception efforts outside of wartime except matters such as weapons development programs that can be kept secret even in peacetime.

Once the deceiver has decided on his own strategy, the deception operation must induce an opponent to take a complementary course of action. In wartime, this may be obvious. Having decided to land at Normandy, the Allies wanted the Germans to concentrate their forces somewhere else. In peacetime, a deceptive rising power might want its target to relax its defense efforts (on the assumption that the rising power is weaker than it really is) or, alternatively might want the target to be anxious to conclude an arms control agreement (on the assumption that the rising power is stronger than it really is.)

Understanding the Adversary

Having decided how it wishes its target to act, the deceiver must understand the target well enough to know what kinds of misinformation are likely to deceive and lead the opponent to act in the desired manner. In particular, the deceiver should understand the target's likely biases, and hence know what exploitable proclivities the target has toward self-deception. This may be the most important piece of information, since it is much easier to confirm opponents in a belief that they already possess than it is to convince them to change their minds. In any case, the deceiver must understand the target well enough to know what false pictures of the world will appear plausible, and whether or not they coincide with his existing preconceptions. This need to understand the opponent well for deception to succeed highlights the importance of good intelligence in deception operations.

In addition, the deceiver must have some sense of how the target, assuming he swallows the bait, will react. Thus, if a deceiver wishes to portray himself as weaker than he in fact is, he must have some confidence that the target will react as desired and will relax his vigilance rather than in some other manner deciding to take advantage of the deceiver's supposed weakness to demand concessions. As the deception proceeds, the deceiver must have some way of understanding how it is affecting the target's behavior and making any necessary adjustments. This highlights the importance of "feedback."

Organizational Infrastructure for Deception and Security Measures

Deception involves coordinating messages on many channels. Thus, once a deception effort has been decided upon, the group within the deceiver's government charged with implementing it must have the bureaucratic clout to orchestrate the deception effort, using other agencies of government as necessary. The lead group must itself have extremely good security, which implies that it should be relatively small. Information about the group must be carefully controlled and compartmented. A leak that a deception operation is under way could alert the target to the true situation. Again, this may be a much more difficult requirement to fulfill in peacetime than in wartime, especially for democratic governments. The deceiver also must be able to prevent the target from learning the true state of affairs; this implies generally good security measures concerning the relevant information. It also means that the deceiver must have good counterintelligence capabilities to be aware of what correct information the target may be able to obtain using his own intelligence sources and methods.

While the requirements for these conditions appears clear in theory, historical evidence suggests that some deceptions succeed even in their absence. Perhaps the best example is Germany's deception of the Soviet Union with respect to its 1941 attack on that country (BARBAROSSA). Although the Soviet Union received numerous true signals indicating an attack, Stalin was so convinced of his reading of Hitler's mind that he tended to dismiss the true signals as fakes. He sometimes attributed information indicating the Germans were about to attack to a plot launched by the devious British who would, of course, have wanted to embroil the Soviet Union and Germany in a conflict.

Channels to Reach the Adversary

The deceiver must have available some information channels to reach the adversary. These may include double agents, the adversary's own intelligence sources and methods, agents of influence, and overt sources. This implies a good knowledge of the target's intelligence collection efforts. To further the deception effort, it may be possible to create decoys and false radio signals that will be picked up by the adversary's technical intelligence collection.

The deceiver should have the imagination to develop new channels on an "ad hoc" basis, such as the British use of a corpse ("The Man Who Never Was") to impersonate a downed courier, carrying supposedly sensitive official documents.

To the extent that the deceiver has good security, the number of uncontrolled channels from which the target can receive information can be reduced. This gives the deceiver two important advantages: first, it increases the relative importance (to the target's analytic process) of those channels that the deceiver is exploiting to pass false signals. Second, it makes the target more eager to develop new channels, hence facilitating the deceiver's ability to dangle double agents and otherwise induce the target to establish, and believe in the validity of, new channels that are in fact subject to the deceiver's control and manipulation.

Feedback

The deceiver must have some way of knowing whether the target has taken the bait, and how the target assesses the misinformation he has acquired. This allows the deceiver to know which pieces of information have been missed by the target, which channels are considered by the target as particularly fruitful and trustworthy, and, most important, what overall picture the target is constructing on the basis of the information collected. Using this knowledge, the deceiver can adjust methods as necessary, and adapt cover stories to what the target appears inclined to believe. The deceiver can take advantage of chance events by reinforcing any misinterpretation of the situation that the target may have reached on his own from *unplanted* items of information that he has acquired.

Good feedback may be the single most important requirement for a successful deception operation. World War II deceptions by the Allies benefited greatly from the window on German thinking that their decryption successes gave them. But feedback need not involve an intelligence channel. The target's overt actions may be all that is needed to know whether a deception is succeeding. In particular, those attempting to conduct a peacetime deception operation against a democracy might be able to rely on the public statements of government officials and others to gauge how well their operation was working. Thus, for example, if the Soviet Union had been engaged in deception operations about weapons systems that were covered by arms control treaties, the constant public debate within the United States concerning Soviet compliance (as well as diplomatic discussions of compliance issues) would have provided useful feedback.

Notes

1.   In jokes, at least, one may attempt to create a false picture by telling *only* the truth, as in this classic:

Two merchants, fierce competitors, happen to meet one morning at their town's railway station. "Where are you going?" asks the first merchant. "To Minsk," replies the second. "Aha!" exclaims the first triumphantly, "You *say* you are going to Minsk so that I'll *think* you're going to Pinsk; but I happen to *know* you are going to Minsk, so, you see, it doesn't pay to lie to me."

Or, on a more elevated plane, this story from a medieval Arab philosopher, Alfarabi:

[A] certain abstemious ascetic was known for his probity, propriety, asceticism and worship, and became famous for this. He feared the tyrannical sovereign and decided to run away from his city. The sovereign's command went out that he was to be searched for and arrested wherever he was found. He could not leave from any one of the city's gates and was apprehensive lest he fall into the hands of the sovereign's men. So he went and found a dress that is worn by vagabonds, put it on, carried a cymbal in his hand, pretended to be drunk early at night, and came out to the gate of the city singing to the accompaniment of that cymbal of his. The gatekeeper said to him, "Who are you?" "I am so and so, the ascetic!" he said in a jocular vein. The gatekeeper thought he was poking fun at him and he did not interfere with him. So he saved himself without having lied in what he said.

Alfarabi, *Plato's Laws*, translated in *Medieval Political Philosophy: A Sourcebook*, Ralph Lerner and Muhsin Mahdi, *eds.* (New York: Free Press, 1963).

2.   This opens up the important question of the role of self-deception in the overall context of deception, which will be discussed more thematically below. Although deception is a hostile act on the part of the deceiver, it paradoxically depends on some "cooperation" by the target; in some cases, this can be merely intellectual (i.e., the target deduces the incorrect picture on the basis of the false signals he has received), but in others, there can be an emotive aspect as well (i.e., the target "wishes" in some sense to be deceived).

3.   As portrayed, for example, in the play *The Front Page* by Ben Hecht and Charles MacArthur (1928).

Commentary

Richards J. Heuer, Jr.

In the 1980s, some saw Soviet deception as pervasive, and as the key to understanding Soviet policy. In their view, arms control agreements were the product of Soviet duplicity, and U.S. intelligence agencies had become channels for Soviet disinformation. Others argued there was actually little evidence of successful Soviet deception, and that Soviet deception rarely had a significant impact on intelligence analysis. I recall these opposing views being expressed at two conferences at the time.

I left each of those events with the strong impression that the differences between the two sides were greatly exacerbated because each focused on a different type of deception. The debaters did not communicate very well, because people were not specific about what form of deception they were talking about. There seemed to be an assumption that if perception management and agents of influence were common, then disinformation through technical sensors also would be common.

When I taught the CIA training course in deception analysis back in the 1980s, I always emphasized at the start of each course that there is very little worth saying about deception in general. Virtually everything that one might conclude about deception—whether it is pervasive or uncommon, a major threat or not, how best to deal with it, even whether deception requires secrecy to be successful, all that and more—depends upon what kind of deception one is talking about.

Deception is an umbrella concept that covers many different activities. The first step in examining any new field of inquiry is to develop a taxonomy, a system for classification of phenomena within that field. Most of us learned in high school that modern biology began with Linnaeus' classification of animals by species, genus, and family. More recently, when scientists first began to study avalanches, they identified more than 120 different varieties of snow, each behaving differently under different conditions.

The many different varieties of deception also function differently under different conditions, and a taxonomy of deception would help sort that out. There are a number of conceptual categories we can use. Strategies of denial *and* deception can be thought of as separate types of operations. A distinction also has been made between strategic and tactical deception. We can distinguish military deception from political deception, or peacetime deception from wartime deception. We can further focus on the nature of the perpetrator: authoritative regimes versus democratic regimes and nonstate actors. All these categories of deception are useful. But from the intelligence community perspective, I believe the *most* useful distinction is based on the target of the deception. Deception aimed broadly at policymakers, opinion-makers (including intelligence analysts), and the general public on one side, is fundamentally different from deception aimed specifically at the intelligence collector or intelligence analyst.

Deception aimed at policymakers, opinion-makers, and the general public has sometimes been called perception management, although the term itself is no longer in vogue. It includes self-serving or deceptive statements by leaders or arms control negotiators, deceptive statements during diplomatic interchanges, placement of articles in newspapers or journals, forgeries, and agents-of-influence. By contrast, what I call intelligence deception is deception aimed at intelligence collectors and analysts that includes cover and concealment from technical sensors and feeding controlled information through human or technical collection channels.

The distinction between perception management and intelligence deception is useful for two reasons. First, it focuses attention on an issue of prime interest to intelligence analysts. Rightly or wrongly, analysts tend to think they can see through the various forms of perception management. Their main concern is whether the human and technical collection sources they assume to be valid are, in fact, being manipulated. Second, the distinction is important because perception management differs from intelligence deception in so many fundamental ways. Different channels are used to reach different targets. In some countries, perception management may be handled by the country's political or diplomatic organs rather than by the intelligence service. Perception management may be the most common form of deception in peacetime, while intelligence deception may dominate in wartime.

Within the Central Intelligence Agency, I understand there is some discussion over who should be responsible for deception analysis. Should it be the country analyst or a special deception analysis unit? That, too, depends upon what kind of deception one is talking about.

The country analyst should be able to deal with most forms of perception management. The country analyst should be trained to recognize circumstances when deception is either more or less likely and, therefore, when consultation with a deception specialist may be useful. By contrast, analysis of deception through intelligence channels requires specialized knowledge that is often not available to the country analyst. It requires information on our technical collection capabilities and what information about these capabilities may have been compromised to various foreign intelligence services. It also may require access to extremely sensitive counterintelligence operations. That is best handled by a special deception analysis unit.

The most important questions one asks about deception are different for perception management and intelligence deception. For perception management, there is no question about its existence, only its impact. What is its impact on U.S. policymakers? Does it also influence intelligence analysts or the intelligence product? I suspect that it does, in ways that may not be recognized by the analysts themselves.

For deception fed through intelligence channels, the key questions concern both its existence and its impact. Is deception of technical intelligence collection systems limited to passive cover and denial, or is there active manipulation of information fed through these systems? If limited to passive cover and denial, does it, nevertheless, bias the intelligence product? If there is active deception, through which channels, how, for what purpose, and with what success?

In the future, effective communication research may be facilitated if we can avoid the general term deception, and speak instead of the more specific forms of activity that fall under this general umbrella. When we make a generalization about deception, we should be careful to specify the type or types of deception to which it applies and the circumstances under which it applies.

Commentary

Nina Stewart

We still make artificial distinctions between what information we think is classified or "secret" and what is not. While this may be useful from a procedural standpoint, it is losing some degree of usefulness today. When you ask an agent from a foreign intelligence service about this classification distinction, the answer will likely be "We don't care what your classification is, we care about how useful the information is to us. Often what you think is unclassified is extremely useful to our government." When we talk about "denial" and what it means today, we have to include other kinds of information that need protection. Because of globalization and information technology, some of this information may be outside the strictly defined "classified" arena. Security programs increasingly have to deal with sensitive but unclassified information and proprietary data. This information might be about troop movements, health records, or breakthroughs in technology, and could be of strategic importance. We need to look at the value of the information from the standpoint of other nations, and adjust our training programs to detect denial and deception accordingly.

Abram Shulsky describes the difficulty in distinguishing strategic from tactical denial and deception efforts, a situation that is even more difficult in peacetime. He suggests that the best way to define what is strategic may be in terms of the intended target of the deception. Often, however, the intended target itself is not clear, especially where propaganda is used as a tool. Or the intended targets may be multiple officials at multiple levels of authority. Nonetheless, attempting to establish the target of a denial and deception campaign is an absolute necessity, despite how hard it may be to pinpoint key decision-makers with accuracy. In some cases, an analyst must role play, discern the various levels of targets likely influenced, and finally, use his or her own best judgment in identifying the targets of a denial and deception campaign.

Even using the given examples, there are instances where the lines blur between strategic and tactical deception. General Schwarzkopf's "Hail Mary" feint to divert Iraqi attention from the main axis of U.S. attack was briefed and cleared by the Joint Chiefs and the Commander-in-Chief. A double agent may be so high-ranking or important that his *bona fides* may be of personal interest to the National Security Advisor. Is this, in and of itself, a strategic deception? What if the fact of the deception itself was of such magnitude that it portrayed a condition of the target country? With the trend toward nonstate actors establishing new, heretofore unseen complex alliances, the distinction blurs further. For example, the *Aum Shinrikiyo* sarin gas attack in Japan might be considered strategic because their motivations were allegedly global.

Shulsky aptly describes the different channels whereby information reaches an audience, and how much more complex it is today in industrial democracies to discern the paths this information takes. Cross-border travel and communication systems have become ubiquitous, but global business relationships and alliances are redefining and shaping paths as well. These "mini global economies" make it difficult to determine motivations, determine origins, and trace authenticity in denial and deception operations. The proliferation of business and trade contacts puts great pressure on analysts to track the fine details of industry in ways not absolutely necessary before.

The long-running Cuban double-agent program against the United States reportedly is one example of how effective a country can be in controlling channels. In some instances, however, limiting channels might also work against the deceiving country. If only one or two channels of communication are open, and relations between the two countries are bad, one might argue that even legitimate assets have no chance of effective communication because the target country might become reluctant, even paranoid, about accepting any channels of information from the deceiving country.

Few would dispute Shulsky's assertion that "the mere transaction of diplomatic business implies a certain willingness to believe" between diplomats, even when the fundamental hostility of a government is obvious. "Clientitus" is a real danger in the diplomatic corps. The use of deception via this channel, however, may be difficult to sustain over time. Once a target feels abused, relations can be ruined for some time, and would-be deceivers have to calculate the probability that efforts to exploit diplomatic contacts will be discovered into their calculations.

The use of separate channels for diplomacy, as well as for other high-level government contacts, does add to the deception analyst's burden when it comes to detecting deception. Senior officials of every U.S. administration often bypass intelligence analysts, believing that they have better insights into the country in question. Often, however, these high-level communications—if important and disputatious enough—tend to get aired in national security or intelligence community forums. If this occurs, these private communications will be weighed against other information collected through other channels. This is especially true where disputes arise among government officials about the "meaning" of a country's actions.

The deduction made is that counterdeception analysts in the intelligence community either need access to diplomatic channels or that the National Security Council (NSC) and State Department analysts need to develop their own counterdeception skills. NSC officials have argued before, however, that counterdeception analysts are not the only ones capable of detecting deception. State Department officials point out that separate channels could, in some instances, enhance counterdeception detection simply by having a variety of eyes interpreting data obtained from different information channels.

As Shulsky noted, much has been written about the formation of "virtual communities" of similarly minded people who are located throughout the world. These virtual communities can spread misinformation on a grand scale. The same information technologies available to us with the Internet potentially will enable new counterdeception and information security tools as well. For example, with more Internet commerce comes greater pressure to develop information security tools that before had few clients and, thus, few producers. Now, more businesses need information assurance, such tools as verification, intrusion detection, and authentication. New collaboration realms and network security advances are already garnering a larger market share, and will become far more prevalent in the future. Big information technology firms are recognizing this trend and actively pursuing the purchase of start-up companies specializing in state-of-the-art information security tools. Additionally, short-range goals such as voting via the Internet and virtual banking are driving advances in Internet security services and technology.

The denial and deception portfolio has received varying levels of attention in past years, resulting in a few peaks and a number of valleys for those committed to its analysis. Often, it has been held hostage to the preferences of individuals. In the future, the issues surrounding denial and deception need long-term sustained attention. This, in turn, implies that denial and deception analysis needs to find an institutional home within a well-established intelligence patron and be provided with funding to sustain a viable training and awareness program. Whether it remains a separate discipline or becomes a part of every analytic branch is a separate question. There are pros and cons to both approaches. My preference is for a little of each approach. Denial and deception analysts might come to resemble counterintelligence professionals. A separate career track might be developed for dedicated D&D experts, but education about denial and deception for all intelligence analysts could be provided throughout their careers. Clearly, D&D analysts need to have better tools in their toolbox to measure, analyze, and forewarn, and this should be a focus of research and development.

3

Conditions Making for Success and Failure of Denial and Deception: Authoritarian and Transition Regimes

Bart Whaley

The Use and Abuse of Historical Case Studies

Political-military deception is a psychological process that back dates to when human cortexes first turned their thoughts to politics and war. Deception also is as unchanging as human nature, modified only by the technological means used to transmit or detect deceptive messages. Consequently, historical case studies can teach us almost as much about how to deceive as can any current operation. In practice, the advantage of historical examples is that they tend to offer nearly complete and accurate data about how the deceivers planned and carried out their operations and how the intended victims perceived and reacted to them.

Most of the little deception theory that we have proceeds from anecdotal evidence drawing on individual analysts' casual recollections of a few case examples that happened to be handy. Any theories or generalizations drawn from this procedure are, at best, highly suspect. When deception theory is weak, we risk drawing misleading conclusions from case examples, whether historical or current.

Useful military deception theory and valid general statements must be based on at least a fairly good database. The first was the Liddell-Hart database of 1929, which drew on a survey of 280 military campaigns from antiquity to 1914. The second study with any pretension to statistical validity was the Whaley database of 1969 of 168 battles from sixteen wars during the period from 1914 through 1968.

My raw data, analyses, and extensive conclusions, titled *Stratagem: Deception and Surprise in War,* were published at MIT in 1969 in nearly 1,000 pages. (Later drafts expanded the number of cases to some 230 without any substantial changes in results.)

Deception and Its Detection in Closed and Transitional versus Free Societies

The distinctions between closed authoritarian and free democratic states are useful when considering the practice of strategic deception, but not absolute. Overlaps exist. Even the most repressive of states, such as Stalin's Russia, Hitler's Germany, Mao's China, or Saddam Hussein's Iraq, has small areas of freedom. Examples include the tiny but influential "*samizdat*" free press in the old Soviet Union, the various "Resistance" movements in Nazi Germany, Mao's brief "Let a Hundred Flowers Bloom" policy, and the Kurds in Iraq.

Similarly, even the most advanced democracies such as the United States and Great Britain have certain institutions and groups that operate more or less along authoritarian lines. For example, censorship of the media during World War II worked almost as well in Britain and America as it did in Germany, Russia, and Japan. Thus, the ultimate distinction that must be made in considering deception is between the open subsystem and the closed subsystem that coexist within all states. A case in point is the highly successful covert and illegal German rearmament between 1919 and 1933 while the democratic Weimar Republic was in power. After Adolph Hitler became Reichschancellor in that latter year he merely continued the existing policy of secret rearmament until 1935. At that point he unilaterally abrogated the Versailles Treaty and openly displayed the results of the previously hidden military developments.

Case Examples

The following case examples have been selected for their exceptional characteristics rather than their typical ones. Thus, they exemplify the outer limits of deception operations as practiced in closed societies.

1. German Covert Rearmament and Public Bluff, 1919-1939[1]

The German example is given in more detail than the others because it has the greatest relevance for contemporary problems, as we will see when comparing it with the case of Iraq.

Disarmament, 1918-1920. From 1918 until 1920, Germany was forcibly disarmed. Then, in January 1920, the Armistice was superseded by the Versailles Treaty. The formal constraints on German war potential were severe. The right bank of the Rhine was demilitarized. The strategic Kiel Canal and several rivers were internationalized. All overseas colonies were forfeit. Chunks of German territory were ceded to France, Belgium, and Poland. The Saar, Danzig, and Memel were placed under League of Nations supervision. In addition, Germany was to pay huge reparations, a sum later set at $33 billion.

The German military was emasculated, conscription forbidden. The Army was limited to 100,000 troops (4,000 officers and 96,000 men). To prevent the build-up of a reserve, officers had to sign on for twenty-five years, and enlisted men for twelve. The Army was denied tanks, heavy artillery, and poison gas. The Great General Staff was abolished and staff colleges and military academies closed. The Army was forbidden to have a field command echelon higher than that of a corps. The Flying Corps was abolished and aircraft prohibited.

The Navy was limited to 15,000 sailors (1,500 officers and 13,500 ratings). It was left with obsolete warships, and was forbidden to build replacements of more than 10,000 tons. Nor could the Navy have aircraft, or possess or build submarines. All production or importation of arms was prohibited, as well as the sending of military missions abroad. Even police were regulated, the national police force being restricted to 150,000, all of whom were to be lifetime employees to prevent the building even of police reserve units.

Germany was not trusted to keep the solemn Treaty provisions that applied to disarmament. As a defeated nation, she was required to accept on-site inspection to assure compliance. The official body set up for this purpose was the Inter-Allied Control Commission, established in September 1919 under the presidency of General Charles Nollet. The Control Commission comprised representatives of Great Britain, France, Italy, Belgium, and Japan. It reported to and received higher policy direction from the specially created Allied Conference of Ambassadors that met irregularly in France. At the outset it numbered 373 professional military officers. This already impressive number was increased in 1920 to 383 officers and 737 men. (However, in the summer of 1921, the staff was reduced by almost half, leaving only 174 officers and 400 men.) Nor were these mere desk-bound bureaucrats: more than 800 on-site inspections, for example, were conducted in a six-week period in September/October 1924 alone.

The Control Commission settled into Berlin's palatial Hotel Adlon. Headquarters staff comprised nine senior officers: four French, two British, one Italian, one Belgian, and a Japanese colonel. The three subordinate echelons had responsibility for oversight, respectively, of armaments, personnel, and fortifications. These echelons worked through twenty-two district commands covering all of Germany. Each district command was weighted in personnel: eleven for armaments, eight for personnel, and three for fortifications. It was a simple, hierarchical structure, functionally well-suited to its mission.

Unfortunately, the Control Commission committed a major strategic political error at the very outset of its work, a blunder that was recognized and admitted by Generals Nollet, Morgan and their colleagues, only when it was too late to reverse. This self-made trap was their own demand that the Germans provide a liaison committee to coordinate the disarmament process. The *Reichswehr* was astounded. It had assumed that the Control Commission would simply sweep into Germany in force, arbitrarily and ruthlessly confiscating, destroying, and punishing any infractions of its orders. Instead, the *Reichswehr* was being *asked* to comply with military dictates and was handed the quite unexpected opportunity to appoint what, from its standpoint, would be a committee of obstruction. Accordingly, the German Defense Ministry created the Army Peace Commission *(Heeresfriedenskommission)*. Prussian General von Cramon, a vehement opponent of the *Versaillesdiklat* in all its onerous aspects, was carefully selected to be its head. At the very first joint meeting with the Control Commission on 29 January 1920, Cramon demonstrated his intention that liaison did not mean cooperation, but rather power games, obfuscation, and general obstruction.

The key to German rearmament was the arms industry, and the key to the German arms industry was the giant industrial empire of Krupp. The Allies, fully aware of its crucial role, had ordered the destruction of Krupp's heavy arms production lines. Legal arms production was sharply restricted in numbers and closely watched by the Control Commission. Thus, Krupp was limited in 1921 to a single type of gun and could produce only four of these each year. Its production of armor plate, ammunition hoists, gun mountings, and cannons for the Navy was limited to replacement of worn-out components in obsolescent warships.

To survive Krupp diversified, introducing peacetime lines that ranged from baby carriages and typewriters through motor scooters and optical instruments, up to such heavy gear as dredgers, agricultural machinery, and locomotives. The government placed orders and generously covered some of the deficits. The more skilled and trusted engineers and workers of Essen were kept on or transferred to subsidiary plants throughout Germany and the world, ready for the day when Krupp could return to making arms.

Both the government and the Reichswehr applauded this effort. Thus, immediately after the Armistice, the Army Chief, General von Seeckt, recognized that "There is only one way in which we will be able to provide for the arming of great masses of troops [and that is to make] suitable arrangements with the industrialists of the nation."

Personal initiative combined with discreet government support to preserve Fokker's famous aircraft factory. His superb F-7 biplane fighter was the only category of German equipment singled out by name in the Versailles Treaty for destruction. Thus forewarned, Tony Fokker immediately began plotting to save his fortune and his factory. His plan was to smuggle them out of Germany to his native Holland. His cash horde (nearly a quarter of his liquid assets) was eventually brought out in two consignments; one by sailboat and the other by rail in a decrepit suitcase concealed among privileged foreign diplomatic baggage. But rescuing the contents of his doomed Fokker-Flugzeugwerke mbH at Schwerin in northern Germany was another matter.

In a race against time and the Control Commission inspectors in 1920, Fokker personally supervised the removal and concealment of over half his factory inventory in numerous remote barns, cellars, stables, and sheds scattered over the surrounding countryside. The remaining planes, parts and equipment were left on open display for the Allied inspection team to find when they arrived at the factory. The inspecting officers did not realize they had been outwitted.

Fokker's next problem was to get this large inventory out of Germany. For that, he needed export licenses and transportation. Accordingly, his export manager, F. W. Seekatz, visited the Trade

Ministry in Berlin. There he argued frankly that if this large stock of military aviation were transferred to Holland, it would be in a country that could be trusted to remain neutral. Germany would get much-needed licensing fees and the Allies would be thwarted. The Trade Ministry officials agreed and quietly handed over export permits for nearly a half-million dollar's worth of material.

The transportation scheme was suggested, planned and arranged by Fokker's transportation department chief, Wilhelm Hahn. He won cooperation from the state railway by a mix of appeals to patriotism, reminders of past favors and much outright bribery. Nearly a sixth of the hidden inventory was collected in trucks by trusted Fokker workers and driven to the waiting railway freight cars.

With Hahn aboard, the train pulled out of the siding at Schwerin on the first stage of its 350-mile journey to Holland. The train was exactly sixty cars long, a length suggested by the bribed German railway customs officials who helpfully pointed out that they could then plausibly pass it directly through to Holland. Because the sidings at the frontier town of Saltzbergen could accommodate a maximum of only forty cars, to hold up Hahn's extra long train would block the main line. Other careful arrangements were made to avoid delays so that no unwitting railway or customs official would have a chance to investigate. As the train neared Saltzbergen station, a report reached the joint Allied-German border patrol that a smuggling attempt was underway, but at a station further down the border. The report was true, but a ruse, nevertheless, as Hahn had arranged for a diversionary party to lay a false trail. This simple diversion worked and the train crossed the border unchallenged.

In the next five weeks, five more trains managed to move the bulk of Fokker's hidden equipment. The precious, stripped-down airplane fuselages were carried on some thirty open flatcars in the last train; Fokker had not previously dared risk sending airframes because of their distinctive shape. Although camouflaged with wooden boards "and metal tubing and covered with tarpaulin," the tarpaulins were boldly marked "Fokker-Flugzeugwerke" and "Schwerin," for Hahn had run out of unmarked covers. Even so, this last shipment got through without unwanted notice.

The entire operation, from initial planning to final delivery, had taken less than seven weeks. Hahn had managed to smuggle out some 350 railway carloads carrying an amazing total of 220 airplanes (including 120 of the proscribed D-7 fighters), more than 400 engines and considerable other material worth nearly $8 million. In all, Tony Fokker had salvaged enough cash and goods to reopen business in Holland as Nederlandische Vliegtuigenfabriek N.V., ready to play a continuing role in Germany's efforts to evade the *Versaillesdiktat.*

Throughout the 1920s, Germany was substantially disarmed. But, if the letter of Versailles was being more or less observed, the intent was not. The potential for rapid rearmament was present and growing and so was the desire for it. The desire to rearm was a common bond between German politicians, soldiers and industrialists. The political leaders resented the constraints placed on their power. The senior officers of the *Reichswehr* saw a need for an Army strong enough to back German foreign policy. The industrialist heads of Krupp, Stinnes, and I.G. Farben cherished continuing profits. And these purely professional desires and goals were complemented in no small measure by simple patriotism.

The various chancellors, chiefs of the *Reichswehr,* and captains of industry had various motives for their desire to see a rearmed nation-state. Some, such as General von Seeckt, realistically feared aggression by Germany's new eastern neighbor, Poland. Others, such as industrialist Gustav Krupp von Bohlen, deeply resented a Treaty that he believed was designed to keep "the German people...enslaved forever." Still others saw armaments variously as profits, national honor, a means to regain the surrendered German lands (perhaps even the colonies), and a renewed chance to gain predominance in Germany and the world. But whatever their separate motives, all shared the slogan "military freedom" (*Wehrfreiheit).* Whatever its final purpose, all saw as its instrument a strong German Army and not the pathetic ersatz one of the detested *Versaillesdiktat.* This shared desire of 1919-20 quickly led to secret collaboration to evade the Treaty and rearm. This goal was so strongly held that it even overrode personal animosities (such as that between the cold aristocrat Seeckt and the outgoing commoner Stresemann) and the bitter infighting of bureaucracies (such as the continuing power competition between the *Reichswehr* and the Foreign Office).

Covert Arms Evasion, 1920-1926. The period of disarmament from 1918 to 1919 was followed by one of arms control evasion. Throughout this new period, which lasted from 1920 to 1926, evasion was covert because it coincided with the presence of the large Inter-Allied Control Commission with its right of on-site inspection. The Chief *(Chef)* of the *Reichswehr* was fifty-four-year-old Colonel-General Hans von Seeckt. Seeckt set out to circumvent Treaty limitations in every way possible. The central control of the Imperial Army, the Great General Staff, had been abolished by the fiat of Versailles (Article 160) and was not to be reconstructed in any form. General von Seeckt neatly evaded this requirement in the low profile guise of the Troops Office *(Truppenamt)*, ostensibly charged with overseeing *Reichswehr* organizational affairs. The *Truppenamt* had four sections: T-1, operations; T-2, organization; T-3, foreign armies; and T-4, training. Among those subsequently prominent officers who received their early general staff experience in this disguised General Staff, were Werner von Blomberg (later War Minister), Colonel Freiherr von Fritsch (later Commander in Chief of the Army), Colonel Walther von Brauchitsch (who also became Commander in Chief of the Army), and Colonel Wilhelm Keitel (later Chief of Hitler's Supreme Command). Conscientious observance of the twelve- and twenty-five-year-old enlistment requirements (for officers and enlisted men, respectively) would have meant the Army could not even begin to build a trained reserve until after 1932, and even then only with troops all over thirty years old and officers over forty-three. But the *Reichswehr* was able to accumulate a small but forbidden reserve quickly by simply taking in a number of short-term enlistment recruits, the so-called *Zeitfreiwillige.*

Padding extended even to the police. The national police force exceeded the 150,000-man limit stipulated by the Allies. The police also introduced semi-military training and accumulated a trained reserve by adopting the *Reichswehr's* twelve-year enrollment policy in the face of an Allied lifetime employment requirement intended precisely to prevent development of a police reserve. Moreover, they managed to accumulate 25,000 of their forces in barracks, as virtual light-infantry ready-response units. The Allies were aware of all these measures. They complained, but the German government fought a successful delaying battle of negotiation.

The *Reichswehr* was allowed an Intelligence Service of sorts. The Versailles Treaty did not explicitly prohibit it; indeed, the Treaty made no mention of the subject. Upon the Armistice, Section IIIb became the Intelligence Branch of the caretaker General Staff. Following general demobilization, it was reduced to an Intelligence Group. Colonel Nicolai, its head, was dumped into permanent leave status and replaced in 1919 by IIIb veteran Major Friedrich Gempp. Following the Treaty of Versailles, Gempp's unit simply followed the Great General Staff into its camouflaged form within the Troops Office. For similar reasons of disguise, the Intelligence Office was renamed the *Abwehrabteilung* (Defense Section) or, for short, *Abwehr.*

Gempp's tiny *Abwehr* had only four officers. Initially it developed intelligence on the Russian civil war and Russo-Polish wars then raging uncomfortably close to Germany's eastern frontier. It went on to develop espionage networks, presumably against the main enemy, France.

Although the Versailles Treaty explicitly permitted the signals detachment of each *Reichswehr* division to include a radio intercept unit, the Control Commission prohibited any cryptanalytic capability. At the beginning of 1919, however, twenty-four-year-old ex-Lieutenant Erich Buschenhagen, who had worked in the Army radio intercept service during the Great War, went ahead on his own to set up a small intercept intelligence unit for one of the Free Corps in Berlin. He called his unit the "Volunteer Evaluation Office" and quietly installed it on the Friedrichstrasse. In the beginning, it merely translated plaintext intercepts from French, British, American, and Russian sources as well as press reports sent by radio. But by May, after Buschenhagen had acquired his first few cryptanalysts, the unit was distributing some decodes, at least of Russian material. In February 1920, his twelve-man team was absorbed into the *Abwehr* as the Cipher Center *(Chieffrierstelle),* moving into the Army headquarters building on the Bendlerstrasse. Then, avoiding Control Commission inspectors just in time, the Cipher Center moved again to nearby Grunewald where it disguised itself as a newspaper translation and study group.

In 1921 the *Reichswehr* secretly ordered expansion of the intercept service *(Horchdienst),* and assigned it to the Cipher Center. By late 1925 when Buschenhagen was transferred elsewhere, the Cipher Center had expanded to a staff of thirty-two, plus twenty radiomen operating six radio interception posts, three or four of whose receivers were being monitored around the clock.

The *Reichswehr* supplemented its limit on troops by secretly equipping or funding several of the many private paramilitary organizations that sprang up in the politically troubled times immediately following the Armistice. These groups were lightly armed to be sure, but soldiers nevertheless. Seeckt himself made only the narrow distinction between "soldiers" and "*Reichswehr* soldiers."

The secret transfer of large quantities of arms, equipment and ammunition from the *Reichswehr* to the paramilitaries was made possible by the long interval of fifteen months between the time when the provisional *Reichswehr* learned of the 100,000-troop limit in the Versailles Treaty and the deadline for its implementation. The Allied Supreme Council originally intended to grant the provisional *Reichswehr* only three months (until summer 1919) to cut down to 100,000 troops and hand over its surplus war material, but the German delegates at the Treaty negotiations raised the quite real bogey that such speed risked a civil war in which a defenseless Weimar Republic could easily be swept away by Bolshevism. The British military delegation accepted this argument and urged it on the reluctant French, who yielded the point in the Supreme Council. Accordingly, the final Treaty provisions permitted the provisional *Reichswehr* to demobilize by stages, keeping 200,000 until 10 April 1920 (Article 163), that is, until three months after the Treaty went into effect. But this Article conflicted with another (Article 160) that set a deadline of 31 March 1920 for the *Reichswehr* to cut back to its final quota of 100,000. To resolve this dilemma, the Supreme Council, on 19 February 1920, extended the deadline to 19 April for the 200,000 quota and to 10 July for the 100,000 quota. The overall effect of putting off these deadlines meant that the original summer 1919 deadline for reduction to the 100,000 figure was delayed until the following summer. The *Reichswehr* was quick to take advantage of this windfall to conceal and transfer material to the paramilitaries in proportion as it gradually reduced its own force.

The Allies rejected the German request to retain a single operational air squadron and eight airfields for internal security purposes and required the disbanding of the seven police air patrol squadrons established in 1919 by the provincial government. The Kaiser's Flying Corps had been abolished in 1920 by an ostensibly stern order of General von Seeckt, but Seeckt never intended that the Flying Corps die, only disappear, scattered and concealed in various guises until a time when it would be safe and politic to reconstitute it.

The first order of business was to maintain a hidden reserve of trained pilots, aircrew, and ground staff. The *Reichswehr* itself sheltered 120 former Army and twenty Navy officer pilots, although it proved much more difficult to keep together the NCOs and ground personnel. The second order of business was to maintain a viable aviation industry and keep it occupied with military research and development. Seeckt also saw to it that his secret General Staff included an Aviation Staff, which was disguised as the Army Command Inspectorate of Weapons Schools. The Inspectorate was headed by Captain (later General) Helmut Wilberg, the very same air officer who had drafted Seeckt's order abolishing the Flying Corps.

The aircraft construction moratorium and Control Commission depredations combined to close most of Germany's thirty-five aircraft companies and twenty airplane engine manufacturers. When the moratorium was belatedly lifted in 1921, only four aircraft companies had survived: Junkers, Heinkel, Albatross, and Dornier. In 1922 Dr. Adolf Rohrbach opened the Rohrbach Metal Aircraft Company in Berlin with private finance and government subsidies. A branch office was established in Copenhagen, specifically to evade the Control Commission.

Many of the German airplane designers welcomed their secret orders from the *Reichswehr* as part of a battle of wits as well as profits. Adolf Rohrbach was one. Ernst Heinkel was another. Thus, Heinkel recalled that fulfilling a 1923 order from Major Kurt Student to build his first military plane involved "an extremely risky game of hide-and-seek with the Allied Control Commission .., and I am bound to admit that it was a game that was bound to appeal strongly to a man who was given to taking risks." To build his reconnaissance plane (the HD-17) and later military prototypes, Heinkel rented a workshop hangar outside his regular factory at Warnemünde. The Allied Control Commission inspectors only saw this hangar empty, because hours before each inspection, all aircraft and components were loaded onto trucks and driven to hidden spots on the heath or among nearby sand dunes.

During the 1923 Franco-German crisis in the Ruhr, the angered German government considered the possibility of military resistance to the threatened French occupation of the Ruhr. Accordingly, Captain Wilberg of the *Reichswehr's* covert air staff placed an immediate secret order for 100 fighter planes with the pro-German Fokker aircraft firm in Holland. By the time they were ready for delivery, the crisis had passed (and the German government had decided against any military resistance). Fokker sold half these planes to Rumania, but the other fifty units eventually were shipped in 1925, via Stettin and Leningrad, to the secret German air base established in Russia the previous year.

The Ruhr Crisis also prompted the Defense Ministry's naval department to order ten seaplane fighters for the Navy. The components were designed and built at Heinkel's factory at Warnemünde, then shipped to Sweden for assembly. There, the ten Heinkel He-1 seaplanes received their British-built Rolls-Royce Eagle IX engines and were test flown with Swedish markings before being packed in enormous crates and stored in bond by a Stockholm harbor warehouse firm owned by ex-German Navy Commander Bücker.

The German commercial airlines merged, at the beginning of 1926, to become the state controlled monopoly airline Deutsche Lufthansa. Prompted by General von Seeckt, the *Reichswehr* immediately began to blend in the desired military component. World War I pilot Erhard Milch became managing director and, working closely with the *Reichswehr,* soon built up a small reserve of combat airmen by including military instruction in Lufthansa's training program.

Some of the more restrictive provisions of the Versailles Treaty, as they applied to aircraft, were modified in the Pact of Paris of 1926. This kept the absolute ban on military aviation, but allowed the German aircraft industry to build, under strict inspection, limited numbers of "aircraft conforming to the aeronautical performance of current types of fighter aircraft" for use exclusively for flying competition and record-breaking. This, of course, was ideal for the *Reichswehr* because it permitted the public design, building and testing of the highest performance aircraft. Of course, some camouflage was still needed, but only to hide the more obvious signs of the intended military use of these aircraft. Thus, the Navy's Seaplane Experimental Station was concealed within the civilian German Airlines Federation.

Under this provision, Willy Messerschmidt developed his Bf-108 "sporting monoplane," which was the immediate forerunner of the superb Bf-109 fighter of World War II. Hugo Junkers developed and sold large numbers of his Ju-52 trimotor that was designed as a bomber but went on to become the workhorse transport of the *Luftwaffe*. Ernst Heinkel introduced his high-speed, slim and beautiful He-70 as a four-passenger mail carrier. It had been designed, however, as a two-seater military reconnaissance and bomber plane, the forerunner of the He-111 medium bomber that would later smash Guernica and London.

The Pact of Paris further relaxed the Versailles Treaty to let the *Reichswehr* and Navy have a total of six officers receive flying instruction and serve as airmen. The Defense Ministry immediately took advantage of this opening to pad out the aviation ranks by secretly ordering that some forty officer candidates per year receive flight training *prior* to call-up.

The relaxation of restrictions on commercial aircraft and sports planes after 1926 had the equally important side benefit of permitting the open training of large numbers of pilots. The rudiments of flight were taught to large numbers of young men who now flocked to join glider clubs and graduated to the growing numbers of civilian flying schools. At least six of these included camouflaged military training facilities operated by the *Reichswehr*. All fully trained pilots and observers were then grouped together in so-called Publicity or Advertising Squadrons *(Reklamestaffein)* that, in addition to hiring out their services for commercial skywriting and advertising, also helped out at *Reichswehr* maneuvers by target marking, reconnaissance, and liaison. These Advertising Squadrons were the first truly operational units of the new German air force. By 1933, the *Reichswehr* had around 550 fully trained pilots, ready to man the air staffs and regular formations that would soon be established.

Although the successive Chiefs of the Treaty Navy lacked Seeckt's single-minded loathing for the *Versaillesdikt*, the Navy did manage similar, if smaller-scale, evasions. It lightly padded the 15,000-sailor limit and built a forbidden reserve by taking short-term volunteers and by integrating Naval organizations into "civilian" ones. It also created secret arsenals and used proscribed weapons. Evasion initially involved duping the national legislators during the annual naval budget fight in the Reichstag. The ruse used was vastly to overcharge for all items of equipment. This deceit was possible only with the collusion of the successive Weimar chancellors, defense ministers and certain other key senior government officials. The surplus obtained was then used to fund the Navy's numerous illegal projects.

Holland was the main haven for German U-boat development during the early 1920s. This took place in a Krupp subsidiary, the Siderius-owned shipyard of Ingenieur-Kantoor voor Scheepsbouw (I.v.S.) in The Hague, and was worked out jointly by Krupp, von Seeckt, and Admiral Behncke, the Chief of the German Navy. Krupp initially sent thirty naval architects and engineers, accompanied by two German navy officers, to Holland to start production. I.v.S. sold submarine plans to Japan, Spain, Finland, Turkey, and Holland itself. Additional German naval officers and marine engineers passed through The Hague to supervise construction in these other countries. Production began in Finland on the prototype of the German 250-ton submarines (U-1 to U-24) that would be used in World War II. Simultaneously, I.v.S. negotiated a secret contract with Spanish dictator Primo de Rivera to construct in Cadiz a 740-ton U-boat that became the prototype for the World War II flag subs, U-25 and U-26. Also Spain, Turkey, and Finland let German commanders and crews put the submarines through their sea trials. This, as admitted later, permitted "the training of camouflaged German naval personnel without diplomatic unpleasantness for the Reich."

Work in the shipyards of Finland, Holland, and Spain had one even more remarkable and direct effect on the future German submarine fleet. By 1934, the prefabricated frames and parts for no less than twelve U-boats had been smuggled into the German naval base at Kiel, awaiting only the order to commence assembly.

The Navy also managed to build a small air arm. It succeeded in purchasing six wartime seaplanes (Friedrichshaven FF-49s) before they could be seized by the Allies as reparations. For cover purposes they were maintained and serviced by the private air transport company of Aero-Lloyd (later Severa) at Kiel and Norderney. They were used by the Navy for anti-aircraft gunnery practice, camouflage exercises, target towing and pilot training. The last of these ancient airplanes remained in service until 1934. From 1924 on, in great secrecy, the few former Great War naval pilots still in the Navy were able to take refresher flight training with Aerosport Company at Warnemünde.

The Versailles Treaty (Article 171) flatly prohibited tanks and, except for police use, armored cars as well. Consequently, the *Reichswehr* ostensibly contented itself with simulated tanks in its maneuvers—to the vast amusement of the foreign press, which featured photos and descriptions of these wood, canvas, and cardboard makeshifts. The undercover reality was less comical, as the *Reichswehr* and German industry were busily designing, building, and testing tanks and armored cars throughout this period.

The few armored cars permitted to the German police were of several makes but all of similar (and antiquated) design. Then the Boulogne Note of 23 July 1920 permitted an increase in number to 150 armored cars for police use and allowed a total of 105 for the *Reichswehr*, fifteen for each motor transport battalion attached to each of the seven infantry divisions. Vehicle design was to be approved by the Control Commission and construction was to be subject to their inspection. These provisions insured that the Daimler and Erhardt models of 1919-21 were obsolete when built. In any event, the Germans did not cheat in the armored car category until after the withdrawal of the Control Commission in early 1927.

Although Seeckt was committed to mobile warfare, he favored cavalry over armor to achieve mobility for German land forces. Still, he and the *Truppenamt* gave limited support to mechanized development, perhaps simply because it was forbidden. Accordingly, as early as 1919, the *Truppenamt* established a small special section to study armored warfare. By 1921 the Inspectorate of Motorized Troops coordinated and directed all mechanized units, including the shadow tank forces.

The pioneering work by Joseph Vollmer, Germany's only significant designer and manufacturer of tanks during the Great War, and that of the Krupp designers were summed up in a later Krupp memo: "With the exception of the hydraulic safety switch, the basic principles of armament and turret design for tanks had already been worked out in 1926." In that same year a German engineer named Ernst Kniepkamp joined the *Heereswaffenamt* for the express purpose of coordinating the various industrial firms engaged in secret armored research and development (R&D).

Designs now gave way to prototype production and the scene shifted to Russia where rigorous field testing could take place behind a curtain of secrecy. The site was the Red Army's tank center at Kazan. After a reconnaissance there by a German officer in 1922, at the very beginning of the Russo-German military collaboration, German technicians were permanently stationed at Kazan from 1926 on. Beginning in 1927, several types of tanks and armored cars were tested there.

Secret orders were placed with German industry in 1926 for the production of tank and armored car prototypes. Ford and Opel were explicitly excluded as potential manufacturers because their American affiliations were thought to make them too insecure for such a delicate undertaking. Production began in earnest and many of these prototypes were immediately smuggled to Kazan for their equally secret testing. First off the mark was Daimler-Benz in 1927 with its so-called Grosstraktor 11 (Heavy Tractor), a "concealed purpose" name to disguise this heavy tank as a hunk of agricultural machinery. Designed by Dr. Ferdinand Porsche, the tank was noteworthy for its large 75mm turret-mounted gun. Rheinmetall and Krupp were next, in 1928, with their VK.3 1 "Light Tractors" of 9.5 tons mounting a 37mm gun in a Swedish-type turret.

Armored cars were produced in the same period. Daimler-Benz Bussing and Magirus entered the field first in 1927. Maffei joined the next year, BMW in 1929, Rheinmetall in 1932 and Demag in 1934. (Krupp did not enter the armored car race until 1936.)

The Swedish Army collaborated secretly with the German covert General Staff on tank development just as it had earlier with aircraft. Thus, in 1929, at the age of forty, Major Heinz Guderian, now with the Transport Section of the Operations Department of the *Truppenamt,* drove his first tank as a guest of the Swedish Army's lone tank company. Appropriately, his machine was one of Vollmer's smuggled ex-German alias M-21s.

As Sweden had proved a safe and discreet haven for German rearmament, Krupp acquired a second dummy company there in addition to its Bofors cannon subsidiary. The new Krupp affiliate was the old machinery firm of A.B. Landsverk, located at Landskrona in southern Sweden. It produced its first tank design by 1929 and its first production tank, the fine 11.5 ton L-10 light tank with a 37mm gun, appeared in 1931 and entered Swedish service in 1934. A succession of excellent tank and armored car models flowed from Landsverk which now dominated Sweden's armored vehicle industry. These models foreshadowed several of the features that would later appear in the tanks of Germany and Russia, clear proof of the fruitful collaborative German-Russo-Swedish cross-fertilization

The Control Commission ended its long surveillance of the Krupp works when it withdrew from Essen in March 1926. Foreign Minister Stresemann now pressed hard for the withdrawal of the Control

Commission from all Germany. His timing was excellent for his French and British counterparts, Aristide Briand and Austin Chamberlain, both welcomed an accommodation. They were impatient with the intelligence from their military advisors that Germany was violating numerous points of disarmament. Briand declared he "had no intention of bothering with such petty detail"; he wanted to focus only on the larger issues. Stresemann deliberately dragged out these negotiations to avoid as many concessions as possible. His delaying strategy succeeded. On 11 December, Briand and Chamberlain decided to withdraw the Control Commission the following month, despite their own ambassadors' reports the previous day that Germany was not meeting its disarmament obligations.

On 31 January 1927, as scheduled, the Inter-Allied Military Control Commission was withdrawn from Germany. The Commission's final, detailed report concluded that: "Germany had never disarmed, had never had the intention of disarming, and for seven years had done everything in her power to deceive and 'counter control' the Commission appointed to control her disarmament." This report was deliberately ignored and suppressed.

Allied efforts had sometimes penetrated German camouflage. As early as May 1921, only fourteen months after Krupp had taken its first steps toward covert rearmament, U.S. Army Intelligence officers concluded from a study of Krupp patents that twenty-six were for artillery control devices, eighteen for electrical fire control apparatus, nine for fuses and shells, seventeen for field guns and fourteen for heavy railway cannon. Although the U.S. Secretary of War made these details available to the press, they were ignored.

If the Control Commission's snoopers were occasionally successful in ferreting out evidence of evasions by German industry, foreign journalists were not. As Gustav Krupp gleefully put it, the visiting foreign correspondents had been hoodwinked to a man. If they had pooled their individually meager investigative resources, they might have noticed suspicious patterns. For example, all saw various parts of Krupp (after all, it was huge) but none saw certain corners. Moreover, those who brought cameras subsequently found their film rolls overexposed. Before leaving the Krupp works, they had been graciously treated to a luncheon snack at a particular canteen, part of the always *gemütlicher* reception that so impressed journalists such as the *Literary Digest*'s correspondent. While they dined, their cameras were irradiated. Krupp's security men took this extraordinary precaution, not because they feared that the visitors would see, much less understand, anything embarrassing (their conducted tour avoided *those* parts), but because their photos may have inadvertently included drawing board plans that experts at home might recognize for what they actually were.

The Control Commission had the power to inspect, including "snap" or spot inspections, and the skilled personnel to do this. However, the *Abwehr* (and/or Krupp's own security staff) had penetrated the Control Commission and gave ample warning of unannounced snap inspections so that embarrassing paperwork could be hidden. Only rarely did German counterintelligence fail to warn of snap inspections. Once, for example, Control Commission inspectors managed a genuine surprise visit to the Rohrbach aircraft factory. Unable to remove a Rohrbach "Roland" experimental three-engine "transport" (i.e., a bomber) in which machine guns had been installed in extra long engine pods, the workmen had only time to move it to the center of the hangar and clutter it up so much with dust covers, staging, ladders and other bits of gear, that it looked like a pile of discarded equipment. The inspectors passed it by without notice.

Some exposés of these numerous Versailles Treaty evasions did appear in the world's press. The earliest serious effort to enlighten the British public about the threat of German rearmament was a long article published with official permission by Brigadier-General Morgan in late 1924, immediately after his resignation from the Control Commission. As might be suspected, some Control Commission inspectors had been mere time servers or, as in the case of certain British members, actually welcomed German rearmament as a counterweight to France. Thus, one of the senior departing naval inspectors, Commander Fanshawe, told retired Lieutenant Renken, his German opposite number: "It is now time for us to separate. Both you and I are glad that we are leaving. Your task was unpleasant and so was mine. There is one thing I should point out. You should not feel that we believed what you told us. Not one word you uttered was true, but you delivered your information in such a clever way that we were in a position to believe you. I want to thank you for this."

Had arms inspection failed? Did the numerous evasions escape the notice of the Control Commission? Clearly not. The memoirs of

Brigadier-General Morgan, for four years a member of the Commission, make plain that much was noticed and the rest suspected, at least by some perceptive members of the Commission. French military intelligence, the famed Deuxième Bureau, also was reporting many evasions. So, too, was British military intelligence, particularly from Holland; the military attaché there, A. C. Temperley, was able to piece together a general picture of the Versailles evasions during his four-year tour (1920-25) in his listening post at The Hague.

The failure had been one not so much of the Control Commission itself, much less of intelligence services, but rather of apathy on the part of the Allied governments behind the Commission. As Winston Churchill later commented, strict enforcement "was neglected while the infringements remained petty, and shunned as they assumed serious proportions." Nobel Peace laureate Philip Noel-Baker, summing up this sordid episode of treaty evasion, concluded that it proved *"Not* that the system of inspection failed in Germany, but simply that after 1925 it was never enforced."

Clandestine Rearmament, 1927-1935. The Inter-Allied Control Commission had left Germany at the beginning of 1927 and the Conference of Ambassadors sent its final report to the League of Nations Council on 22 July. Henceforward, the League Council would be the only agency authorized to inquire into German disarmament violations. But the League of Nations could only inquire and complain; the Germans easily dragged such matters out by protracted debates and negotiations. Without Control Commission inspectors, the League was blind; without an Army of Occupation, it was powerless.

The withdrawal of the Control Commission did not, however, mean that Germany could immediately begin rearmament; the political climate was not yet ripe. It only meant that design, testing and training could proceed under thinner, less hampering cover. Having surrendered their rights of inspection and verification, the Allies were henceforward limited for information to their small, interwar intelligence and espionage services. German counterintelligence and security could cope with much of that, and a judicious mix of official lying and thin cover stories usually sufficed to deceive the foreign press and diplomatic corps.

Krupp now launched a period of so-called "black production" *(Schwarze Produktion)*. Manufacture was stepped up on self-pro-

pelled guns, torpedo launching tubes, periscopes, armor plate, remote control devices for naval guns and primitive rocket design.
The prototype of the magnificent 88-mm AA/AT gun emerged from
the drawing board. According to one interoffice memo, "Of the guns
which were being used in 1939-41, the most important were already
fully developed in 1933." This also was the case with tanks, which
went into production in 1928. Except for the hydraulic safety switch,
all other tank components had been worked out by 1926. Artillery
test firing ranges were going full blast in 1929. And Krupp acquired
an enormous, 15,000-ton press, suitable only for making giant cannons.

The *Abwehr* remained under the command of Gempp until 23
June 1927 when he was promoted out and succeeded by Major
Günther Schwantes, a cavalryman who had been in the *Abwehr* only
a year. Then, the conniving empire-building inside the Defense Ministry by General Kurt von Schleicher led the Ministry to grab the
Abwehr from the *Truppenamt*. First, in 1928, appropriately on April
Fools' Day, Schleicher persuaded his boss, Defense Minister General Wilhelm Groener, to create an *Abwehr* Branch as "the Defense
Ministry's sole intelligence-acquisition post." This centralized service combined the *Abwehr* and its Cipher Center, appropriated from
the *Truppenamt*, and the small naval intelligence section, appropriated simultaneously from the Navy. The next year, on 1 March 1929,
the *Abwehr* Branch was incorporated, along with several other Ministry offices, into a newly created Minister's Department headed, not
surprisingly, by the ambitious Schleicher himself. This administra-
tive shuffle made the *Abwehr* the supra service military intelligence
agency that it henceforward remained.

To ensure his closest control over the flow of information,
Schleicher relieved Schwantes as head of the *Abwehr* Branch and
replaced him at the end of 1929 with Lieutenant Colonel Kurt von
Bredow, a trusted friend and protégée whose only other qualifica-
tion was that he had briefly served as an *Abwehr* field officer eight
years earlier. Bredow somewhat reorganized and enlarged the *Abwehr*
Branch, recruiting employees of German arms firms as agents and
traveling to France and Belgium.

Bredow remained chief of the *Abwehr* Branch until June 1932
when Schleicher, who had become Defense Minister, moved Bredow
up to replace him in the Minister's Department. Three days later, on

27 June, Schliecher broke with a sixty-six-year-old tradition by appointing a naval officer to head military intelligence. This new Chief of the *Abwehr,* Commander Conrad Patzig, had been head of the *Abwehr's* naval group since 1929.

An unusual contribution, literally above and beyond the call of duty, to the *Abwehr/ Reichswehr's* secret capabilities was made at this time. Theodor Rowehl had been a reconnaissance pilot in the Great War, credited with several cross-Channel missions to observe England. Now, he became concerned by the possible threat posed by the new fortifications that Poland was building along the German and East Prussian frontiers. A 1929 treaty between Germany and Poland expressly forbade unauthorized military or civilian overflights of each other's territory and required special permission for aerial cameras. Nevertheless, Rowehl decided to attempt to photograph the forts at a sufficiently high altitude; he hoped to avoid detection. As a twenty-six-year-old civilian, entirely on his own, he hired a private plane on Sundays and holidays and flew it over the prohibited areas at 13,000 feet. The flights went unchallenged. When he believed that he had obtained adequate photo coverage, Rowehl presented his intelligence to astonished government officials. He argued that he could do much more, if money were given to supplement his own slender, private means. The officials were delighted to arrange this service and in 1930 the audacious young patriot became a civilian contract employee of the *Abwehr.*

Rowehl promptly chartered a singularly suitable aircraft. It was the unique Junkers W-34; the very plane that had the previous year (26 May 1929) set a world's altitude record of 41,800 feet. For the next four years Rowehl flew this superb machine along the Polish border taking oblique photos; and over the target country itself, covering mainly forts and harbors. As before, these sorties attracted no attention and Rowehl's successive *Abwehr* chiefs, Bredow and Patzig, winked away this violation of the 1929 German-Polish agreement.

Adolph Hitler was appointed Chancellor by President Paul von Hindenburg on 30 January 1933. His views on "revenge" against the so-called *Versaillesdiktat* were well known to his intimates, and quiet, verbal understandings were sufficient substitutes for blatant contracts between government officers and arms companies. In anticipation of arms orders, the production of steel soared and stockpiles of strategic metals grew rapidly, including imports of Brazilian zircon ore used only for gun steel.

With the experimental and training air bases in Russia closing down, Germany cast about for a suitable substitute. Mussolini agreed to permit selected German fighter pilots to train with the Regia Aeronautica, at that time one of the world's largest, most modern and efficient air forces.

The first group of the selected pilots already was serving in Lufthansa. They traveled secretly in 1933 to Italy and, posing as South Tyrolean soldiers, were escorted to various Italian Air Force airfields. There they were issued Italian Air Force uniforms and enrolled as students in combat aviation. One of these young pilots, the twenty-one-year-old Adolf Galland, was the future General of Fighters in the *Luftwaffe*.

Training was intensive and included realistic ground attack and support exercises held jointly with the Italian Army. When the course ended a half-year later, in fall 1933, the now highly trained fighter pilots returned to Germany as Lufthansa commercial pilots. Early in 1934 they were placed on the German Air Force active list and a year later, most, including Galland, were commissioned officers in the *Luftwaffe*. The bases in Italy had only been a brief stopgap to bridge the closing of air bases in Russia and the large-scale opening of new bases in Germany now about to take place.

Conscription into the *Reichswehr* was, of course, forbidden by Versailles, but the Treaty said nothing about a National Labor Service because it did not exist. In 1934, Hitler created the National Labor Service *(Reiclisarbeitdienst)* and made it obligatory for all eighteen-year-old males to spend six months in this rigidly disciplined, mass national organization, complete with close-order drill with shovels. A reserve Army also was prohibited, but in July 1933 Hitler authorized the *Reichswehr* to take military jurisdiction of the private, paramilitary Stalhelm and the Nazi SA and SS organizations. Specifically, the *Reichswehr* undertook to train 250,000 SA members as an army reserve.

In April 1933 the Reich Commission for Air Transport became the Ministry of Air Transport *(Reichsluftfährtministerium)* and Hermann Göring was appointed Air Transport Minister, a title designed to perpetuate the fraud that it was a purely civilian occupation, although within a month the Army began handing over its secret military aviation component. The Paris Air Pact (1926) had relaxed the provisions of Versailles to permit Germany to have "air police" units and aerial defense. Göring now invoked this to create the German Air Defense Union, which gave him control of anti-aircraft artillery, and civil air-raid defense.

Hitler wanted something to whip up popular support for his rearmament plans, something that would simultaneously seem to justify to the world the German need for increased arms, albeit "defense" arms. Göring needed something similar that could give him a military role in the air. The imaginative Propaganda Minister, Dr. Joseph Goebbels, therefore, manufactured a suitable "big lie," an aerial equivalent of Hitler's political "Reichstag Fire" hoax. Accordingly, on 24 June 1933, the official Nazi newspaper, *Völkischer Beobachter,* banner-headlined "FOREIGN AIRCRAFT OVER BERLIN!" The lead story, which covered the front page, told a dramatic tale of how, the previous day, a formation of several unidentified foreign bombers had violated German airspace, penetrated to Berlin and circled the German capital, dropping insulting leaflets before making their return flights to the east. The implication was that the warplanes were Soviet Russian. The article pointed out that interception had been impossible because the Air Police had no aircraft. Göring, feigning outraged innocence, complained to the British Embassy of Germany's defenselessness against air attack, and pleaded that Britain grant export licenses for enough engines to equip "a few police planes." As a result, the Armstrong-Siddeley works shipped more than eighty-five engines from England. By early 1934, the secret air force was operating forty-four units from forty-two airfields throughout Germany, disguised by civilian cover names.

In January 1934, Hitler astonished the world by signing a ten-year non-aggression pact with Poland. A secret clause of the pact enjoined each party not to engage in espionage on the other's territory. The *Abwehr* Chief, Navy Captain Patzig, summoned his department heads to apprise them of the secret clause, but concluded with the remark: "It goes without saying that we continue our work."

Thus, Rowehl's overflights of Poland continued unnoticed until October, when Defense Minister General Werner von Blomberg made an inspection visit to Kiel-Holtenau Airfield. There he innocently asked about an aircraft standing outside one of the hangars and was told it was an *Abwehr* plane used for photo-reconnaissance over

Poland. Appalled to learn of flights that risked disrupting Hitler's cherished pact with Poland, Blomberg immediately terminated Rowehl's operations against Poland and soon dismissed Patzig as *Abwehr* Chief.

At this point Rowehl had collected five aircraft and about as many pilots and formally joined the *Reichswehr* as an officer. His small *Abwehr* unit was given the camouflage title of Experimental Post for High Altitude Flights and transferred from Keil-Holtenau to Berlin-Staaken. Prohibited from overflying Poland, Rowehl turned his cameras on other potential *Luftwaffe* targets. By the end of 1934 his aircraft had begun photographic cover of the USSR, penetrating to the Kronstadt naval yard at Leningrad and the industrial regions around Pskov and Minsk. Other flights were soon exploring the fortified border regions of France and Czechoslovakia.

The armed forces were now given a blank check, the *Wehrmacht* and Navy being told to prepare their own budgets, the government undertaking full responsibility to find the money. An order was placed for six submarines with a sub-a-month program to follow. The naval architects and craftsmen who had been squirreled away in Dutch shipyards returned. Tractor-drawn, quick-firing howitzers were tested and manufacture of armor plate and the great guns was begun for the Navy's battleships whose keels were now laid.

On 4 April 1934 Hitler secretly ordered rearmament, creating the Central Bureau for German Rearmament to coordinate the effort. This not only helped assure the fidelity of the *Reichswehr* chiefs, but also firmly cemented his relationship with German industrialists. But camouflage was still the order of the day. Amidst a fanfare of Goebbels' orchestrated propaganda about Hitler's 5.4 billion-mark public works program, the 21 billion for arms went unmentioned. This enormous rearmament budget was skillfully concealed by Economic Minister Hjalmar Schacht's elaborate financial legerdemain. The "Old Wizard's" main trick was to pay the industrialists special IOUs, called Mefobills, that were accepted in Berlin by a dummy corporation, Metallurgische Forschungsgesellschaft, GmbH, representing four private concerns and two ministries that were, in turn, backed by the national treasury. Since the Central Bank eventually rediscounted all the Mefo IOUs, all creditors were paid without a single mark appearing on the record. From 1934 through 1937, Schacht's Mefobills totaled 12 billion marks, all used to finance rearmament. This amount constituted 33 to 38 percent of the total military expenditures in that crucial period.

Hitler now placed an order with Krupp for the first hundred new tanks, all light models, to be delivered by March 1934 with 650 more to follow a year later. The German engineers and foremen who had been serving quietly with Landsverk in Sweden were recalled. The blueprints were brought out of hiding, the Krupp truck assembly line at Krawa shut down to retool and tank production began. By October 1935 the first three Panzer divisions had come into existence, a fact duly reported by agents of French military intelligence.

By withdrawing their arms inspectors early in 1927, the Allies had cut themselves off from their best source of intelligence about German military developments. The foreign press corps was hardly a paragon of aggressive investigative journalism. The international business community contributed little information because the German arms industry limited its foreign contacts to German-controlled companies (as in Holland and Sweden) or ones that benefited from continued secrecy (as in Spain, Finland and Russia). Leaks to and public disclosures in the Reichstag also diminished. And the *Reichswehr* and its collaborators in industry and government had improved their security following the occasional embarrassing disclosures of the early 1920s.

The Allies and other concerned governments were left with only two regular sources of information on German arms: official German statements and their own intelligence services. But these various interwar organizations were understaffed following demobilization in 1918 and under-budgeted after the start of the Great Depression in 1929. Only the Russians maintained large services, but their size was not reflected in efficiency and, besides, they targeted mainly Britain and the United States. The French maintained perhaps the best services and their reduced effort was at least concentrated on Germany. The British services also were highly professional but were very thin on the ground in Germany. The Americans operated mere skeleton services, dependent for data on military attachés and foreign service political officers who, with very rare exceptions, lacked intelligence training. The Poles operated a centralized intelligence service (the world's first), but it was targeted on Russia as well as Germany. Czechoslovak military intelligence had only twenty men, $120,000 per annum and no current intelligence on Germany. Consequently, even when suspicions about German activities were raised by rumors, reports or leaks, the various intelligence and espionage services were seldom able to mount the sort of intensive search necessary for verification.

With the Allied inspectors gone, the task of maintaining security eased considerably for the Germans. It was no longer necessary to work under such deep cover, or to hide plans and documents. A bold *"Geheim"* (Secret) stamped on the papers usually sufficed to keep them from prying eyes. For example, after 1932 the Reich Defense Ministry simply stopped publishing its lists of active military officers. Unlike British, French and American practices they now treated this list as secret information. As well they might, for these lists contained two forbidden facts: one, the services had exceeded the 4,000 *Reichswehr* and 1,500 *Reichsmarine* officer limits (albeit by only small amounts)—British military intelligence suspected this but could not prove it; and two, rapidly increasing numbers of officers had received pilot training. The overworked French military intelligence had been trying to monitor precisely such biographical detail but was, henceforward, severely hampered by the lack of these officer lists.

Occasional intelligence coups, however, were still possible. For instance, the French Deuxième Bureau was able to learn from close study of the German government budgets that the *Reichswehr* and *Reichsmarine* were being permitted to overspend their already large proportion (40 percent in 1929-30) of government funds. Valuable inputs to these fiscal analyses were supplied by the published texts of speeches made by opposition deputies during Reichstag debates. Other Versailles evasions, such as the training of pilots in Russia, also were partly known to the British and French Intelligence services and duly reported by them to their governments. However, the governments themselves chose to keep most of this intelligence secret.

A secret French dossier reported the *Reichswehr's* concealed short-service enlistments, the enormous (technically legal) proportion of NCOs, of whom there were something like one for every two privates, the illegal General Staff *(Truppenamt)*, the large numbers of militarized police in barracks, the training and equipping of various paramilitary units, the secret arming with forbidden weapons, the covert training of pilots in Russia and the existence of the "Black Luftwaffe." The dossier also outlined the scheme of industrial mobilization. Despite such comprehensive and credible intelligence, political considerations prevailed and on 8 September 1926 Germany was admitted to the League of Nations.

Overt Rearmament and Bluff, 1935-1939. In the spring of 1935, Hitler took the political decision unilaterally to abrogate the Versailles Treaty and publicly to display German rearmament. This did not mean, however, that deception was at an end. It only changed its form.

On Saturday, 16 March 1935, the eve of Germany's Memorial Day, the Fuhrer decreed universal military conscription and proclaimed his intention to build up the existing ten-division, 100,000-man Army to thirty-six divisions with a strength of 550,000. Two months later, Hitler secretly promulgated the Reich Defense Law. The *Reichswehr* was superseded by the Wehrmacht. The *Truppenamt* came out of hiding to become publicly the *Generalstab.* The naval *Reichsmarine* was renamed *Kriegsmarine.* And the Defense Ministry became the War Ministry. The defense forces were now openly a war machine.

Göring soon took jealous note of the impressive successes of the *Abwehr's* photo-reconnaissance unit headed by Theodor Rowehl. Accordingly, in 1936 Rowehl and his small unit were plucked whole from the *Abwehr* and placed in the *Luftwaffe* General Staff as the Special Purposes Squadron of the Fifth (Intelligence) Branch. It quickly grew in size to a full squadron of about a dozen planes with improved cameras, photo-interpretation staff and handpicked aircrew. Rowehl also had his choice of aircraft types and the superb single-engine He-70 "Blitz" was soon replaced by the He-111 that Heinkel had just unveiled as the world's fastest passenger aircraft. With a crew of four, this fine, twin-engine machine had a cruising range of 2,000 miles and a ceiling of 28,000 feet. They flew against Czechoslovakia and England in violation of air treaties with those two countries and against France and Russia as well. Rowehl's planes flew disguised as commercial aircraft, their crews in mufti. Over public targets, such as cities, they operated at normal altitudes while pretending to test possible new commercial routes; against military targets they flew at maximum altitudes to avoid detection and, if detected (by sound or condensation trails), identification. Even when one He-111 went down in the USSR, the Russians did not complain; perhaps its "civilian" disguise enabled Stalin to avoid embarrassment.

The year 1935 marked a new stage in German propaganda policy. It produced a new myth and introduced a period of bluff. The myth was that the *Luftwaffe* had been conjured into existence out of nothing but the sheer will of the Führer and the genius of Göring and German industry and engineers. The more than fifteen years of careful, secret preparation (design, prototypes, testing, recruiting and training) was officially forgotten. The sole purpose of this myth was to exaggerate the achievement and potency of Hitler's Third Reich at the expense of the solid progress under the Weimar Republic. Henceforward, there was no fear of publicizing the existence of the *Luftwaffe* and Army.

The only German fear, now that the Army and *Luftwaffe* were brought into the open, was that they would be seen for what they were, weak instruments of Hitler's aggressive foreign policy. The *Wehrmacht* timetable estimated 1942 or 1943 as the first year when it would be ready to go to war. Consequently, deception was continued. Now, however, it switched from dissimulative deception that concealed the facts of secret preparations to simulative deception that concealed weakness.

Hitler's policy switch from shy concealment to intimidating bluff in the diplomatic arena was coordinated with Göring, who paralleled it in public announcements. Just as Hitler used Anthony Eden as his channel, Göring used Mr. Ward Price as his. Price was the bemonocled roving correspondent for Lord Rothermere's London *Daily Mail*. Göring had chosen well, as both Price and his newspaper proved most accommodating to the Nazi regime throughout the mid- and late 1930s, uncritically publishing all the disinformation that the top German leaders were pleased to provide them. In the first state, in February 1934, Göring told Price and his readers that Germany possessed a grand total of only 300 aircraft, of which many were obsolete and none were capable of being used in a military role. He added that the aviation industry was so weak that at least two years would be required before it would even be possible to start building an air force, one that he assured Price would be purely defensive. Only thirteen months later on 9 March 1935, Göring summoned Price to give him the scoop of the year, proclaiming the existence of the *Luftwaffe*. That same day, Göring also summoned the British and French air attachés to give them, officially, the same news.

The sharp contrast between these two successive policies of concealment and bluff is epitomized by Hitler's personal assurances to Anthony Eden, who was then Lord Privy Seal. In February 1934, on the occasion of Eden's first meeting with the German Chancellor, Hitler flatly asserted that Germany was defenseless in the air. Hitler also stated that Germany was not aggressive, had no need of offensive weapons, and was prepared to renounce all military aircraft if other nations would do the same. He promised to limit the *Luftwaffe* to 30 percent of the number of planes of its combined neighbors, but in no case to exceed 50 percent of the French Armée de l'Air and to comprise purely short-range defensive aircraft, no bombers. Then, just thirteen months later, on 26 March 1935, only sixteen days after Göring had publicly unveiled the *Luftwaffe*, Hitler informed Eden that the *Luftwaffe* had already achieved parity with the RAF. To illustrate this, Hitler displayed a table that put British air strength at 2,100 machines, including reserves. Knowing that actual RAF first line strength in Britain was only 453, and 130 auxiliaries, the Foreign Office queried the German Air Ministry about the precise meaning of Hitler's claim to parity. The disturbing reply was that Germany had 900 planes. Foreign Secretary Sir John Simon read this as 30 percent superiority for the Germans.

The essence of the new propaganda was bluff, to portray a force far stronger than it was. Accordingly, it was shown off at its best: in photo magazines that caught the world's attention; at the vast Nazi rallies at Nuremberg; by entering souped-up, prototype aircraft in international air shows (1936-39); and by giving carefully conducted tours to visiting British, French and American experts (1936-38). Military attaches and selected foreign dignitaries were invited to the first, full-scale maneuvers (1937) that, along with tours, were specially designed to imply more than was shown. The Condor Legion fighting in Spain (1936–39) was publicized to prove the excellence of German "volunteers" and equipment.

The new *Wehrmacht* was a gigantic bluff, but a bluff that served Hitler's purposes superbly. His immediate goal was to recover the borderlands that had been lost at Versailles; and for three-and-a-half years, from early 1936 until final confrontation in late 1939, the *Wehrmacht* gave him a series of bloodless victories over stronger armies.

Hitler's first target was the Rhineland demilitarized buffer zone. On 7 March 1936, in violation of both Versailles and the Locarno

Treaty, the *Wehrmacht* re-occupied the Rhineland. This coup was achieved by the *Wehrmacht's* single division of infantry, marching under strict orders to retreat literally on the mere first sight of any French Army patrol. Such extraordinary orders were based on wisdom, not cowardice, for although Hitler had threatened publicly to send six extra divisions into the Rhineland, the *Wehrmacht's* entire combat strength mustered only four brigades against thirty French *divisions*. (The *Wehrmacht* originally had ten divisions, but they were broken up five months earlier to provide the cadre for the projected thirty-six-division Army.)

Although the *Wehrmacht* had deployed only its one division and placed three battalions, totaling 3,000 men across the Rhine, British Intelligence showed four divisions totaling 35,000 troops on its Rhineland enemy order-of-battle map. William L. Shirer, Berlin bureau chief for Universal Service, accepted a figure of four divisions, or about 50,000 men. Incredibly, French intelligence believed the German strength *inside* the Rhineland to be 265,000.

On their part, the French simply stood back, their Army refusing to march unless the British marched with them. Britain refused. It was an astonishing victory. As Hitler later admitted, "we would have had to withdraw with our tails between our legs, for the military resources at our disposal would have been wholly inadequate for even a moderate resistance." Among the most astonished were the *Wehrmacht* commanders who had expected defeat.

Luftwaffe deployment comprised three squadrons of fighters (armed, but with unsynchronized and, therefore, useless guns) and three squadrons of dive bombers (newly organized and inadequately trained). However, Galland's view that it was a bluff force still holds. The British were still deluded by Hitler's year-old claim that the *Luftwaffe* had achieved parity with the RAF.

Beginning in the fiscal year 1935-36, the *Luftwaffe* was ready to begin mass production. The budget had grown rapidly from $30 million in the fiscal year 1933-34 to *$52* million in the fiscal year 1934-35. Now, in the fiscal year 1935-36 it was allotted $85 million in its official budget. However, that year it also received $750 million in a special black fund financed by interest-bearing notes sold secretly by the government to the *Reichsbank*. This elaborate scheme to circumvent public debate in the Reichstag was the invention of *Reichsbank* President Schacht. His intention was to keep these transactions secret to escape both inflation inside Germany and loss of confidence in the Reichsmark abroad.

Göring's Air Ministry understood that efficient mass production required selecting a few promising types from among the numerous aircraft prototypes currently being test flown. For its medium bomber, it chose Ernst Heinkel's He-111, which had its first test flight on 24 February 1935. Like its He-70 predecessor, it was a bomber camouflaged as a civil transport. In this mufti version, the He-111 carried ten passengers, four forward and six aft, separated by an empty compartment amidship that Lufthansa advertised as a smoking lounge. In fact, it was the bomb bay. Series production began, but the first ten proved unwieldy in flight and were rejected by the *Luftwaffe*. (Heinkel later sold them at a handsome profit to Chiang Kai-shek.) An improved version quickly followed that was accepted by the *Luftwaffe* and serial production started in earnest.

The civil transport version of the He-111 was unveiled to the public at the Berlin-Templehof airfield in January 1936. Lufthansa, however, was not destined to receive this high-performance aircraft. Instead it went to Theodor Rowehl's secret, high-altitude, photo-reconnaissance squadron of the *Luftwaffe* as replacement for its He-70s.

At this point, the Air Ministry decided to adopt the He-111 as its main medium bomber and mass production was ordered. Accordingly, Colonel Fritz Loeb, from Colonel Wilhelm Wimmer's Technical Office, informed Ernst Heinkel that the Air Ministry wanted him to build a separate factory that would produce exclusively He-111s and at the then prodigious rate of 100 per month. The astounded Herr Heinkel balked at the enormous cost, coming as it did before he had paid off his new factory at Marienehe. Colonel Loeb, aware of the secret funds available in the 1935–36 *Luftwaffe* budget, announced that the *Luftwaffe* would underwrite the entire costs of Heinkel's new plant. It was to be ultramodern with carefully dispersed sections to minimize its vulnerability to enemy air attack, its own air raid shelters, and a self-contained fire department. When Heinkel pointed out that dispersal reduced production efficiency and hence lowered profits, Colonel Loeb merely answered: "Don't worry about it, it isn't your money." Heinkel agreed, and a suitable site was found at Oranienburg. Plans were completed at the beginning of April 1936 and ground was broken on 4 May.

Exactly one year later, on 4 May 1937, the first Oranienburg-built He-111 bomber taxied off the assembly line to be greeted by a cheering throng of thousands of workers and guests. Oranienburg was, henceforth, the public display model of the new German aircraft industry. The *Luftwaffe* used it freely to impress, and intimidate, foreign visitors.

Göring, with Hitler's permission, took the occasion of the Fourth International Military Air Competition held at Dübendorf, Zürich, Switzerland, in the last week of July 1937, as a fine opportunity to propagandize his new *Luftwaffe*. The crowd, which included air force observers from many countries, was awed by the apparent display of German aerial strength. The superb little combat observation and liaison Fiesler "Storch" hovered at 32 mph without stalling, but it was merely a pre-production model. The beautiful, streamlined Heinkel He-112 fighter flashed past, but it had already been rejected by the *Luftwaffe*. A team of five Messerschmidt Me-109s easily captured first, second, and third places in the 228-mile race; took first in the 31.4 mile circuit and another first in the climb-and-dive contest. A sleek, silver, twin-engine Dornier Do-17 "Flying Pencil" medium bomber, complete with military markings won the Alpine Circuit with a 280-mph performance, an amazing 30 mph faster than any non-German fighters present. It seemed to be an uncatchable bomber. The stunned French and British observers did not know the crucial fact that this "bomber was only a handmade, specially souped-up, single plane;" the real production models were being turned out with smaller engines that gave a top speed 30 mph under that displayed at Zürich.

The Air Ministry had conducted a series of comparative test flights at Travemünde, back in October 1935, to determine the one fighter plane that would be adopted for mass production. The winner was Willy Messerschmidt's easy-to-assemble Bf-109. It was a clear choice over the runner-up He-112, which was a more promising performer but grossly over-engineered with 2,885 separate parts and 26,864 rivets. This defeat for his He-112 spurred Ernst Heinkel, who considered Messerschmidt an upstart, to go back to the drawing board and return with a winner. The result was the magnificent He-100. It had only a third as many parts and half the rivets of its He-112 forebear. It was first flown on 22 January 1938 and on 5 June, with the head of the *Luflwaffe's* Technical Office, General Ernst Udet at the controls, it set a new world air speed record at 394.6 mph; a spectacular 50 mph faster than the then current record held by Italy.

The next day every major newspaper in Europe featured the German air triumph. Some careful readers were no doubt alarmed that Propaganda Minister Goebbels' press release had declared this custom-built, experimental model to be the production version of the long-discarded He-112 or the "He-112U," a design that, in fact, existed only in Goebbels' imagination.

Hitler's best opportunity to portray the illusory German might was offered in 1936 by the Civil War in Spain. It also enabled the *Luftwaffe,* Army, and Navy to give their pilots and other military specialists some combat blooding and to battle-test their latest equipment. It was a showcase operation, but one that represented a proportionately far greater drain on Germany's available strength, a point not widely appreciated. Moreover, because she made a recognized contribution to Franco's victory, and because Russia ended among the losers, Germany received a grudging recognition from the fearful world that she was a major military power.

In addition, the *Luftwaffe* and *Wehrmacht* gained nearly 14,000 pilots with combat experience, aircrewmen, tank men and anti-aircraft crewmen in the thirty-two months of battle. They tested a number of new weapon systems, such as the Messerschmidt Bf-109 fighter, the Junkers Ju-87 "Stuka" dive bomber and the superb dual-purpose 88mm anti-tank/anti-aircraft gun. All these would become major weapons in the upcoming World War II. They tried out several new tactics, such as air-ground support and "carpet" (saturation) bombing. And commanders learned some strategic lessons, as when in 1937, Condor Legion Commander "Sander" (General Hugo von Sperrle) gutted the Basque town of Guernica with his He-111 medium bombers. This was the same weapon and tactic that three years later, as General-Field Marshal commanding Air Fleet 3, he would deploy against London.

While the Spanish Civil War continued with German aid, Hitler launched a further series of land grabs. In each case the then current mix of allied states possessed a combined strength quite sufficient to have called Hitler's bluff with relative impunity. But, mesmerized by the German propaganda that exaggerated the strength of the *Wehrmacht* and *Luftwaffe,* and hoping to appease Hitler's appetite, they failed to move. Hitler did so instead. In March 1938 he annexed Austria by a bloodless invasion. In September, at the Munich meeting, he bulldozed France and Britain into surrendering the Czechoslovak border region to Germany.

Munich not only was a failure of Anglo-French nerve, but it was an enormous failure of intelligence. We now know two things that were, at best, uncertain at the time. Hitler himself was not bluffing. At this juncture he fully intended to invade Czechoslovakia. But the *Wehrmacht was* bluffing; it almost certainly could not have succeeded against Czechoslovakia and France, even without Britain and possibly the USSR joining in. The French Deuxième Bureau counted ninety German divisions (plus thirty reserves) when, in fact, the *Wehrmacht* had only forty-two divisions (plus seven reserves). The French had sixty-five (plus thirty-five reserves) and the Czechs a crack, well-entrenched force of thirty-two (plus six reserves). Thus, French intelligence reported an uncomfortable parity when the real order of battle gave the Allies a better than two-to-one advantage. Similar Allied intelligence miscalculations applied to the *Luftwaffe* and armor, to deployments and mobilization levels. The Allies succumbed to a combination of fear, self-delusion, and German deception.

Two specific examples can be given to show how the Germans directed their campaigns of disinformation by using visiting experts to carry back tales of German invincibility. The primary targets of intimidation were the French. Accordingly, in August 1938, as the Czechoslovak crisis was heating up under Hitler's pressure, Hermann Göring invited the chiefs of the French Armée de l' Air to an inspection tour of the *Luftwaffe*. General Joseph Vuillemin, Chief of the Air General Staff, promptly accepted and brought along several key members of his staff. His guide, General Milch, showed Vuillemin huge and well-furnished *Luftwaffe* barracks. A mass bombing display was laid on. He took him to Berlin-Doberitz to view the pampered Richthofen Wing, where Vuillemin was walked past long rows of brand new Messerschmidt Me-109 fighters; their tall, stern pilots in full battle dress drawn up at attention by their planes. All this was mere conditioning for the final act of the tour, one in which the Germans had laid a careful trap.

Vuillemin and his staff were now conducted about the busy, ultramodern Heinkel works at Oranienburg by Milch, Udet and Heinkel himself. Dozens of He-111 medium bombers were flowing off the mass production assembly line. He saw the immaculate air-raid shelters, deep underground with "everything in readiness, even down to ten sharpened pencils on every desk." He watched a He-111 pushed to its limit on a single engine. Udet then took Vuillemin up in his personal courier plane to view the sprawling factory. As Udet brought the slow plane in at near stalling speed, the moment he had carefully planned with Milch and Heinkel for his passenger's benefit arrived. Suddenly a Heinkel He-l00 streaked past at full throttle, a mere blur and a hiss. Both planes landed and the Germans took their startled French visitors over to inspect the sleek "He-112U." Milch explained that the aircraft (one of only three He-l00s ever built) was the *Luftwaffe's* latest production fighter. "Tell me, Udet," Milch asked with feigned casualness, "how far along are we with mass production?" Udet, on cue, replied, "Oh, the second production line is ready and the third will be within two weeks." Vuillemin looked crestfallen and blurted out to Milch that he was "shattered." Later, in the privacy of their limousine, Vuillemin confided to François-Poinçet that he was depressed by what he had seen of the *Luftwaffe* and glumly predicted that: "should war break out as you expect late in September, there won't be a single French plane left within a fortnight!"

The French air delegation returned to Paris with the defeatist word that the *Luftwaffe* was unbeatable, but this opinion was not fully shared by the resident Deuxième Bureau officer in Berlin, Assistant Air Attaché Paul Stehlin, who observed that: "The Germans set out to make a great impression on him [Vuillemin]. They succeeded and Vuillemin's opinions had more effect than they deserved upon the decisions of our government." Stehlin was less gullible, but Vuillemin had the rank and influence.

The other noteworthy instance of German disinformation was directed against American and, indeed, world opinion. The unwitting instrument was Colonel Charles A. Lindbergh who, beginning in 1936 made three trips to Germany at the request of American military intelligence. Lindbergh was brought in by U.S. military attaché Truman Smith specifically to ferret out better intelligence on the *Luftwaffe*. On its part, the *Luftwaffe,* from Göring and Milch and Udet down, were charming hosts. Literally charming, for Lindbergh accepted their false production figures, future plans that were never fulfilled and their pretense that the *Luftwaffe* was already, in 1936, the world's most powerful air force. After his second visit to the Reich, in October 1937, Lindbergh reported that the *Luftwaffe* had a vast air fleet of 10,000 (of which 5,000 were serviceable bombers) and was building between 500 and 800 planes per month (with a capability of 20,000 per year); statistics that, he pointed out, made the *Luftwaffe* "stronger than that of all other European countries combined." The truth was that the *Luftwaffe* then totaled only 3,315 aircraft (of which only 1,246 were serviceable bombers). During the Munich crisis, the *Luftwaffe* was actually able to mobilize only 1,230 first-line aircraft (including 600 bombers and 400 fighters). Production was, in fact, far below 300 planes per month. But Lindbergh's misinformation circulated on the eve of Munich throughout the United States, Britain and France, where it was accepted credulously by such persons as French Air Minister Guy la Chambre, French Foreign Minister Georges Bonnet and U.S. Ambassador to Britain Joseph P. Kennedy. When British Prime Minister Neville Chamberlain flew to Germany the week before Munich, he carried a summary of Lindbergh's report. Two weeks after Munich a grateful Göring presented Lindbergh with the Service Cross of the German Eagle.

During March 1939 the *Wehrmacht* occupied the rest of Czechoslovakia, again without resistance. Later that same month the port city of Memel was simply annexed from Lithuania by the German Navy. In June the Danzig Free State was virtually occupied by German forces thinly disguised as local, volunteer "Free Corps."

At 4:45 a.m., dawn on 1 September 1939, the *Wehrmacht* launched its surprise invasion of Poland. Despite the existing Anglo-French treaty guarantees to Poland, Hitler still hoped that France and particularly Britain would remain as irresolute as they had over Czechoslovakia. In his speech delivered at 10 a.m. that same day to the Reichstag and simultaneously broadcast to the world he said: "For more than six years now, I have been engaged in building up the German Armed Forces. During this period more than ninety billion Reichsmarks were spent building up the *Wehrmacht*. Today, ours are the best equipped armed forces in the world, and they are superior to those of 1914. My confidence in them can never be shaken."

Hitler's 90 billion Reichsmarks claim was a gross exaggeration, if not a deliberate lie, to encourage his people and to overawe his enemies. Nonetheless, it was widely credited. Although the amount is not entirely fictitious, it is a misrepresentation. Actually, it was the approximate *total* government expenditure for the period, about 50 billion Reichsmarks of which had been spent on armaments. One postwar German economist remarked: "Public views of the scale of armament were very much exaggerated. The German government at the time did nothing to contradict the exaggerated ideas; on the contrary they were desirable propaganda, producing the illusion of a warlike strength which in reality was not available on that scale."

Hitler's luck in bluffing appeared to have run out with the Polish invasion in September 1939 when the Poles chose to fight and, after two days of ragged indecision, Britain and France joined the battle. His luck still held to the degree that the powerful Franco-British forces limited themselves to mere pinprick attacks. Incredibly, they still thought they could do business with Hitler during the half-year period they called the "phoney war." Meanwhile, the *Wehrmacht* had six months' grace to build its strength at a more rapid rate than either Britain or France.

Finally, in April 1940, Hitler invaded Denmark and Norway, and the following month, by his all-out onslaught into France, shattered the last illusions about his aggressive intentions. But only those illusions concerning his intentions were shattered, for the illusion of *Wehrmacht* might was actually enhanced by the blitzkrieg victory in France.

Even that late in the German rearmament program, Germany had only just managed to reach overall parity with her combined enemies in order of battle. French military intelligence reported a total of 190 German divisions in April when, in fact, five months later the *Wehrmacht* had managed to mobilize only 157 divisions. In reality, German production began its prodigious growth only after mid-1942, when Albert Speer took over as an effective Minister of Armaments. By then it was already too late, as Allied production had been outstripping that of Germany since 1939. Even the shaky French war economy was catching up in the race with Germany after having slipped suddenly behind after 1935; British aircraft production also was gaining on that of Germany and would achieve parity the following year. And in naval warship construction, British, U.S. and even French production exceeded that of Germany by 1939.

How had this situation, one that boded ill for German hopes of victory, come about? It arose from two circumstances: deliberate policy plus self-deception. Hitler's policy was, from the outset, to portray the maximum of publicly visible strength, even when this portrayal was at the price of real military strength. In other words, the bluff policy required that armament depth, that is, long-term investment in strategic raw material stockpiles, expansion of military production capacity and buildup of military spare parts, take a lower priority than armament breadth, that is, the stress on sheer numbers of planes, tanks, guns, troops, divisions, etcetera, that would show up most impressively on the order of battle charts of Germany's opponents. The consequence of choosing this latter option was that on the outbreak of war in 1939 the *Wehrmach* had only enough ammunition for six weeks of war. The *Luftwaffe* had bombs enough for only three months, and the war economy as a whole, had raw material stockpiles for only nine to twelve months.

By opting for show over substance, Hitler deliberately made the better choice for a strategy of bluff but the poorer one in the event of war. Success, initially in bluff and later in quick battlefield victories, fostered hubris that insidious arrogance fed by excessive pride. Convinced of his own infallibility, Hitler finally overreached in 1941, attacking Russia and then declaring war on the United States. In the end, it seems that the German leadership had succeeded also in deceiving itself.

Lessons Learned

The story of secret German rearmament contains seven main lessons:

1. National political leaders tend to be unwilling to heed intelligence that has awkward political implications.
2. Negotiators, having negotiated a difficult agreement to mutual satisfaction, tend to place unwarranted faith in that agreement. They lose the skepticism that is part of vigilance.
3. Arms limitation agreements tend to leave out automatic sanctions that would significantly raise the costs of any evasion. Credible and potent sanctions might better deter evasions and swiftly punish those that do occur.
4. Technical experts tend to discount intelligence suggesting that their opposites have accomplished something that they, themselves, have not achieved or have not thought of doing. In such cases, the technicians and engineers may not be the best judges of enemy intentions and achievement.
5. Intelligence services tend to be under enormous bureaucratic political pressure to report (or at least stress) data that is in line with the prejudices and needs of their clientele and to suppress (or at least deemphasize) that which is not.

6. "Money," as British Major General Temperley concluded from his long experience with the German case, "is the key to increased armaments and a careful scrutiny of any upward trend would justify a demand for explanations." Any such economic analysis, however, must go beyond publicly professed budgets to probe deeply for fiscal deception. Not only must the target government's books be opened to skilled auditors, but also those of plausible or suspected contractors including those in other countries.

7. Evidence of arms evasion is likely to be ambiguous to some (perhaps a large) degree—the familiar problem of signal to noise ratios. Though it is possible to find evidence of sharp and strikingly prophetic judgments in a retrospective examination of the intelligence data presented to decision-makers of the period, it is likewise possible to find grossly inaccurate assessments and facts. In such a situation, the preconceptions of the decision-makers together with other (e.g., domestic) considerations loomed more significant than the evidence before them.

By failing to understand the first two lessons, the national leaders were easy prey for deception. By failing to demand rigorous verification of alleged infractions they showed apathy. By failing to apply sanctions when intelligence did occasionally bring undeniable proof of infractions to their attention, they showed themselves impotent as well. And the opponent's perception of this impotence was a spur to ever more audacious infractions.

2. German Surprise Attack on the Soviet Union, June 1941[2]

All military and political intelligence systems receive vast numbers of pieces of information. Usually, only a small proportion of this great bulk is relevant to a current problem such as predicting whether an attack is planned by one country against another. Even the small proportion of relevant information is seldom both complete and accurate. Most is a jumble of information that is accurate but incomplete or from a dubious source, unintentionally distorted or misleading, well-intentioned but wholly wrong, or deliberately deceptive. The task of the strategic information analyst is to construct a mosaic of these separate pieces, picking the accurate scraps, correcting the distorted bits, and discarding the false ones. This eternal labor of the intelligencer is made Herculean when the information system is flooded with disinformation (information intended to deceive), particularly when that disinformation is fed in as part of a systematic deception campaign.

This section will describe the types of misleading and deceptive information that perturbed the correct evaluation of intelligence on BARBAROSSA.

German Deception Operations. Having decided to initiate war, the national leader faces a dilemma: how to mobilize and deploy his martial means without sacrificing surprise, much less drawing a pre-emptive attack. The pedestrian answer is "security." But, as BARBAROSSA shows, it can be most unrealistic to expect conventional passive security measures to guard against ample disclosure of secrets. Only the most naive, preoccupied, witless, incompetent, or unlucky enemy will remain un-warned. But the cunning leader can interject one special type of counterespionage activity that will enhance his chances of gaining surprise. That is stratagem—a coordinated campaign of deception to mislead the victim's analysis.

Deception has, of course, been used by occasional clever leaders in politics and war since antiquity. But evidently the Germans were the first to institutionalize it when, late in World War II, the Great General Staff created a Disinformation Service that contributed to the occasional and rather crude German deception operations in that war. In the 1920s surprise and deception were preserved in German military doctrine and training by General von Seeckt, and by the mid-1930s the Abwehr had restored the specific organizational machinery for deception. This machinery was the D Group (Gruppe III-D), one of the half dozen main divisions in Colonel von Bentivegni's military security section (Abteilung III). Group D (subdivided into two geographic desks) was responsible for developing deception operations in coordination with the Army, Navy, and Air Force general staffs and for providing disinformation suitable for dissemination by the Abwehr's counterespionage (III-F) and other services. Its functions, although less centralized, were similar to the later British "Double-Cross Committee." However, the broad guidelines of strategic deception planning were centered in Hitler's personal military staff, the OKW, specifically in the operations staff (WFSt) under Jodl and in the latter's plans section (Abteilung L) under Warlimont during the BARBAROSSA planning. The Abwehr mounted rather primitive but more or less successful deception operations in connection with the Spanish Civil War in 1936, the takeover of Austria in early 1938, and the pressure on Czechoslovakia later that year. Finally, since at least as early as 1940, deception was made standard procedure in the OKW *Timetable* coordinating each of Hitler's surprise attacks. Thus, during the BARBAROSSA buildup, deception was a practiced, institutionalized, and routine part of Hitler's strategic planning. Indeed, these ruses of war were generally initiated by the Fuhrer himself.

Thus, Hitler would devise the broad outline and even specify the main themes of each strategic deception operation, leaving it to his personal military staff (usually Keitel or Jodl) to coordinate the detailed planning and directives with the appropriate segments of the military, propaganda, and foreign affairs bureaucracies. Hitler, with his intelligence and propaganda chiefs, wisely anticipated that the many highly visible preparations for BARBAROSSA would not go unnoticed. They also understood that enemy intelligence services and leaders could easily interpret these as signaling the intended invasion. Conventional passive security procedures were deemed inadequate. Consequently, the Germans very deliberately launched what they themselves termed the "greatest deception operation in the history of war" to mislead their enemies about the very intention to invade Russia, and to conceal the time, direction, and strength of the blow.

The deception campaign was conducted from 31 July 1940 until the invasion on 22 June 1941. During that period the Germans launched four distinguishable deception themes. These themes overlapped in time, were mutually supporting, and were well calculated to fit the preconceptions of their enemies at each stage of the developing operation. These themes went on to achieve almost complete believability within the intelligence services of Russia (and Britain, the United States, Japan, and other countries).

Invasion of Britain. The first deception theme launched by the Germans was that their military buildup on the eastern frontier (Operation AUFBAU OST) was merely part of the preparations for the widely heralded invasion of Britain (Operation SEA LION). Originally conceived by Hitler himself and ordered into effect by him on 31 July 1940, this theme was maintained all the way through to B-day itself. A variety of plausible arguments were advanced in connection with this cover story. For example, the buildup was explained as a training maneuver, held well out of range of British bombers and reconnaissance aircraft.

Indeed, throughout early 1941 the Wehrmacht units in the east were not organized for attack: most lay well back, with only the original negligible force screening the frontier itself. They were widely dispersed and engaged in training programs. Leave was generously apportioned; and no more senior headquarters than that of Günther von Kluge's Fourth Army in Warsaw was east of the German border. The posture was that of a peacetime army, but a "peacetime" army fully mobilized and quartered within striking distance of Russia.

On 15 February the OKW generated a special twist in this deception theme by touting BARBAROSSA to the *Russians* as itself a "deception diversion" to mislead the *British* about SEA LION. That rare double bluff was sustained until at least as late as 5 June. Then, on 24 April, von Brauchitsch ordered a major deception operation—Fall HAIFISCH (Operation SHARK)—to involve military activities from Scandinavia to Brittany. A series of "secret" notices was sent in early May to the German military attachés in Moscow, Berne, Tokyo, and six other embassies, lying that the rumors of war were false and that some eight German divisions would soon be withdrawn from the Russian border. Clearly, this widely distributed false information was expected to leak to Soviet intelligence.

Propaganda Minister Goebbels, privy to BARBAROSSA by June, contributed his personal bit of fakery. He wrote an article "disclosing" that the invasion of *England* was imminent. It was published on 13 June under his own name in the *Völkischer Beobachter* and ostentatiously withdrawn by the police as soon as copies were known to have reached the foreign press correspondents. Delighting in his own cleverness, Goebbels then even placed himself in simulated disgrace to complete the masquerade. This brief public "disgrace" was accepted by the foreign press corps as the final proof that the article did represent a genuine "leak."

As absurd as this cover story has seemed in retrospect to historians, the "big lie" that BARBAROSSA was SEA LION not only apparently worked against the Russians but, suitably modified, almost completely deceived British intelligence until 1942, nearly a year and a half after Hitler had, in fact, abandoned his intention to invade Britain.

Defense against Russia. On 6 September 1940 Hitler added a second major deception theme when he directed the Abwehr to mask the eastward troop transfers as a contingency shield against any hostile Russian moves, particularly into the Balkans, specifying that this cover story be fed to the "Russian intelligence service." Subsequently, on 18 December, Hitler further specified that BARBAROSSA planning and deployments be explained to subordinate German commanders as mere contingency planning and "precautionary measures in case Russia should choose to become more hostile. This plausible lie was kept afloat until at least as late as 4 June 1941." By 19 March 1941 this cover story was modified slightly to present the eastern deployments as a "defensive measure" in response to the then apparent Russian buildup. That specific lie was maintained at least as late as 5 June. Moreover, during April and May the Germans introduced the momentarily appropriate theme that the Wehrmacht's eastern deployment formed a "rear cover" for their then current Balkan invasion.

In accord with this cover story, relevant OKW orders often carried a preamble explaining their purpose as purely defensive in case of a possible Russian attack. Since this tale was believed at Army Group staff level, it should not be surprising that Russian intelligence also credited it.

Buildup against Balkans. When, during April and May 1941, the Wehrmacht's blitzkrieg thrust through the Balkans, that operation was made to do double duty as cover for BARBAROSSA. Thus, on 3 February 1941, Hitler added the planned invasion of Greece to the BARBAROSSA camouflage list. On 12 May, after the Greek enterprise had been liquidated, Crete was substituted on the list.

Impending Ultimatum. Sometime shortly before 17 May 1941 the Reich Foreign Ministry invented (or at least first utilized) the cover story that German actions were determined by Russian conduct. This crucial lie was picked up by the OKW on 25 May and further propagated by them. This became the main and most crucial set of rumors during the final weeks before the invasion. Because I have been unable to establish conclusively the official inspiration of most of these particular rumors, I have discussed them in the following section on rumor.

Other Aspects. The Gestapo's intelligence service (the SD) had a major part in these deception operations. In addition to its partially successful efforts to cut Russian intelligence off from sources of authentic information, the SD contrived to pass them considerable misleading information prepared by the Wehrmacht, including material about renewed preparations for SEA LION.

The German psychological warfare factories also busily contributed to the mass of rumors that were circulating in early 1941 about

German plots and troop movements in the Mediterranean. Many of these themes, such as German "tourists" controlling the French air and naval bases in Morocco in February; 6,000 German troops in Morocco in March; 60,000 German troops massing in Spain in May to attack Gibraltar and Morocco—simply vanished with the invasion of Russia on 22 June. These and similar baseless tales were widely credited, for example, by the British and American Economic Warfare boards, the British ambassador in Washington, the American consul-general in Algiers, the British embassy in Lisbon, and the Foreign Office in London. Such rumors were effective not only in diverting attention from Eastern Europe but also in placing a great strain—and embarrassment—on all other intelligence and diplomatic services, as Robert Murphy has so well described.

This elaborate rumor campaign was orchestrated at least in Spain by the German press attaché in Madrid, Hans Lazar, who simultaneously was playing out a private game by disclosing BARBAROSSA to Polish intelligence.

An odd smoke screen, which evidently originated in early 1941 with Nazi propagandists, were the letters from German soldiers to their families. They bore faked Russian postmarks and contained false descriptions of Wehrmacht operations in conjunction with the Russians.

A major part of Hitler's effort to lull Russian suspicions was the maintenance of normal economic and diplomatic ties. In this case, "normal" meant those intimate commercial negotiations and deliveries flowing from the Nazi-Soviet Pact of August 1939. This relationship involved the exchange of strategic goods, mainly Russian raw materials (such as oil and grain) for German machine tools, prototype weapons, and other military-industrial manufactures, as well as negotiations over minor delineations of frontiers. For example, on 30 March 1940 Hitler ordered that the deliveries of war materials to Russia receive top priority, over that of the Wehrmacht itself, which he knew to be on the eve of its assaults on Denmark, Norway, Holland, Belgium, and France. However, on 14 August, following the conquest of France, Hitler specified that punctual deliveries to the Russians would continue only to spring 1941. Göring conveyed this order to General Georg Thomas, chief of the OKW's Economic and Armaments Branch and himself one of the conspirators against Hitler in the so-called "Generals' Plot," adding that thereafter "we would have no further interest in completely satisfying the Russian demands." It is odd that the interests of logistic efficiency were allowed to take precedence over BARBAROSSA security, which would have required that the first order canceling deliveries would have been the accomplished fact of the invasion itself. As it happened, the Russians did receive some of their war warnings through security leaks about these reallocations in German industry.

The Soviet Invasion of Manchuria, 1945. Since V-E Day on 8-9 May 1945, Stalin had been formally bound by Russia's allies to wage war on Japan and invade Manchuria by August 10. But the Japanese knew only that Stalin intended to attack sometime in the future. At this juncture the Japanese government invited the Soviet Union on June 24 to become a party to negotiating a conditional surrender between Japan and the Anglo-American Allies. The Japanese clearly signaled that, in return for his good offices, they were prepared to pay Stalin a high territorial and political price. Stalin quickly seized this opportunity for secret bargaining and strategic deception to explore his diplomatic options and to influence Japanese perceptions about Soviet intentions and schedules for invading Manchuria.

Intent. Through both his Foreign Minister in Moscow and the Soviet Ambassador to Japan, Stalin managed to arouse Japanese beliefs that he was, indeed, seriously interested in negotiating with them. The overall effect of this secret diplomacy was to reinforce, in the weeks before the planned attack, official Japanese illusions that Stalin was prepared to negotiate tolerable terms for an end to the war. The Japanese government expected on 8 August that the Soviets would soon deliver a specification of terms, an ultimatum perhaps but not a declaration of war. Ironically, this illusion was both the one that the Japanese had tried to foster with the Americans immediately before 7 December 1941, and the one that Hitler had induced in Stalin immediately before the Nazi invasion of Russia on 22 June 1941.

Although surprise of intent was at least partly achieved in this manner, it is doubtful that it had great material effect. The Japanese military potential was by then so denuded by combat with the Americans, British, and Chinese that an overriding strategic decision had already been taken in Tokyo to concentrate on defense of the home islands. Consequently, even had the central authorities recognized the imminence of the Manchurian operation, it is unlikely that they would have reinforced the Kwantung Army. The commanders and staffs of the Kwantung Army, moreover, were effectively insulated from or immune to the psychological effects of Soviet diplomatic deception. Thus, strategic surprise was only minimally due to the Soviets' concealment of their intent.

Time. Even when an attacker's intent to move is expected, strategic surprise can still follow from a defender's failure to anticipate the time of attack. As with all other forms of surprise, surprise of time is either self-induced or can be induced by deception. The Russians achieved the latter by tactfully exploiting certain Japanese preconceptions.

At the Teheran Summit Conference in late 1943, Stalin had committed the USSR, by agreement with its allies, to attack Japan as soon as possible after the defeat of Germany. Not only did he make this promise to the Americans and British, but he also ordered the Soviet army immediately to start stockpiling munitions in Far Eastern depots—a process that continued until the invasion.

At the end of September 1944, four months after the Allies opened the second front in Western Europe and the Soviet summer offensive had succeeded, Stalin told the General Staff to begin preparing estimates for the movement of troops to the Far East, explaining simply that "Apparently they will be needed soon." The consequent General Staff estimate, which was completed about the beginning of October, scheduled the transfer of troops to start "early" in 1945, but the unexpected requirement for forces on the Russo-German front during the winter of 1944-45 delayed this schedule.

Preoccupied with the Wehrmacht, the Soviet General Staff did no further strategic planning for the war with Japan from November to February. However, other Soviet plans were in process that determined the Manchurian timetable. From November through January, Stavka and General Staff plans anticipated the capture of Berlin and V-E Day by 5 March. These plans changed about February 1 with Stalin's decision to cancel abruptly the final Soviet offensive against Germany in mid-course. Then, on 11 February, Stalin committed the Soviet Union to enter the war against Japan "in two or three months after Germany has surrendered." The only conditions were specified territorial claims.

At exactly midnight on 8-9 May, Germany's surrender was effected and 9 May became V-E Day. Henceforth, 9 August would be

Manchuria D-day for the few who knew what Soviet commitments had been established at Yalta. Weather remained a consideration in setting a date for the attack. July and August were generally considered undesirable months to initiate ground operations in Manchuria, while September, October, and November were thought best. Japanese authorities shared these professional assessments with their Russian counterparts.

By 13 June the General Staff's timetable called for the last troop units to reach the Far East between 1-5 August. And by 18 June, the timetable specified that D-day be between 20-25 August. The target date was subsequently moved forward until, finally, on 3 August, Marshal Aleksandr Vasilevskii reported to Stalin that all fronts and units were ready and in position to go into action as early as 7 August. Given this circumstance, together with the suddenly and unseasonably improved weather, Vasilevskii urged that the battle be joined no later than 9-10 August, that is, one or two days earlier than the most recently projected D-day of 11 August. Stalin soon approved this revised schedule and immediately notified Vasilevskii, although he did not actually sign the order until 1630 hours on 7 August Moscow time, that is, fifteen hours after the Americans dropped the atomic bomb on Hiroshima.

Until the very hour of the Soviet invasion, on 9 August, the Japanese government, Imperial Army General Staff, Kwantung Army HQ, and their respective intelligence services expected that even if the Russians attacked they would and could not do so before September at the earliest. The fact that Japanese troops working on deep defensive lines were deployed forward on warning increased rather than reduced the effectiveness of strategic deception because it exposed Japanese forces to a well-prepared attack while they were moving, vulnerably, toward defensive fortifications. Thus, given adroit Soviet reinforcement of their enemy's own preconceptions, the Japanese were very surprised by the early timing of the Soviet invasion.

Direction. The choice of direction or axis of the main Soviet attack was of major concern to both the Soviet and Japanese planners. The former sought to mislead Japanese expectations as to the main source and angle of attack while the latter sought to detect Soviet deployments and plans.

The Japanese correctly foresaw Manchuria (rather than Inner Mongolia, Korea, or the Japanese home islands) as the main theater of Soviet action. Since late 1940 the Kwantung Army had considered the potentially most dangerous Soviet axis of attack to be a drive from the Transbaikal toward central or southern Manchuria, even though that axis crossed the Greater Khingan Range. This assessment was based not on secret intelligence but rather on simple geographical and logistic calculations: the proximity of urban, rear staging areas and of strategic reserves in European Russia made the Transbaikal the most defensively secure and offensively efficient base in the Soviet Far East.

Moreover, General Georgi Zhukov's victory at Khalkhin-Gol in 1939 had already demonstrated to the Japanese the Soviet ability to mount a large-scale attack from Mongolia. Hence, when the invasion finally materialized, the Kwantung Army was not completely surprised that a blow was staged from that quarter. The Japanese, however, were utterly stunned by the sudden strength and sustained speed generated by Marshal Rodian Malinovsky's Transbaikal Front.

Strength. Although Japanese estimates of the overall build-up of Soviet strength in the Far East were approximately correct for strategic planning purposes, Soviet security, cover, and deception measures prevented the Japanese from discovering the location of these forces within the theater. The intelligence sections of both the Kwantung Army and the Imperial Army General Staff had good estimates of total Soviet strength in the Far East but very poor estimates of its distribution. The only deployment that the Kwantung Army could confirm was in two sectors on the eastern front that had apparently been reinforced, but the size of these reinforcements remained unknown. In retrospect, a Japanese historian, Colonel Saburo Hayashi, correctly speculated that "this detected build-up may have been a ruse to draw the Kwantung Army's attention to the eastern front." Indeed, Meretskov's First Far Eastern Front had created false formations to dissimulate its strength in relation to the other two fronts.

Japanese intelligence had identified and located only seven of the twelve ground armies (plus the Soviet-Mongol Group) in the Far East. All those identified had been established by 1941. This was very old intelligence. The Japanese failed to detect either the arrival of four entirely new armies or the formation of another, together with the Soviet-Mongol Group. Moreover, they also failed to detect the transfer of the 16th Army from the west (Transbaikal Front) to the north (Second Far Eastern Front). Consequently, the Japanese were working from base figures that implied distribution among the western, northern, and eastern fronts of, respectively, 30 percent, 30 percent, and 40 percent, when the real distribution was closer to 40 percent, 25 percent, and 35 percent. The gross maldistribution of Japanese defenders confirms the success of this operational deception.

Lessons for the Model

The Manchurian campaign is exceptional in Soviet experience because strategic and operational surprise was won from an enemy that was continuously receiving and correctly evaluating a substantial amount of authentic intelligence. The Soviet deception campaign was moderately sophisticated; it employed most of the ruses or channels that could have been used to supply credible disinformation to the enemy, and it adroitly directed these misleading data to the most receptive and influential Japanese institutions and individuals. Significant surprise was thereby effected in each of its main dimensions, but in varying degrees. With respect to Soviet intentions, it was moderate; for the timing of the attack, it was very high; for the direction, strength, and method of attack, it was fairly high; and the overall intensity of strategic surprise was quite high. Yet, the strategic success of Soviet deception planners in the Manchurian campaign was won from an opponent that was unusually vulnerable to deception due to its primitive intelligence services and its gullible foreign minister.

The Soviet deception effort was both systematic and substantial. It developed Japanese misperceptions of Soviet military preparedness and plans and thereby diverted Japanese defense efforts away from the area of the main effort. To accomplish this result, it employed extensive military and discrete diplomatic means. The stocks and movements of pre-positioned supplies and equipment were effectively camouflaged.

Invasion plans were restricted to a few top commanders and chiefs of staff who used field disguises and pseudonyms. Forward reconnaissance and deployments were strictly limited before the time of attack. Intense patterns of normal "defense" activities, communications, training, and construction were established well beforehand. Carefully simulated concentrations, false movements, and misinformation were presented to effective sources of Japanese intelligence, and special plans for final deployments at night on the eve of attack were worked out and rehearsed in advance. In short, the achievement of surprise was the deliberate result of Soviet designs to aggravate inevitable Japanese mistakes and weaknesses.

The modern significance of this historical case has been explicitly affirmed or commended by Soviet analyses of the campaign's strategic design. Indeed, one of the most important lessons of this campaign for the future is that "it is possible to attain complete strategic surprise in executing the first operations at the beginning of the war." It is not only of theoretical interest, but, as main authorities assert, "this experience can be of practical interest for planning modern operations." Moreover, from the data and testimony of Japanese authorities, this case demonstrates that less-than-complete surprise can be gained at limited cost and used to great advantage. Thus, it successfully illustrates a variety of principles and techniques that Soviet officers have professional interest in implementing by more modern means.

When Deception Fails: The Theory of Outs

"If the performer knows enough outs, he will never fail to bring a trick to successful conclusion."
—Jerry Mentzer, *Card Cavalcade*

Deception fails only if the target takes no notice of the offered data, notices but judges it irrelevant, misunderstands its intended meaning, or detects its method. In most cases, the deception game ends at that point. However, both the successful analyst and the persistent deceiver can, if they have prepared, continue the game one stage further. Elsewhere I have discussed the strategies available to the successful detective of deception. Here I describe those steps the deceiver can take to rescue success from impending failure.

Among all types of deceivers, only confidence tricksters and magicians have developed any standard operating procedures for recovering from the unfortunate effects of discovery of their deception. The others leave themselves only the option of hasty flight, if even that. Some academic military deception specialists have taken the odd view that the risk of a failed deception is so great that it is better to have no deception at all. This is overly pessimistic advice. In *Stratagem*, I found historically that deception operations usually have substantial payoffs and never backfire.

Neither soldiers' manuals nor generals' war plans tell them what to do when their deception operations fail. The usual attitude is, "Well, we tried." Because, as seen earlier, deception seldom costs much; most commanders just write it off as a small loss and either abort the real operation or, more likely, charge on in without the advantage of surprise. In either case, the logic is that a failed deception is no worse than not having tried at all. I agree with the logic but would hope for a more creative solution. I know of only two cases where military officers overcame their self-crippling sense of helplessness and redesigned their deception plans to take positive advantage of the new situation.

Sometime around mid-1942, Major Oliver Thynne was a novice planner with Colonel Dudley Clarke's "A" Force, the Cairo-based British deception team. From intelligence,[3] Thynne had just discovered that the Germans had learned to distinguish the dummy British aircraft from the real ones because the flimsy dummies were supported by struts under their wings. When Major Thynne reported this to his boss, Brigadier Clarke, the "master of deception," fired back:

"Well, what have you done about it?"

"Done about it, Dudley? What could I do about it?"

"Tell them to put struts under the wings of all the real ones, of course!"[4]

Of course? Hardly. A commander with a straightforward mind, having recognized a telltale flaw in the dummies, would have ordered the camouflage department to correct it. But Clarke's wonderfully devious mind immediately saw a way to capitalize on the flaw. By putting dummy struts on the real planes while grounded, enemy pilots would avoid them as targets for strafing and bombing. Moreover, it would cause the German photo-interpreters to underestimate the number of real RAF planes based locally and falsely conclude that many of the real ones must be based elsewhere. Clarke had the wit to see the "out" as a general principle. One of his favorite maxims that he taught his staff was: "When you put over a deception, always leave yourself an escape route."[5]

The second example of a necessary military out that worked was an audacious and risky one, a last minute improvisation forced upon the deception planners by sheer urgency.[6] Operation OLIVE was

Field Marshal Earl Alexander's decisive offensive to break the German line across central Italy in summer 1944. In early June, Alexander planned his main attack with his American and French divisions to go through the mountainous center, with a feint by his British divisions along the eastern flank on the Adriatic. On 5 July Alexander learned that London and Washington had decided to strip him of many of his American and all his French divisions, sending them away for the amphibious invasion of South France. Consequently, on 4 August, he reluctantly decided to make the real attack up the Adriatic coast with his British troops, leaving the denuded American force to conduct the feint at the center, in other words, the very strategy that the current deception operations were communicating successfully to the Germans. This reversal of strategy now required a plausibly readjusted deception. Moreover, with OLIVE D-day set for 25 August, Alexander's deception planners had only three weeks to reverse the enemy's perceptions—a feat that military history shows to be very rare indeed.

The essence of the new deception plan was to work a double bluff by having the Germans now believe that the old "evidence" fed them had been and still was the Allied deception operation. This was carried out by a new and elaborate program of radio deception. As far as I am aware, this is the only case where a military deception plan was turned back on itself, a stratagem to attempt to discredit earlier disinformation by exposing it for the deception it had been. In the event, the new deception was successful enough to gain surprise of place, strength and of timing. Two German divisions were tied up in reserve for a *possible* attack at the center, one division at the point of real attack was caught being relieved, and both the field commander and a key divisional commander were still off on leave.

The "out" works in military deception because of the "principle of security of options."[7] Deception, by its very nature, provides its own best security. Although the term "security of options" was original with me, the concept was only a generalized extension of Liddell Hart's principle of "alternative objectives," first formulated in 1929.[8] Alternative objectives mean simply that every football play, most military offensives, and so forth, can have two (or more) goals.

If the deception operation succeeds in anticipating the preconceptions of the victim and playing upon them, deception security is absolute. In that case the victim becomes the unwitting agent of his own surprise, and no amount of warning (such as security leaks) will suffice to reverse his fatally false expectations. Even if the deception plan runs counter to or fails to play upon the victim's preconceptions, the very fact that it threatens alternative objectives will usually assure enough uncertainty to delay or defuse or otherwise blunt the victim's response.

The worst possible case would occur if the deception plan itself were prematurely disclosed to the victim. While such potentially disastrous disclosure is rare in general and so far unknown in war,[9] even if it were, all would not necessarily be lost. First, the disclosure itself would have to be believed. Second, if the deceiver knows or even suspects disclosure, he can actually capitalize on this by switching to one of the alternative courses of action or simply adopting a new deception plan to reverse appearances. This is what Field Marshal Alexander did to breach the German Gothic Line in Italy in 1944 when he reversed an already successful deception operation by deliberately disclosing the first one. Even if the direction or objective of the attack has been compromised, the planner can still manipulate the victim's perception of the timing or strength or even the intent or style of the attack.

I did not learn until much later that this modern notion of a military deception "out" had been anticipated by magicians back in 1785, in Henri Decremps' second Rule. Confidence tricksters and other hustlers also have developed a standard systematic technique to buy enough time for a safe escape just before the victim sees the operation for the scam it is. This technique is called "cooling out" or the "blow-off." It is built into the final stage of the operation and is itself a deception. I have described these two nonmilitary "outs" at length elsewhere in "The Maverick Detective" (draft, 1999).

Notes

1. For extensive documentation on the German case, see Barton Whaley, *Covert Rearmament in Germany, 1919-1939: Deception and Misperception* (New Brunswick, NJ: Academic Press, 1983). A condensed version appeared in the *Journal of Strategic Studies*, Vol.5, No. 1 (March 1982), pp. 3-39. A fine memoir of one of the disarmament inspectors is J. H. Morgan, *Assize of Arms* (New York: Oxford University Press, 1946).
2. For an extended discussion and documentation of the German deception against the USSR preceding the 1941 invasion, see Barton Whaley, *Codeword BARBAROSSA* (Cambridge, MA: MIT Press, 1973).

3.	David Mure, *Master of Deception: Tangled Webs in London and the Middle East* (London: W. Kimber, 1980). Although Mure does not give the source of this intelligence, it was probably ISOS, the British intercepts of German Military Intelligence (the *Abwehr*), which they were reading along with the better known ULTRA. The ISOS codebreaking was first made public in the British official history by F. H. Hinsley, *British Intelligence in the Second World War*, Vol. III (London: Her Majesty's Stationery Office, 1981).

4.	Mure, *Master of Deception*, 1980. See also J. Barton Bowyer (pseudo. J. Bowyer Bell and Barton Whaley), *Cheating: Deception in War & Magic, Games & Sports, Sex & Religion, Business & Con Games, Politics & Espionage, Art & Science* (New York: St. Martin's Press, 1982), p. 223.

5.	Mure, *Master of Deception*, 1980.

6.	Barton Whaley, *Stratagem: Deception and Surprise in War* (Cambridge, MA: MIT Press, 1969), pp. A414-A418.

7.	First stated in Whaley, *Stratagem*, pp. 225-226.

8.	The concept of "alternative goals" or "alternative objectives" was first stated by B. H. Liddell Hart in *The Decisive Wars of History: A Study in Strategy* (London: Bell, 1929) pp. 141-158. See also Hart, *The British Way in Warfare* (London: 1932); *Strategy: The Indirect Approach* (New York: Praeger, 1954), pp. 161-164, 333-372; and *Memoirs*, Vol. I (London: Cassell, 1965), pp. 166-168. See discussion of the evolution of this concept in Whaley, *Stratagem*, pp. 128-139.

9.	The closest to this was during the Battle of Midway in 1942 when faulty security permitted the U.S. Navy to see *around* the primitive Japanese deception operation and set an ambush. See Whaley, *Stratagem*, pp. A-286- A287. A recent example from strategic international politics was the disclosure in 1986 of the CIA's disinformation campaign against Libyan leader Khadaffi. At less exalted levels, we see this in "tipoffs" of con games and other scams and commonly in "poison-pen" letters that reveal marital infidelities.

4

Conditions Making for Success and Failure of Denial and Deception: Democratic Regimes

M. R. D. Foot

"...willing to overcome by fraud those whom he desired to subdue, because he was wont to say that it was the victory that brought the glory, not the method of achieving it."
—*Machiavelli*, on Castruccio Castracani, dictator of Lucca ca. 1325, *The Prince*

Introduction

This look at British deception begins with a glance back to Sun Tzu, Machiavelli, Marlborough, and Wellington, but deals mainly with the Second World War of 1939-45. In this conflict, General A. P. Wavell was the inspiration for a deception system whose central feature was to persuade the enemy that allied forces were much larger than they really were. In May 1944 the Germans believed that there were seventy-nine divisions waiting in England to invade Western Europe; in fact there were fifty-two.

Deception in the Mediterranean was run by Brigadier Dudley Clarke, and by Colonel J. H. Bevan in London. Their triumphs included *Mincemeat*, which persuaded the Germans that Sardinia, not Sicily, would be attacked next after the fall of Tunis; and *Fortitude*, which led them to believe that the Normandy landings were a diversion to draw troops away from a later main assault on the beaches south of Boulogne. Ultra secret intelligence provided an indispensable control over how well these plots were working.

A sub-plot of *Fortitude* was *Titanic* in which a handful of parachutists succeeded in decoying away the reserve regiment opposite

Omaha beach. The Germans wasted the whole morning of 6 June 1944 hunting down the decoys instead of counter-attacking the forces of General Bradley. An eyewitness account of the origins of this deception is provided here. *Fortitude North* was aimed directly at Hitler himself, and played on his liking for Andrew Thorne, the Grenadier Guards colonel who had been British military attaché in Berlin in 1932-35. By 1943, Thorne had been promoted to the rank of general and was commander-in-chief, Scotland. Hitler was persuaded, mainly through double agents, that Thorne intended to invade Norway. He kept 300,000 troops locked up there uselessly until the end of the war.

The principal lesson learned from these efforts was the need for absolute secrecy. This sits uneasily with parliamentary, congressional, or media government, but is essential for success in this type of war. Access to enemy ciphers was an additional asset that is unlikely to be available in the future. It also was a help to have the business run by officers from similar backgrounds who shared a common outlook, and it was indispensable for all the secret services involved to cooperate, thinking only of victory, and disregarding private service advantage.

Deception

Deception is far older than warfare. It is almost as old as combat, which goes back to before the Stone Age. The first primitive man or woman who thought how to feint when fighting a fellow human being originated a device now in common use by boxers, fencers, and footballers. It is strange that it should be regarded as something extraordinary by journalists and under-informed commentators on war.

Sun Tzu laid down, centuries before Christ was born, that "All warfare is based on deception," and that no general could accomplish anything worth doing without it.[1] Today, Sun Tzu's general principles of strategy seem to gain warm approval from staff colleges the world over. Developments in technology have made wars, especially between industrially developed powers, more devastating than they used to be; but the principles of how to fight them have not altered much in two and a half millennia.

"To such a name no praise can be high enough," says the epitaph on Nicolo Machiavelli's grave in Florence. In the early sixteenth century, Machiavelli put deceit high among the characteristics that would be necessary to a successful ruler; and even though he has become a byword for immorality, he remains favorite reading for those who seek greatness in politics—of which strategy is a part. Indeed, we have Churchill's word for it that at the summit, politics and strategy are one.

Marlborough and Churchill

The history of warfare is littered with examples of deception, most of them successful. There seems to be no limit to the credulity of bad generals. Yet, in a paper that concentrates on modern British deception efforts, one example from Queen Anne's reign is too striking to omit. In the summer of 1704, Marlborough finally secured the agreement of the Dutch to move his combined Anglo-Dutch army where he wanted, to defeat the French forces in Bavaria. He set off up the right bank of the Rhine, and so confused the French highest command about where he was really heading, that he was able to catch Marshal Tallard unreinforced at Blenheim and to inflict a severe defeat on him.[2] In a sub-continent where Churchillolatry is rife—I have affectionate recollections of the Other Other Club at Madison, Wisconsin—it is worth drawing attention to the huge stroke of luck for the free world that Churchill was out of office for ten years from 1929. He spent several years pondering the career of his great ancestor Marlborough, about whom he wrote a four-volume life. Working on this, he went through all the problems of coalition war, and its manifest advantages and disadvantages. He thus prepared himself, unconsciously, for the task that was to fall to him in May 1940. In what he regarded, in his childhood, as the Great War— the war against revolutionary and Napoleonic France—there had been ample scope for deception. For instance, in the mid-1790s Pitt flooded France with forged *assignats*, as a means of destabilizing the young republic's currency and thus bringing it down. However, this is perhaps an example of subversion, rather than deception.

Wellington

Wellington was certainly ready to deceive his enemies when he could. As the allied army formed up on the heights of Busaco on 27 September 1810, Sergeant Hamilton of the 43rd Light Infantry found his whole battalion required to change their coats with the Portuguese battalion beside them. Massena's scouts who came forward to reconnoiter allied movements encountered Wellington's attempts to confuse him about where the weak spots in the allied line were. In both Wellington's great sieges of Ciudad Rodrigo and of Badajoz in 1812, a false attack was mounted at the same time as the main assault to confuse the enemy garrison. This succeeded in both sieges.

The First World War

Churchill himself had had some practical experience of high command during the Great War of 1914-18. He was the politician in charge of the Royal Navy when it began. He was at least familiar with the Navy's arrangements for deceiving enemy fleets in battle; later he plunged himself deep in the controversies that followed the apparently inconclusive battle of Jutland (31 May-1 June, 1916) in the early 1920s, in which feinting had been among the many maneuvers used. The German High Seas Fleet, for instance, had left its W/T call sign operating as usual in harbor, to conceal the fact that it had actually gone to sea.

During World War I, deception was attempted in land warfare also, but the conditions of trench warfare were such, on the western front at least, that it was hardly possible to deceive the enemy about where any major blow was to fall. The concentrations of ammunition and men that were necessary to attempt any serious assault on the trench line that ran from the North Sea to the Swiss border were so vast that they were bound to be spotted. If air reconnaissance, which camouflage might baffle, did not pick it up, then spies, who could see beneath camouflage, could give ample warning to prepare countermeasures. Similarly, the attack on the Dardanelles, finally mounted on 25 April 1915, had been preceded by so many preliminary reconnaissances and bombardments that it forfeited surprise. Ludendorff, with the advantage of interior lines on the western front, tried all the same to bemuse Haig and Foch, and sometimes succeeded, but not for long.

The Interwar Years

The 1920s and 1930s were not the grandest years for the Foreign Office. Officials did their best to follow the principle laid down by Arthur Balfour, a former prime minister, when he was foreign secre-

tary during Woodrow Wilson's presidency: "Open covenants, secretly arrived at." But in their secret negotiations, British diplomats
were too often victims of German deception. They were profoundly
mistaken, for example, about the real strength of the Luftwaffe in
the middle 1930s. This was only sorted out when ultra secret intelligence about German capabilities in the air came on stream in late
spring 1940. In the autumn of 1939, the entire British high command, right up to the war cabinet, was taken by an ingenious
Sicherheitsdienst ploy. They believed they were in touch with a body
of German generals disaffected from the Nazi high command, and
successfully impersonated by Major Walter Schellenberg. It was he
who kidnapped the British secret intermediaries at Venlo on the Dutch-
German border on 9 November and accused them of having tried to
blow up Hitler the day before. The sour taste left by the Venlo incident was probably the reason why, all through the war, the British
resolutely rejected any approaches made to them by German diplomats or intelligence staff who were trying to bring the war to an end.

Two other major peacetime deceptions should be noted. They were
in progress in 1934-38 while Churchill's *Marlborough* was coming
out, and their results still resound today. One was orchestrated by
that master of propaganda, Dr. Joseph Goebbels. It convinced most
of the German people, and then a substantial slice of the populations
of Europe and of North and South America, that the Nazi regime
was doing wonders for Germany, particularly for its youth. In
Goebbels's imagery, the Führer of Nazi Germany was the mildest,
gentlest, and most benign of dictators. The horrors of the Holocaust
persuaded most of us otherwise. Yet even today there are fanatics
who deny that the Holocaust ever took place, and look back fondly
on the antics of the Bund deutsches Mädel and on how kind Hitler
was to children.

Lenin, too, was wonderful with children, and Lenin's disciple Stalin
brought off the second, simultaneous feat of worldwide deception,
rivaling that of Goebbels. Many of my own English contemporaries,
and many a few years older than myself, were captivated by the
prospect that Stalin was building a new society, the like of which
had never been seen before, and which would establish the equality
of mankind. The 1936 constitution he set up for the USSR looked
marvelous; nobody outside Russia noticed that little clause which
gave the Communist Party of the Soviet Union the right to override

everything and everybody, if need arose. Of course, the methods by which the Bolsheviks had come to power had been coarse, but the rough edges, surely, would soon be smoothed out by time and care. The horrors of Beria's Gulag, which rivaled those of Himmler's concentration camps, were still more of a closed book to the outside world, and for much longer. (The Bolshevik ascent to power also included a nice stroke of deception. At the critical moment on the night Trotsky took over Petrograd, the cruiser Aurora fired only blanks. Live ammunition was withheld until the Winter Palace had fallen, by which time it was no longer needed.)

The perceptions of key players played a pivotal role during the Munich crisis of September 1938. The only moment at which there was any trace of faltering on the German side was when it was announced that the Royal Navy had mobilized. Chamberlain had no desire to go to war that autumn; but the mere impression that he might made his putative enemies ponder. It also is worth recalling that the personal impression made on Hitler by Chamberlain and Daladier at the Munich conference was of men so feeble that thereafter he felt confident that he could outface them and get his way. He strode ahead on his determined path; the next world war followed.

The Second World War

The immediate cause of World War II was a deceptive measure by Hitler known as the Gleiwitz incident. "I will provide a propagandistic *causus belli*. Its credibility does not matter," he told his generals on 22 August 1939. Several Abwehr and SS parties were told to raid various parts of the German-Polish frontier. One of the raids was carried out on the night of 25-26 August, when Hitler had originally wanted the war to begin. Six nights later, the radio station at Gleiwitz (now Gliwice), which was then well inside the German frontier, was raided by SS men in Polish uniforms. They pretended to be Poles taking it over. They broadcast a few inflammatory phrases, in Polish; and left some corpses behind (concentration camp prisoners, who could easily be spared) to impress the United States correspondents who were summoned next day. This provided a final excuse for the German invasion of Poland early that day, 1 September 1939.

Early in the war, the Royal Navy was able to bring off a deceptive stroke that was old in Admiral Nelson's day, but sufficed to deceive a Reichsmarine commander less versed in naval history. Captain

Langsdorff took the pocket battleship *Admiral Graf Spee* into Montevideo after an indecisive action with three British cruisers on 13 December 1939. The least damaged of the cruisers hovered off the port, exchanging streams of flag signals with a supposedly more powerful friend over the horizon. There was no more powerful friend, but Langsdorff believed he would be outgunned if he came out, and sank his ship at the mouth of the River Plate, thus presenting the British with a badly needed victory.

Wavell and Clarke

As the war developed, British soldiers and policymakers settled down to organize deception seriously, inspired by the war's most intelligent, though not its luckiest, high commander, General (later Field-Marshal Earl) A. P. Wavell. Wavell had long pondered how best the British Empire, weakened as it had been by the scrapping of the Grand Fleet (at Churchill's insistence) in the 1920s, could stand up to the growing menaces of Bolshevism, Fascism and Nazism. He had concluded that trickery would have to be used as a substitute for strength, until real strength could be built up again.

Why was Wavell so devoted to deception? Because, as a member of General Edmund Allenby's intelligence staff, he had watched a now famous example of its use against the Turks in October 1917. Beatrice Webb's nephew Richard Meinertzhagen had succeeded in misleading the Turks around Gaza about which flank Allenby was about to attack, by dropping a bloodstained haversack full of false documents.

While he was commander in Palestine in 1936 (then a British mandate under the League of Nations), Wavell earmarked three young officers for special duties in the event of another major war. One was Orde Wingate, who later became famous on his way to his heroic, accidental death on the second Chindit expedition into Burma. The second was Tony Simonds, who died early in 1999. He organized wartime escapes from Eastern Europe to the Near East. The third, Dudley Clarke, wrote a book, *Seven Assignments*,[3] about the less interesting parts of his war, which included the formation of the commandos during the summer crisis of 1940. He never said anything in public about his role as Wavell's deception officer.

Late in 1940, Wavell secured Clarke at his own elbow in Cairo, where he had become commander-in-chief, Middle East. Clarke took over the running of deception, keeping Wavell informed by word of mouth about what he was up to. He called his own tiny staff "A Force," which meant nothing, as it was intended to do. Italy had by this time run to the help of the apparently invincible Germany. Clarke's main preoccupation was to convince these two enemies that Wavell's forces were substantially bigger than they were. Inflating the enemy's view of one's own order of battle was central to British successes on the deception front all through the rest of the war; it succeeded admirably. For the supreme instance, by May 1944, the Germans believed that there were seventy-nine divisions waiting in England to invade Western Europe, when in fact there were fifty-two.

Clarke was aided in tactical deceptions by a small team of camouflage experts of unusual skill, headed by Jasper Maskelyne. In the 1920s and 1930s, one of the main delights for a child in London had been to visit Maskelyne and Devant's conjuring theater. Jasper Maskelyne packed up his full skills and took them to the western desert. He could transform tanks into trucks, or trucks into tanks in a few minutes of wrestling with hoops and painted canvas. He even created inflatable warships, right up to battleship size. This caused no end of confusion to the Italian and German intelligence staffs trying to make sense of British strengths and dispositions. Coming from the world of entertainment, Maskelyne had no reservations about going public. He chronicled his achievements in an enjoyable book, *Magic-Top Secret,* published in 1949, long before academic inquiries into this sort of subject started.

Camouflage is not always impenetrable to air reconnaissance. Several times over, each side in the desert noticed that it was being deceived. Both the Royal Air Force and the Luftwaffe used to cherish the anecdote of the dummy aircraft that were bombed with wooden bombs.

Two examples of successful deception in the eastern Mediterranean are worth mentioning. While Montgomery was preparing for the second battle of El Alamein, in autumn 1942, his engineers built some fifteen miles of dummy water pipeline across the desert, running towards the southern end of his defensive line. The pipeline was clearly visible to German air reconnaissance. German engineers judged, as they were meant to, that it would be completed by mid-November. So Rommel went on leave, and was absent from his front when Montgomery's attack was launched against the other flank of

the Axis army on 23 October. The second example was longer last-
ing. Through double agents and captured agents' sets played back,
the British convinced the Germans that they had a sizeable army
assembling in Syria, Lebanon, and Iraq that would invade the Balkan
peninsula. They thus kept several more German divisions tied up on
garrison duties in the Balkans than the realities of war would have
justified.

Central Organization

A start had already been made in Whitehall with the organization
of a central deception service, a group called the Inter-Service Security Board (ISSB), whose cover task was to allot code-names for
impending major operations. Jo Holland, who from 1938 to 1940
worked in the war office on methods of irregular warfare, set up the
ISSB, which formally was a sub-committee of the Joint Intelligence
Committee (JIC). He also found the man to run it, Major E. E. Coombe.
Coombe was a regular engineer, born in India in 1897, who had
won the Distinguished Flying Cross on the Salonika front during the
Great War, had been wounded in Dublin during the Troubles, and
had been given his war office post to do research on any subject he
chose because he had failed a medical examination for promotion to
lieutenant colonel. In two years, he founded the escape service, the
commandos, the Special Operations Executive (SOE), the subversion service, and the deception service, and organized the stay-be-
hind parties who were to disrupt the German invasion of England
that (thank goodness) never happened. His health was re-established
and an ordinary battalion command in his regiment fell vacant. As a
regular soldier he thought he ought to take it. So he bowed out of the
secret war early, but he had made his mark.

Sir Michael Howard, in the decisive and indispensable book on
British deception policy, *Strategic Deception* specifies that strategic
deception was originated by one man: Wavell.[4] In the now quite
large literature devoted to deception, much of it trivial or inaccurate, or both, Howard's book, the fifth volume of the series edited
by F. H. Hinsley, shines like a beacon on a dark night. Howard's
work, and it is almost the only one, bears witness to what was actually done, because it is founded on such archival material as the
wartime deception service left behind, as well as the writer's unusually well-developed historical insight.[5]

Secrecy

Howard finished the draft of his book some years before it was allowed to appear in print. A few words in defense of secrecy may be allowed, in a country where the political public seems to believe nothing ought to remain secret for fifty minutes, let alone fifty years. Mrs. Margaret Thatcher (as she then was) refused to pass the book for publication, having learned as a young woman when she was a clerk in a solicitor's office, that it was always a mistake to reveal to the other side any weighty point that might be usable in court, unless the rules of court compelled one to do so. As Wavell had noticed, deception could become a powerful weapon in the armory of a weak power. Great Britain was no longer as strong as it had been in Mrs. Thatcher's girlhood; she saw no reason to explain to potential enemies how Britain might fight them. Once she had left office, the book could appear.

Wavell certainly insisted on the need for absolute secrecy where A Force's work was concerned. He carried this doctrine to India with him, when he became commander-in-chief there in July 1941. He set up an equivalent to A Force under Peter Fleming (elder brother of Ian, creator of James Bond), and let Fleming do what he could to deceive the Japanese. Like Clarke, Fleming told nobody anything he did not need to know. His main difficulties were caused by the incompetence of the Japanese intelligence staffs against whom he was working. They were often reluctant to take the bait he held out to them.

The London Controlling Section

Clarke visited London early in October 1941, and explained what he was doing to the chiefs of staff. They warmly approved, and at once placed Coombe's ISSB under a more senior personage: Colonel Oliver Stanley, MC, MP, a recent secretary of state for war, younger son of the seventeenth Earl of Derby who was nicknamed "King of Lancashire."

Stanley established that deception was a matter for the operations, rather than the intelligence, staffs to cope with, a vital point that needed to be settled early on. But his heart was not in it, and in May 1942, with Churchill's leave, he went back to full time politics. He was succeeded by Colonel J. H. Bevan, a stockbroker in peacetime, who remained the central figure in British deception planning for the rest of the war. Nominally, Bevan came under the future operations planning section of the joint planning staff. He had a small office directly beside the cabinet war rooms at the southeast corner of St. James's Park, but in fact he ran a virtually independent secret service, which came top in the inter-secret-service pecking order. (The war rooms are now, as part of the Imperial War Museum, open to public inspection.) Anything Bevan asked for, he got; he was too sensible and too honest a man to ask for what he knew would be extravagant or unobtainable.

Bevan's little group was called by another meaningless name, the London Controlling Section (LCS). He belonged, as Stanley did, to the old ruling class. He was the grandson of a former speaker of the House of Commons who had become a viscount, and he was related to many notables. For example, his cousin, the current viscount, had married a duke's daughter, and his own brother-in-law was Field-Marshal Alexander. Moreover, he had known Churchill when working in Paris as a junior staff officer in 1918, after surviving several years as an infantry subaltern in the Hertfordshire Regiment on the western front. The old ruling class had run the secret services for centuries (Walsingham's decipher expert, for instance, had unraveled Mary Queen of Scots); they had traditions of how the work ought to be done, which spread quite widely through the officer class, and formed a dense, and all but impenetrable, security screen. It was long regarded as the depth of bad form to put anything about such matters on paper, let alone discuss them in front of strangers.

Such a community was well placed for dealing with so secret a subject; and was not likely to blab out of turn about what it was doing. Secrecy is a recurring theme here; it has always been regarded, in England at least, as the indispensable condition for adequate deceptions. Peter Fleming perhaps carried the doctrine a shade far at Jellore near Calcutta where the Royal Air Force's special duty aircraft were stationed. When he wanted something done by air on the deceptive front, he came down to the airfield himself, took the relevant flight commander, who himself would fly the operation, out for a walk, explained what he wanted in detail, and made sure no notes were taken.[6]

Coalitions

An awkwardness about coalition warfare needs mention here. If one is conducting deceptions in complete secrecy, what can be said to one's coalition allies? The British practice was to say nothing at all to the various governments in exile in London. That included de Gaulle's still formally unrecognized staffs in London and later in Algiers, and least of all de Gaulle himself, because his political ciphers were leaky. Nothing was said even to the Poles, whose ciphers even the cryptographers at Bletchley Park could not read; and not much to the USSR, on the ground that the Germans could probably read a good deal of Soviet cipher traffic. But the British were more forthcoming to the Americans, once the United States had entered the war. American officers sat on Bevan's small staff, and they, too, learned to keep their mouths shut outside the office.

Bevan was made privy to every secret he asked about. As Fleming once said, "It is impossible, or at any rate highly dangerous, to tell a lie until you know what the truth is going to be."[7] Bevan not only saw all the chiefs of staffs' minutes, but also was aware of the code-breaking achievements of Bletchley, and sat on the XX Committee that MI5 organized to look after the playing back of captured German agents.

Double Cross

All but one of the agents the Germans sent to Great Britain during the war were captured; most of them agreed to cooperate with their captors, while those who did not were tried and executed. The one exception was a wireless operator who committed suicide. His body was found with his unopened transmitter beside him.

The branch of MI5 that handled German agents, called B1a, came under Major T. A. Robertson, another man who never gave newspaper interviews.[8] He set up an inter-service committee to run these double agents, with representatives on it from all three of the armed forces, Combined Operations Headquarters (COHQ), and the intelligence and cipher services. I know from first-hand experience the secrecy surrounding Robertson's operation. I was posted to COHQ for eighteen months from August 1942 as an intelligence officer, and I shared a desk with a fellow-captain, G. G. Rice, who became a close friend (he was my best man when I married in 1945). Only

after his death did I discover that he had been COHQ's man on the
XX Committee. He never breathed a word to me of its very exist-
ence, a further instance of the watertight-compartmented security of
English wartime life.

That the deception, decipher, and security services could all be of
one mind, and work together amiably toward the same end, collabo-
rating with a small sealed knot of officers close to the highest command, provided part of the secret of the British wartime successes in
this field. Emphasis also must be laid on the decipher aspect. Thanks
to the probably unique opportunities offered by the penetration of
the Enigma and *Geheimschreiber* cipher systems, both of which the
Germans regarded as wholly secure, the deception staff could dangle
baits before the enemy, and find out exactly whether and when he
nibbled at them.

"Mincemeat"

One of the masterpieces of the deception service was operation
"Mincemeat" conducted in the summer of 1943. Tunis fell in May,
with a larger haul of prisoners than even at Stalingrad. Obviously,
the Anglo-American force in North Africa was preparing to invade
Europe. Any bright child with a school atlas could see that Sicily
was, equally obviously, the next step. Johnny Bevan decided all the
same to try to make the Germans believe that preparations against
Sicily were only a cover for assaults on Sardinia and on southern
Greece.

The keystone to this deceptive arch was to float a body ashore in
southwest Spain. Dressed as a major in the Royal Marines, he had a
briefcase full of highly secret material, including personal letters to
allied commanders in the Mediterranean from such personages in
London as Mountbatten. Their content pointed unmistakably to
Sardinia rather than Sicily. The briefcase fell into Abwehr hands with
the connivance of the Spanish police. The letters were opened and
re-sealed (a shade clumsily as the British were later able to establish
the fact of opening). The chiefs of staff were able to telegraph to
Churchill, who was in the United States at the time, "Mincemeat
swallowed whole." The Germans dutifully reinforced Sardinia and
the Peloponnese, leaving Sicily alone.

There was a literary as well as a strategic sequel. Duff Cooper, a
minister at the time, became aware of this story, and five years after

the war's end published a novel based on it called *Operation Heart-break*.[9] The secret authorities were alarmed to hear rumors that word was spreading that the novel was in fact a true story. So the admiralty called on Ewen Montagu who had done all the detailed work preparing Mincemeat, and had then gone back to the profession of barrister. Dictating continuously for forty-eight hours, Montagu produced an account of his own, *The Man Who Never Was*[10] that deservedly became a world bestseller and took the wind out of Duff Cooper's sails.

Montagu put nothing in that book that government wanted to remain secret. After Bletchley's decipher operation became public knowledge in the early 1970s, Montagu was able to write a sequel, *Beyond Top Secret U*,[11] in which he explained how heavily the deception service had relied on deciphering Abwehr messages to gauge how well their ploys were really deceiving their enemies.

As for how time passed in the London Controlling Section, much is clear from J. C. Masterman's admirable *The Double Cross System*.[12] More came from the pen of a prolific writer of detective stories, Dennis Wheatley, whose *Deception Planners* gives a detailed account of its work (and includes a good photograph of Bevan).[13] Wheatley, when he joined, was a pilot officer, RAF, the lowest commissioned rank in all the armed forces. Yet, with a decent private income and a London club, he had entrée to the world of the old ruling class and could move among its members as one of them. By the end of the war he was a wing commander (equivalent to an army lieutenant-colonel); as Bevan's secretary, he had earned his promotions. He, too, emphasized that "as few people as possible, having regard to practical necessities, should be allowed into the secret of any deception plan."[14]

"Fortitude"

The main achievement of the LCS was operation "Bodyguard" renamed "Fortitude." The objective, of course, was to deceive the Germans about the time, place, and nature of the start of operation "Overlord," the allied re-invasion of Western Europe in 1944. It is now popularly misremembered as D-day; misremembered, because every operation had its D-day, not just the Normandy landings. Bevan went to Russia in good time, with an American colleague, Colonel William H. Baumer of the United States Joint Security Control, to discuss with the Russian staffs, who were great believers also in the power of deception, how Soviet and Anglo-American efforts were to be combined for the protection of Overlord. They met with the usual maddening delays, but in the end secured useful agreements.[15] Much of the detailed work for Fortitude was done by Roger Fleetwood Hesketh, a Lancashire notable, who wrote a full account of it at the end of the War. This was long kept secret, and was published only after his death with the simple title of the codename: *Fortitude*.[16]

Fortitude was a colossal success. It made the Normandy landings, tough as they were, succeed. Had Montgomery's left flank been counterattacked with vigor in mid-June 1944 by the formidable German forces east of the Seine, the invasion might well have failed. It is now taken for granted that those landings were bound to succeed because they did; in fact, the outcome was far from a certainty. Churchill, in particular, could never forget that at the landing on V beach at Gallipoli, for which he was responsible, the sea had run red with blood for thirty yards off shore on the evening of April 25, 1915. (This was related to me by a man who had been there, as an engineer corporal; he had risen to be quartermaster of my unit at the outbreak of the next world war.) Churchill, who knew this story, offered no guarantees that Neptune, the assault phase of Overlord, would not encounter a similar rate of casualty.

Fortitude prevented a disaster on the beaches by distracting and diverting the defenders. Through double agents and dummy radio traffic, the LCS succeeded in persuading the Germans that General Patton commanded a large, notional United States army in Kent and East Anglia, which was standing by to cross the Channel at the Straits of Dover. The German general staff had picked this as the most likely spot for an allied invasion, because air cover could there be densest. The landing further west, led by Montgomery under Eisenhower's command, was presented to the Germans as a diversion, intended to draw troops away from the threatened area round Calais.

"Titanic"

On the very night of the invasion, 5-6 June 1944, three tactical deceptions were mounted to confuse the enemy even further: "Glimmer," "Taxable," and "Titanic." Glimmer and Taxable were airborne spoofs. Two specially selected RAF squadrons, 218 and 617 (the Dambusters), each ran one of these operations. Their aircraft flew overlapping oblong courses, at a set speed, throwing out bundles of Window foil at precisely timed intervals. On the few German naval radar screens that R. V. Jones had left in action they appeared as large fleets; one heading for Cap d'Antifer, north of Le Havre, and the other for Cap Gris Nez, near Calais. They appeared to move at eight knots from midnight till first light when they were near the coast, and then vanished.[17] I chose the codename for operation *Titanic*, and may perhaps be allowed, for a couple of paragraphs, to appear as witness instead of historian. By May 1944, I was intelligence officer of the Special Air Service brigade, an international brigade made up of two British and two French parachute units, some Belgians, a few Yugoslavs, a few Austrians under Scots cover names, and a Pole who was my assistant. We were forbidden to land before D-day. Our task was to operate, in uniform, well behind the main battle line, disrupting German reinforcements and providing intelligence.

About mid-May, I was telephoned by a stranger: would I scramble? I did. He introduced himself by naming a fellow intelligence officer whom I knew well, on Eisenhower's intelligence staff, and with whom I had been dealing for months on various points. He gave his own extension number, but not his name (he may have been Colonel David Strangeways, a canon of the Church of England who died in 1998). I was to allot a codename to an operation that would take place on the night of D-1 to D-day for Neptune, and was to provide four (shortly reduced to two) parties for it, each consisting of an officer, a sergeant and three other parachutists. He specified that they were to come from the British component of the brigade. They were to report to Tempsford airfield, the base of the RAF's special duty squadrons, by 1800 hours on D-2, where they would be briefed. I checked back with my friend at Supreme Headquarters Allied Expeditionary Force (SHAEF), got the brigadier's approval, and had the parties duly told off. I was forbidden to go with them. Regimentally, Titanic is regarded as a failure, because of the ten men who went only a sergeant and a trooper came back. Tactically, it made a little more sense. The men were armed with Verylight pistols and Victrola gramophones playing recordings of small arms fire, interspersed with soldiers' chat. With each party went 500 dummy parachutists, supposed to explode on landing. The aim was to simulate two major airborne landings. One group landed near Jumièges on the lower Seine, and at least gave the commandant of Le Havre a horrible fright. He telegraphed to everyone he could think of that he had been cut off, and every senior German commander who visited his map room after breakfast on 6 June saw a flag in Le Havre marked *abgeschnittet*, a minor source of confusion.

The other party had a more direct impact. They landed southeast of Isigny, which, in turn, is at the southeast corner of the Cherbourg peninsula, and made such a stir that the local unit rang up divisional headquarters. The duty officer went to wake the general but he was away in Rennes at a senior officers' conference on how to repel airborne attacks. So he woke up the chief of staff instead. This was a regular army officer, brought up to counterattack automatically whenever attacked. He ordered out the reserve regiment of the division, which spent the morning of D-day beating the woods near Isigny for a major airborne landing that was not there, instead of being on hand to put General Bradley's landing at Omaha beach back into the sea.

For several weeks before the landings, as a security precaution, foreign diplomats in London had been forbidden to use their own ciphers. Only the Americans and the Russians (and, in secret, the London-based Poles) were exempt from this ban. On 7 June, foreign secretary Eden sent a message to Eisenhower that he proposed to end the ban at once. He was persuaded with difficulty to keep it going until the end of the month, in order to reinforce Fortitude.

An extra touch was provided, at this critical stage, by one of the star double agents, Garbo. In a report sent by radio on D+3, he drew the Germans' attention to the fact that no formation from the [notional] First United States Army Group had taken part in the landings, and that Patton's divisions were still poised for their assault. At the same time, SOE sent out a call for immediate mobilization to Belgian resistance, in a cipher the Germans read easily. Some German formations east of the Seine already ordered to western Normandy were therefore turned round, and directed towards the Calais neighborhood instead.[18]

"Fortitude North"

Besides the main Fortitude deception, there was a subplot called Fortitude North which deserves attention because it validated one of Bevan's golden rules: go for what you know for certain about your enemy, thus making him act (actions are far more important than beliefs) in the way you want. One of Bevan's friends was Andrew (Bulgy) Thorne of the Grenadier Guards who had been a colonel military attaché in Berlin from 1932 to 1935. As a matter of routine, he attended, in uniform, Hitler's first big diplomatic reception in 1933. Making the rounds, Hitler with his odd eye for detail noticed that Thorne was wearing—after his gallantry decorations—what the army called (after a once famous children's cartoon) Pip, Squeak, and Wilfred, the three main Great War service medals, with the 1914 star. Had he been at First Ypres? He had? Where was he on 30 October 1914? It turned out the two of them had been only about five hundred yards apart that day. Hitler, therefore, marked Thorne down as "ein alter Frontkämpfer," his highest praise, and was disappointed when Thorne was posted back to Aldershot to command the Guards Brigade two years later. One of the many reasons why he hesitated to invade England in the late summer of 1940 may have been because he discovered that Thorne was by then the corps commander against whom his armies would first have to fight upon landing. It was leaked to the Germans, through the double agents and just in advance of the newspaper reports, that by 1943 Thorne had become a full general, a knight, and commander in chief, Scottish command. To anyone in the know, this meant that his career as a field commander was over, but Bevan then took a hand. He leaked more and more bogus information through his controlled agents indicating that Thorne was preparing an invasion of Norway. Dummy landing craft on the east Scottish coast as well as dummy radio traffic, bore this out. Hitler therefore kept a garrison of over 300,000 men in Norway because he was afraid of what Thorne might do. None of these troops was moved to help avert imminent defeat either on the eastern or on the western front, throughout the last winter of the war.

Air Deceptions

Two other routine features of deception, both affecting the war in the air, were undertaken during most of the war against Hitler. To protect the secrecy of Bletchley's successes with the German and Italian codes, it was an inflexible rule that no target found through ultra-secret intercepts could be attacked, until it had been spotted by more usual means of reconnaissance. This often resulted in aircrew being instructed, for no stated reason, to search in a particular direction. Reconnaissance aircrews, though bright, were not unduly inquisitive, and there were no unfortunate repercussions.

Again, once Bomber Command had organized its system of marshaling aircraft over a selected target in a stream of carefully timed attacks, it was usual for a few Mosquito aircraft to go into Germany a few minutes before the main attack, and drop markers on some quite different target. This caused the German night fighter defenses to send their aircraft to the wrong parts of the country, reducing the main bomber stream's exposure to their attacks.

Gulf War

It is no wonder that General Norman Schwarzkopf made decisive use of deception during the Gulf War of 1991, threatening a seaborne attack on Saddam Hussein's left just before he delivered a devastating land attack on his right. Not the least of the general's successes was that he managed this without exasperating the American news media, which since their triumph against President Nixon over the Watergate affair in the early 1970s seemed to have advanced to a position of power.

Counterterror

The principles of deception are as usable against terrorists as they are against more conventional enemies. It is important for intelligence and operations sections to work completely hand in hand, without any reservations. What matters is to persuade the enemy to act to his own disadvantage, rather than to affect his thoughts. Double agents can be used to plant misinformation about proposed security precautions. Terror occasionally can be used against terrorists, so that weak links in their networks can be persuaded to change sides. Ideally, bomb-makers can be arrested as they are getting their bombs ready for use, rather than after the bombs have gone off.

Lessons Learned

The principal lessons learned from the British experience of deception are these:

- Deception is a matter for operational planning, but also needs incessant contact with reliable intelligence staffs and sources;

- Complete secrecy is indispensable, while the deception planners, in turn, must know everything they can about the intentions of their own side and of the enemy;
- It is helpful if the staff in charge all come from a single, cohesive background;
- Deception must persuade the enemy to act, rather than to think;
- All the staffs concerned, both directly and from other agencies, must be prepared to sink their interdepartmental differences and pursue the common aim of victory, without insisting that theirs is the only important contribution.

Notes

1. Sun Tzu, *The Art of War,* tr. Samuel B. Griffith (Oxford, UK: Clarendon Press, 1963 ed.), pp. 66-7.
2. See Winston Churchill, *Marlborough. His Life and Times* (London: George G. Harrap & Co. Ltd, 1934 ed.) 2.332-44.
3. Dudley Clarke, *Seven Assignments* (London: Jonathan Cape, 1948).
4. Sir Michael Howard, *Strategic Deception*, volume 5 of F. H. Hinsley, *British Intelligence in the Second World War* (London: HMSO, 1990).
5. The only other books fit to be mentioned in the same breath are R. V. Jones, *Most Secret War* (London: Hamilton, 1978) and *Reflections on Intelligence* (London: Heinemann, 1978, revised ed., 1989); and *Double Cross* J.C. Masterman, *The Double Cross System in the War of 1939 to 1945* (New Haven, CT: Yale University Press, 1972), a bowdlerized version of his official report to MI 5 at the end of the war. The rest of this paper relies heavily on Howard.
6. See Terence O'Brien, *The Moonlight War: The Story of Clandestine Operations in South-East Asia, 1944-5* (London: Colins (1987).
7. Ibid., p. 28.
8. Obituary, London *Times*, 16 May 1994, p. 19a.
9. Duff Cooper, *Operation Heartbreak, A Story* (London: Hart-Davis, 1950).
10. Ewen Montagu, *The Man Who Never Was* (London: Evans Bros., 1953).
11. Ewen Montagu, *Beyond Top Secret U* (London: P. Davies, 1977).
12. Masterman, *The Double Cross System.*
13. Dennis Wheatley, *The Deception Planners: My Secret War* (London: Hutchinson, 1980).
14. Ibid., p. 35.
15. Howard, *Strategic Deception*, pp. 111-2.
16. Roger Hesketh, *Fortitude: The D-Day Deception Campaign* (London: Little, Brown, 1999).
17. R. V. Jones, *Most Secret War,* 405-6; *Radar: A Wartime Miracle*, Recalled by Colin Latham & Anne Stobbs, and by Men & Women Who Played Their Part in It for the RAF (Phoenix Mill, Far Thrupp, Stroud, Gloucestershire, UK: Sutton Publishers, 1996) 137-40.
18. Masterman, *The Double Cross System*, pp. 156-8.

Commentary

Walter Jajko

M.R.D. Foot has presented us with a fine history of selected instances of Britain's practice of deception while adding some insights and conclusions of his own. In reading Foot's paper, I found one lesson learned that I do not believe is applicable to twenty-first century democratic states, probably including the United Kingdom, and certainly the United States. As a historical statement, however, I cannot disagree with it. That lesson is "that it is helpful if the staff in charge all come from a single cohesive social class." It is based on Sir Michael Howard's similar assertion in the United Kingdom's official history. This assertion is *sui generis* to the British and to the British during World War II. This common denominator of the upper class may be of value as a facilitator in the work of government. In the United States, however, commissioned officers and their civilian superiors come from diverse social backgrounds. Even the Central Intelligence Agency no longer recruits predominantly from the Ivy League. There are more important characteristics than common social background to be sought in deception officers, namely flexible and imaginative minds that can intuit possibilities that conventional minds deem nonexistent, as well as an understanding of how the enemy thinks.

My comments generally address deception and not denial, although denial is an essential and inseparable part of deception. The cumulative effect of persistently poor United States security and spectacularly successful foreign espionage is that it is generally easy for other states to deny the United States the intelligence it seeks. A difficult, complex, and unrelenting effort is necessary for the United States to do the same. Thus, denial, an essential condition for the conduct of deception, is difficult for the United States to sustain.

There are two ways to consider deception and the United States: as deceiver and as deceived. I will make some assertions mostly about the United States as deceiver, having known something about this subject in the past. I will address the conditions that make for success or failure of denial and deception in a democratic regime, in the context of strategic deception by the United States in peacetime.

Abram Shulsky has a useful definition of the term "strategic" which is similar to one that I developed almost two decades ago. It is worthwhile keeping an open mind about definitions and conceptions: what is strategic in practice, at least in military deception, is no longer clear since the strategic, operational, and tactical levels of military operations seem to have merged, as, for example, in the Gulf War.

The United States does not know how to practice systematic strategic deception in peacetime. This is an astonishing inability in the country that spawned Madison Avenue, Broadway, Hollywood, and television, whose products are founded on varying degrees of self-deception if not actual deception. This is an even more astonishing inability in the Department of Defense (DoD) whose thought is about strategy and whose action is about war fighting. After all, deception is at the very heart of strategy and war fighting. Notwithstanding the Department's mission, the practice of deception in the Defense department is underdeveloped. Opportunities to practice deception are not routinely recognized, understood, and exploited.

An inventory of factors that inhibit DoD's systematic practice of peacetime strategic deception can be compiled. A sometime perception among senior officials is that deception is unnecessary and probably more dangerous in its repercussions to the deceiver than the deceived. In part, this fear is related to our scandalous security situation.

Sir Michael Howard's judgment and Foot's concurrence that a common outlook is instrumental, useful, and important to the practice of strategic deception are correct in a larger, but negative, sense with respect to the United States. Values, principles, beliefs, and perceptions held in common are important in forming an ethos, and an ethos is important in informing common action. The strictures of contemporary education, the practice of national politics, and the biases propagated by the media, however, tend to leave Americans with the idea that all values and beliefs are equally meritorious and, therefore, at some levels are either tolerable or irrelevant. Thus, absent an *in extremis* threat, there are few ideas and behaviors of foreign states or groups that are sufficiently stark and serious to merit the consideration of extraordinary, unorthodox exertions such as deception.

Related to this dismissive attitude towards emerging threats is the fact that, except for a few people, the ruling elites in the United

States have never conceived of peace as war fought by means other than combat. The conception of a pervasive and protracted, systemic and systematic struggle with an enemy never was generally accepted by U.S. elites even during the worst episodes of the Cold War. A conviction that the United States now has one or more serious enemies capable of inflicting substantial, if not mortal, damage does not animate the elites. Therefore, the organization of a permanent apparatus for long-range, systematic, strategic deception in peacetime against a variety of potential and actual enemies in a variety of areas of official interaction—economic, military, political, and social—seems an absurdity, even as analysts and pundits proclaim the threat of asymmetric attacks in peace and war. Deception also is regarded as a tool used by the weak to compensate for their weakness. The United States as a superpower obviously has no need to resort to such desperate and perhaps illegitimate efforts. Of course, this is the wrong way to think about deception, and the result is to deprive the nation of a valuable instrument of statecraft.

The institutionalization of deception as a permanent instrument of policy is probably tied peculiarly to the conception of statecraft by subversion. The United States, of course, has no need to resort to such means; after all, the export of popular American culture accomplishes such subversion spontaneously. The United States' view of the world is not conducive to understanding fanatical zealotry, systematic secrecy, sustained sacrifice without the prospect of success, the paradox of defeat as victory, and the determination to deny and deceive.

This same intellectual outlook and psychological predisposition make it difficult for U.S. officials to establish and operate a comprehensive, coordinated counterdeception program. Yet, foreign deception, particularly strategic deception, poses great danger to the United States; foreign strategic deception, not detected, understood, and countered, pollutes U.S. intelligence and policy, neither of which is sufficiently attentive to this threat.

The inability to institutionalize deception, or counterdeception, is a reciprocal reflection of the reluctance to acknowledge, much less address, efforts at deception by others. For example, in the early 1980s, an Interagency Intelligence Memorandum on Soviet Active Measures, including cases of deception, was produced only after some two years of emotional and acrimonious interagency negotiation. This happened in spite of almost seven decades of Soviet practice of deception and almost three decades of the Cold War. Only in the past year, after several years' hiatus, has a National Intelligence Estimate on foreign denial and deception been produced. The inescapable inference is that inattention to deception is ingrained and not inadvertent.

Foot correctly asserts that deception is an operational activity and that it "needs incessant contact" with intelligence. Certainly deception is peculiarly and particularly dependent on and infused with intelligence. Nevertheless, deception is an operational activity, and, therefore, ought to be controlled by the operators, not the intelligence side. This seems obvious, but it has been contested. Categorizing deception as an intelligence activity rather than an operational activity could have far-reaching implications for the Department of Defense. Such categorization would make deception *ex definitione* a special activity subject to Presidential approval and Congressional notification. The Defense Department views deception not as a special activity but as a constituent component of combat, an activity inherent in warfare. Further, the contention that deception is or should be a special activity, if realized, ultimately could interject the director of Central Intelligence into the military chain of command and could interfere with military operations. This confusion over intelligence and operations and how to separate the two in practice occurs throughout the intelligence community. More than one agency has difficulty in seeing the bright line, as the lawyers say, that separates intelligence from operations, particularly in the conduct of information operations. This difficulty may become more contentious and consequential if the conduct of information operations expands, particularly in peacetime. The conduct of deception in information operations will certainly compound the contentiousness.

One must agree with Foot's lesson "that all the staffs concerned with [deception], both directly and from other agencies, are prepared to sink their inter-departmental differences and pursue the common aim...." Such unselfish pursuit of a deception is much easier in wartime than over the long term in peacetime or in a fast-breaking contingency. However, several institutional barriers to the pursuit of a strategic deception exist in the executive branch of the United States government. There is no interagency organization, for example, under the National Security Council that is competent to plan, coordinate, and monitor interagency strategic deception operations. Nor is there a presidential policy on the conduct of such deception. The absence of authority and organization in interagency councils is critical because both are essential to foster the conduct of a sensitive activity. The Department of State is unlikely to countenance and participate in any strategic deception program, because deception is believed to be fatal to diplomacy. Likewise, the Central Intelligence Agency is unlikely to participate in any deception project that includes domestic supporting activities. Coordinating the actions of several agencies to support any sensitive activity is a formidable undertaking; coordinating the actions of several agencies to support a deception, especially if they are not witting, is a problematic undertaking. Further, unlike Britain in World War II, orchestrating public actions to add verisimilitude in support of a deception in Congress or the Fourth Estate is unthinkable with the former and impossible with the latter.

At the policy level, both appointed and career officials are rarely involved in deception except for brief instances when an approval is required for a particular project. Peacetime strategic deception tends to be an exceptional, occasional, and episodic activity with necessarily marginal achievements. The continuity and fidelity in the relationship of a specific peacetime deception to its supported activity is difficult to monitor, particularly in those of longer duration. As a result, it is easy for senior officials to question whether the activity is worth the effort.

Deception that occurs in military operations is confined, as we know from recent history, to the operational and tactical levels of war fighting. Perhaps this is because opportunities for the employment of strategic deception in combat have not occurred—for which we probably should be thankful. The United States armed forces, despite the revolutionary rhetoric of the *National Military Strategy* concerning the information dominance of the battle-space, are predisposed to attack an enemy's capabilities, not an enemy's strategy. Systematic shaping of an enemy's strategy and attacking an enemy's intentions through deception in peacetime are unusual undertakings.

In the United States armed forces there is insufficient education and training in deception, both practical and theoretical, at least above the tactical level. According to Mr. Foot, Sun Tzu's tenets, particularly his dictum that "All warfare is based on deception" gets warm approval from staff colleges, the world over. In practice, the contrary is true in the United States. Although it is stated that deception is valuable and should not be neglected, the war colleges' curricula in strategy are not suffused with a stress on the practice of deception. Deception is presented *en passant* as an exceptional enterprise, not as an expected activity integrated into, fundamental to, and inseparable from policy, strategy, and operations. The subject, more or less, consists of anecdotal episodes without theoretical foundation. Deception is viewed as an unorthodox curiosity proselytized by eccentric enthusiasts and infrequently indulged in by the occasional Great Captain. Students anticipating advancement do not aspire to the stature of either of these and settle for the security of accepted practice. It is intellectually easier and professionally preferable to put iron on the target and kill the enemy, rather than to win by defeating the enemy's strategy through stratagem.

The systematic practice of deception also is hampered by the absence of selective recruitment of personnel who are interested, much less likely to be successful in this art. Deception planners are simply designated or in many instances, are self-selected. The assignment is not a rewarding one; those who serve more than a single assignment make marginal careers in a marginal activity.

As to the functioning of deception planners, Foot says that "the deception planners in turn must know everything they can about their own side's and their enemy's intentions." Foot quotes Peter Fleming, who said, "It is impossible, or at any rate highly dangerous, to tell a lie until you know what the truth is going to be." In the Defense Department, the knowledge of both so-called "blue" and "red" information often is concentrated only at the highest levels. Intelligence officers almost always know more about the other side than they do about their own side. Deception planners usually know more about their own side than they do about the other side.

Foot also writes, "[British Army Colonel John] Bevan, [Chief of London Controlling Section] not only saw all the chiefs of staffs' minutes, but was aware of the code-breaking achievements of Bletchley, and sat on the XX Committee that MI5 organized to look after the playing back of captured German agents." Such an arrangement and such access would be well nigh impossible in the Department of Defense. Americans think of the British as class-conscious, but there is no culture as stratified as the American military in the Pentagon. It is unthinkable that a mere colonel would be entrusted with such a portfolio and granted such wide access to both "blue" and "red" information. The Pentagon is populated by too many horse holders and button counters to permit a phenomenon remotely resembling Colonel Bevan to exist, much less succeed. Then, too, there is the stricture of civilian control that in practice interposes several strata of supernumeraries and impels the intervention of the uninvolved. The bureaucracy of the Pentagon and the rest of the national security community are too elaborate, articulated, engaged, and insistent to be avoidable. Organizations actively enforce their autonomy and the exclusivity and indispensability of their special *arcana*.

As Foot correctly notes, feedback sources are indispensable to the conduct of deception and counter-deception. The Department of Defense is hampered by an inadequate organization to support these missions. There is no integrated Defense Department counterintelligence organization, so a synergistic effort in support of deception and counter-deception is not pursued. Historically, the counterintelligence mission *de facto* has been secondary to law enforcement, so it has been narrowly conceived. Lately, counterintelligence has been reduced to a tactical, defensive, force protection role, so it is narrowly conducted. Moreover, counterintelligence, in collection and production, is poorly, if at all, integrated with the rest of intelligence. Counterintelligence operators have not generally taken the initiative to pay attention to or to become involved in deception and counter-deception. They have lacked a strategic purpose and a long range, offensive outlook.

Understanding the enemy is both critical and essential, and Foot puts the case well with several historical examples. Yet, we do not understand our main enemies and, when we do, we do not know how best to influence their actions in our favor or to their detriment. This ignorance is a failure of intelligence and policy at such a fundamental level that the conduct of systematic strategic deception and counter-deception in peacetime against the most important targets is not viable. In Sun Tzu's schema, for example, we have not "fathomed" the leadership of North Korea after a half century, Iran after a score of years, or China after five decades.

Foot points out that the necessity for secrecy suffuses everything connected with deception. The issue of secrecy is of an exceptional immediacy to the U.S. armed forces in much more than the usual sense. Joint Doctrine prescribes that the United States will rarely fight alone, that is without allies. In 1999, the United States and its NATO allies waged an unprecedented war. The United States may engage in similar operations in the future and will seek allies when it does so. At the very least, it is timely to consider whether we will plan and execute deceptions that require the participation, witting or unwitting, and perhaps even the approval of some, if not all, of our allies in a particular operation. Obviously, the protection of sources, methods, techniques, and technologies remains important, but what other concerns must be considered in a coalition are not yet clear. If we undertake such inclusive enterprises in the future, the most valuable information that we must protect from an enemy is knowledge of our approach to, conception of, style of, and our reflexive reaction to deception, theirs and ours.

Despite the historic organizational and intellectual impediments, one can be optimistic about the future of deception—even in the United States: after all, reality never kept men from self-deception, for which there is ample scope in international intercourse. Moreover, there are the unimagined and untried opportunities for deception in the still unknown universe of information operations. So, there is much promise that deceivers and deceived will not lack for employment.

Commentary

Ilana Kass

Deception is as old as human interaction, as old as war itself. From biblical warriors and kings, through ancient Egypt, China, Greece, and Rome, to the tail end of the twentieth century, deception, often as the handmaiden of surprise, has served as "the strategists' keys to victory."

Throughout history, superpowers and small nations, democracies and authoritarian regimes, have surprised and deceived each other, and fallen victim to deception and surprise, often with devastating results. Yet, as the collected repository of human wisdom, either history has not been a very good teacher or we have not been very good students. Exposure to hostile deception does not provide immunization from being deceived again, either by the same actor who "got you" before, or by someone else. All too often, the deceiver can become the deceived within an amazingly short time frame, falling victim to precisely the same ruses and stratagems that recently delivered a decisive advantage. For example, in the 1956 Sinai Campaign, Egypt, then a revolutionary-authoritarian regime, was surprised and deceived by Israel (which was aided by two other democracies, Britain and France). Egypt, as well as Syria and Jordan, was surprised again by Israel's preemptive strike in June 1967, with even more devastating results. Yet, six short years later, in October 1973, the shoe would be on the other foot, when Israel became the victim of a superbly conceived and executed deception-based surprise attack by its erstwhile victims, Egypt and Syria. This example underlines Bart Whaley's point that even good practitioners can be vulnerable to deception.

Perhaps less dramatic, but still telling is a similar role-reversal during the Falklands/Malvinas War. Britain, the original victim of Argentinean deception and surprise, quickly turned the tables, regaining both the strategic initiative and lost territory through equally well-thought-out deception and surprise. American officials, thoroughly deceived by Iraq and surprised by its August 1990 invasion of Kuwait, went on to win the war through superbly designed and flawlessly executed deceptions of their own. These recent examples also demonstrate that deception is, indeed, an equal opportunity enterprise, universally practiced.

Why haven't we learned better from past experience? Are there ways to make history a better teacher? As for the first question, my own view is rather pessimistic: deception is an integral part of human life. We constantly attempt to spring traps, but we also fall into them, always promising to do better next time. Because deception is inherent in human nature it is bound to happen, our best efforts to the contrary notwithstanding. Determined efforts to surprise and deceive are almost always successful precisely because they exploit and capitalize on universal, enduring human frailties, perceptual distortions and biases. Key among these is hubris, wishful thinking, and mirror imaging. Efforts to learn from our own experience as well as that of others will forever be limited by the over-confident assumption that "this won't happen to me."

Moving to a less existential level, history has not been a good teacher because, as Whaley suggests, it is open to both use and abuse.

On the one hand, we can learn much from historical case studies, because the principles of deception are both enduring and universal. On the other hand, we risk drawing misleading conclusions because, all too often, we merely retell what happened, draw sweeping conclusions from anecdotal evidence, and forget that each case of deception is idiosyncratic. In other words, each case is shaped and defined by a unique set of circumstances concerning time, place, the nature and motivations of the players, and, perhaps most importantly, the interests and objectives that were at stake, as well as the ways and means that were available. Simply put, what worked once may or may not work as well, or even at all the next time. Worse, an approach that succeeded in the past might be used against you, either concurrently, or in some future interaction. Historical lessons can provide only so much guidance for the future.

Equally problematic is the fallacy of retrospective analysis. Looking at any case of surprise and deception with the benefit of hindsight is like putting together a jigsaw puzzle for the umpteenth time. The overall design and the shapes, patterns, and relationships of the pieces are thoroughly familiar, and therefore are relatively easy to fit together. The victim's myopia and terminal stupidity tend to be more striking than the initiator's skill in pulling off the deception. This only reinforces the erroneous notion that a scheme like this would never work against a more sophisticated opponent, feeding into the equally mistaken assumption that "it will never happen to me." Further, retrospective analysis rarely captures the uncertainties, ambiguities, and complexities that face real players, in real-time, especially in high stress situations, with the nation's well being, if not very survival at stake. The old adage that victors write the history books has a particularly ironic twist in this context. There are precious few memoirs with the title "How I Was Deceived and Why." Even the victors tend to emphasize the valor and underplay the guile that combined to assure success; note the vastly differing emphases of British and American analyses of World War II in the European theater.

Given these inherent limitations, how can we make history a better teacher? Fine-grained, nuanced analysis, and care in drawing lessons learned are probably key requirements. A focused effort to identify and isolate the factors that make for success and failure of D&D also is a giant step in the right direction. Yet, if the objective is to develop methods to overcome the threat posed by hostile D&D, the distinction between regime types is only one of several "slices" that make up a well-differentiated analysis. Staying at the gross anatomy level, we should try to integrate and draw conclusions from at least three additional dimensions. First, there is the fairly obvious distinction between national behavior in peacetime and in war, between perception management and intelligence deception.

The second and related dimension is the ends-ways-means nexus, the very essence of strategy, which determines how the various tools of statecraft, including D&D, would be orchestrated and employed to attain national objectives in peace, crisis and war. As the military strategist Carl von Clausewitz said: "The value of the objectives determines the level of effort in magnitude and also in duration."

Third, it would be very useful to underscore the fundamentally different perspectives of the victim and the initiator of surprise and deception. This distinction may be less intuitively obvious than the other two. For the victim, surprise born of deception is an *event*: embarrassing, traumatic, humiliating, and often paralyzing. Having been caught unprepared, the victim must scramble to react in the least favorable of circumstances: the initiative is lost, events are spinning out of control, and recovery is impeded by the self-doubt and recriminations that follow. Thus, the victim learns the makings of the deception only in retrospect. For the initiator, deception is a process: a painstaking, often laborious plan in which everything worked just right and, if surprise were the desired outcome, is now coming together in one concentrated burst of action. Having pulled it off, the initiator has gained a huge, albeit temporary advantage. Having seized the initiative, until the victim recovers, a window of opportunity exists to exploit and reinforce success.

This distinction is important for several reasons. First, behavioral patterns typical of the victim and the initiator cut across cultural and regime diversities. A victim behaves like a victim, whether a society is open or not. Second, a clear distinction between the perspectives of the victim and the initiator underscores the interactive, non-linear, dynamic nature of deception and surprise. Third, the distinction between victim and initiator helps account for the common misperception that democracies are systemically incapable of pulling off surprise and deception. The database is not large because democracies do not fight very often. When they do, it is almost always because they see no other way to defend their vital interests. In those rare circumstances, they behave very much like authoritarian regimes, using the very same tools of secrecy, censorship, manipulation, perception-management, and control—deceiving both friend and foe, including their own public. That was certainly the case for Israel in 1967, just as it was for Britain and the United States in World War II.

Even in less extreme circumstances, when democracies seek to regain lost initiative or redress the strategic balance in their favor, they shift from victim to initiator status by adopting behavior patterns typical of closed-systems, at least as far as deception is concerned. Britain in the Falklands and the United States in Desert Storm are excellent examples of such selective D&D. So, too, are the D&D efforts of both Israel and India concerning their clandestine development of nuclear weapons. It is perhaps the greatest tribute to the strength of the democratic tradition that it can tolerate both a near-total closure for the duration of the national emergency (World War II and 1967), a temporary/selective closure to protect a specific endeavor (Falklands, Desert Storm), or cover a strategic capability deemed critical to national survival (Israeli and Indian weapons of mass destruction and such U.S. breakthrough technologies as nuclear weapons, stealth, or ballistic missile defense components).

D&D is a tool that any state (as well as some non-state actors) has available in its strategic toolbox. Democracies tend to use these particular tools in extreme and usually carefully controlled circumstances to defend what is really vital. In contrast to authoritarian regimes, where deception and secrecy are a way of life, democracies do not engage in D&D as a matter of course. Their selective, infrequent employment should not be taken for lack of capability. Practice, however, does make perfect.

As M.R.D. Foot points out, "Deception is a powerful weapon in the armory of the weaker power." That is what Britain was in World War II and this was how Israelis saw themselves in 1967. The two nations at these particular historic junctures shared many of the attributes that are the key to success in deception ventures. These are coherence and cohesion in design and execution; unity of purpose; freedom of action; single-minded dedication to a common goal; strategic agility and adaptability, matched at the operational level by centralized planning and decentralized execution, with plenty of room for initiative by junior commanders; a culture of ingenuity, improvisation and calculated risk-taking; unlimited access to top leaders and virtually unlimited claim on resources; and, perhaps most importantly, the overarching conviction that failure is not an option, because national survival is at stake. For both Israel and Britain, deception and the surprise it was designed to generate were an essential, integral part of the war plan. They were the cornerstone of success, rather than an afterthought (or a "Deception Annex," such as the U.S. planners today are told to write). In 1967, surprise and deception were the *sine qua non* of victory for Israel, even more so perhaps than for the Anglo-American allies in Normandy. The margin for error was razor-thin. As my commanding officer so aptly put it in the late afternoon of 5 June 1967, with some 420 Egyptian, Syrian, Jordanian, and Iraqi jets in flames and Israeli armor deep into the Sinai, "It worked because it had to."

Strong, secure democracies like the United States lack the incentive to engage in D&D. They rarely have had to stake all on the successful outcome of a single course of action. The mainstream culture in the U.S. military can be summed up as "Why bother with fancy footwork, since we have overwhelming force." The answer is straightforward: "Because it saves lives." And that, perhaps, should be sufficient incentive. Writing about the British military in the wake of World War I, Liddell Hart bemoaned its fostering "a cult of soundness, rather than surprise," and raising a generation of officers who were so concerned about doing something wrong that they forget to compel the opponent to make mistakes. Successful deceptions require a level of "evil sophistication" as well as ingenuity, creativity, and risk taking that are uncommon in today's zero-defects military. These attributes need to be fostered and nurtured. Otherwise, the legacy of Normandy and Desert Storm will simply wither away.

5

Conditions Making for Success and Failure of Denial and Deception: Nonstate and Illicit Actors

J. Bowyer Bell

There are many kinds of nonstate actors: transnational companies, failed states, revolutionary organizations, or religious orders. Many operate secretly and some illegally. Organizations and movements, defined by the recognized and legitimate as illicit, must seek cover to operate. Some organizations are thus partly covert while others, particularly the most illicit, are apt to be mainly if not entirely, covert. For these latter groups to operate, denial is so vital that it becomes a strategic necessity achieved by the creation of a real and conceptual underground. Both rebels and criminals, just like lethal cults or business agents stealing patents, depend upon cover to operate illicitly; but the clandestine world of the terrorist or the criminal is an alternative reality rather than a mere matter of hiding the operations of a journalist or a banker. This denial through the fabrication of a clandestine underground world is a strategic construct for the most illicit organizations. Such strategic denial permits operations to go forward, although at a high cost in efficiency.

Those operating most covertly, in fact, seldom have the resources, time or opportunity for strategic deception planning. Instead they achieve organizational goals by relying on operational surprise, effective denial and the vulnerabilities of the opponent. Only rarely does strategic denial allow strategic deception planning, and then most often to groups with some legitimacy, with havens, with conventional resources, or to those not assumed dangerous by the legitimate. Thus, the more illicit and hidden the group, the more difficulty members have organizing strategic deception. A movement may be assumed to be benign, thereby maintaining denial and deceiving the perceived enemy. But once an asymmetrical conflict arises, the resources demanded by denial, maintenance of the organization, or normal operations absorb most organizational resources.

As a result, the threat of strategic deception rather than strategic denial by illicit organizations is real but rare except on a tactical level. Regimes that seek to co-opt such organizations often find the capacities and discipline of the underground less than anticipated and control elusive. State-sponsored terrorists have state assets while a revolutionary terrorist relies on perceived truth, will and history. Yet, strategic deception does exist and often does threaten national stability, global order, and the innocent—and such deception is hidden by the strategic denial of illicit organizations.

Strategic denial is assured by the creation of a parallel world that both exhilarates and protects, offers haven and enhances the life of the committed. This is as true for the Sicilian Mafias who seek respect, power, money, and at times display as it is for the terrorist who seeks to change the direction of history through recourse to violence. The criminal flourishes in the hidden world protected by denial while the mobster uses denial to get out of the hidden world into legitimate power. In both cases denial is a strategic necessity, not a tactical choice nor a cluster of ruses. A cult may be a secret world of the chosen that is perceived as benign by outsiders until its members commit murder. The known criminal and the potential gunman who focus public attention are the types of individuals who require denial to operate on a day-to-day basis. The Islamic fundamentalists operating in New York in the nineties offer an insight into the dynamics of strategic denial: the creation of a parallel reality as cover and haven.

Strategic deception is rare because of a lack of resources and talent. In the cases of the 1993 Holy Jihad World Trade Center bombing in New York, the Irish Republican Army's preparations for a three-stage campaign in January 1970, and the Sicilian Mafia's covert participation in the drug trade after 1957, the requisite talent and means were available. Most illicit criminal and political organizations, covert and limited, conservatively pursue advantage with violence rather than cunning, with technical and tactical deceit rather than elegant strategic planning. For most illicit organizations, denial is a strategic necessity that can afford protection, continuity, a base and reassurance but rarely tactical assets. Severely limited in most cases by states, illicit organizations can rarely afford time dedicated to strategic deception, are inclined to reveal the truth as they perceive it, and tend to rely on techniques and tactics to purse advantage. Time, tangible assets, and technological skills often will allow strategic deception; but few criminals and fewer rebels have the resources to plan strategically. Yet, potential targets would be deceived if they imagine that such deception is never a threat.

Nonstate and Illicit Actors: The Spectrum of Analysis

In the contemporary global order, states determine legitimacy. They define the way individuals may organize with recognition. How illicit a movement or an organization is usually is a matter of perception and national interests. In Russia in 1999, the Jehovah's Witnesses were perceived by many to be a dangerous, anti-national cult, or else agents of the United States. Proselytizing, if not fully covert, was most discreet. In fact, many organizations, transnational corporations, human rights groups, religious orders, even at times visitors on tour are perceived as hostile and must operate not just discretely but secretly. In other words, even groups that are considered in some states to be legitimate organizations pursuing legitimate goals must use cover and at times deceit to achieve their objectives. Those defined as or suspected of being illicit make conversions secretly, make a profit secretly, investigate torture secretly or simply see the sights secretly.

Various "secret" organizations are mostly visible because they are mostly legitimate and so resort to denial as policy, but only rarely to hide illegality. Secrecy may have charms for fraternities or bring advantage in take-over bids, but such practices seldom are related to a systemic threat, the use of violence or a danger to civil order. The International Red Cross, the Vatican, and Microsoft may use denial, but not to pursue illegal policies as convention. And when they use denial as an instrument in the cause of profit or fostering civil liberties, their legitimacy rarely is eroded. Some covert groups are not easy to define as "illicit" in any case. In Italy a contemporary Masonic order known as G-2 existed covertly, engaged, it was assumed later, in right-wing political conspiracy and in financial deals. Many knew of G-2 but few knew its purpose, and so for years G-2 operated secretly beyond the purview of the law.

Even their members almost always consider some organizations illicit. Some Masonic orders or religious groups may at times operate without authorization and so, like the Sicilian Mafia or the Holy Jihad, need cover. In fact, they often deploy absolute denial in an alien arena. The leadership of the guerrilla army or the dissenting sect may feel its cause is legitimate but still recognizes the power of the legitimate authority. The criminal understands the reality of the law even when exchanging favors with the establishment. The establishment often tolerates potential dissent or criminal activity. Some regimes are without sufficient assets to curtail vice or hunt down guerrillas, while democracies are open to all sorts. A few organizations may appear benign, such as an alternative religion or a radical political movement, but once deployed against state alternatives are deemed illicit. The *Aum Shinrikyo* doomsday cult or the *Brigate rosse* urban terrorists in Italy, that for a time existed on the fringes of society and were tolerated by their host governments, ultimately were deemed illicit once they initiated violence.

Thus many revolutionary movements may be perceived to be illicit only in part or in some places. They may be able to operate legally within a political party or as newspaper publishers, or through volunteers who are known but have not been arrested. Some American militias are assumed to be merely extreme patriots, a residue of the frontier mentality. Vigilantes and some private armies may be encouraged in Latin America. Most revolutionary groups have acceptable structures, political parties, newspapers, and cultural associations.

The Palestine Liberation Organization (PLO) became a proto-state with diplomats, a visible, uniformed army based in friendly countries, and a leader who could speak at the United Nations. All Palestinian *fedayeen* groups were perceived as illicit by Israel and by many in the international community, but the fedayeen, like many revolutionary movements, offered a mixture of structures. The largest PLO-armed faction, Al-Fatah, could be found easily in various exile bases, uniformed, armed conventionally, and on parade. The leadership was willing to use cover and deception to operate but seldom had to exist underground. For a time, Al-Fatah contained a totally covert, deniable strike force, Black September, that in dynamics, deployment and resources more closely resembled a state-sponsored terrorist unit than an illicit, revolutionary organization.

The more the organization is perceived as illicit, the more necessary is denial.[1] What banks hide is accepted as sound practice; what terrorists hide is the dynamics of an illicit movement. In the midst of an armed struggle or during the course of the drug trade, an organization, whatever the motive or however extensive its support, must have absolute cover, especially during operations. The operational part of a movement must be hidden: members, finances, intentions, arms, contacts, and strategy. At times, even the existence of the group must be hidden from the authorities. The political arm of the liberation front marching for the latest martyr, the public ceremonies with the cult's guru, the Sicilian funerals of murdered Mafioso are open to all and are the visible face of conspiracy; but the police or the army, the state or the international community knows that just out of sight is the organization's conspiratorial core.

Only a few revolutionary groups have operated totally underground without legal entities and beyond the reach of potential friends. For example, even potential volunteers could not reach Lehi, the Stern Group, and the Irgun Zvai Leumi in the Palestine Mandate nor Brigate rosse in Italy after the Aldo Moro kidnapping. Sometimes there can be no effective cover. In a brutal and efficient state, the revolutionary and the criminal cannot operate at all. To choose a criminal career in the Soviet Union was to choose to spend half a lifetime in prison or be co-opted by the KGB. To organize dissent in Soviet Russia was to opt for the Gulag. If the state is both efficient and cruel, the security forces imprison, detain, kidnap and murder the suspect and their families and friends to close down potential opposition. Protest is futile and secrecy no defense against the power of Stalin or Mao or even General Augusto Pinochet in Chile.

Much of the world, however, is the province of open societies providing vast areas where dissent can go underground, crime can flourish or cults claim civil liberties. The dissent may organize under cover and deny entry to all but the faithful. Such secrecy makes operations difficult. Secrecy assures inefficiency, so that with total secrecy there is almost no action. The more denial is needed the less effective action there is to deny. Full denial is counterproductive. The problem is that there is no solution to this trade off: denial exacts a price and total denial exacts an unacceptable price. The illicit must hide to exist.

Few organizations actually need absolute denial. To widen the arena for operation, even criminals remove some of the penalties of secrecy. They seek to corrupt government, to find acceptance within the elite, and to achieve tolerance in at least one place to permit the expansion of illegal enterprise. The revolutionary guerrilla may be safe in the hills or operate freely in exile, just as criminals find a haven. Like Chase Manhattan or the Mormons, only part of a subversive group need be hidden, although unlike Chase Manhattan or the Mormons most illicit groups must remain mostly hidden much of the time.

Thus, various organizations on a spectrum of legitimacy may find that operations in hostile societies need real cover. Even in the most hostile societies, there may be acceptance. At times in the safe haven, everyone knows the criminal. The silence—*Omertà*—in Sicily hides the Mafia that everyone knows but out of habit, awe or fear denies. The refusal of the nationalists in Ireland to inform arises not from ignorance or fear but conviction. Everyone knows the IRA gunman or the Mafioso but nothing is said. Clearly, if the Holy Jihad and the Sicilian Mafia do not always need cover, the spectrum of illegality is not a complete one. It depends on both the perception of the threatened and the actions of the clandestine. The Japanese *Aum Shinrikyo* cult, for example, needed only to deny the outside world access to certain programs for the authorities to assume the cult was legitimate, just as the authorities in Sicily assumed the Mafia necessary, and many Arab states find Holy Jihad acceptable in offering Allah as the answer and violence as the means.

There is a spectrum of both legitimacy and cover. In general, the less legitimate need to be more covert. Increasingly, the necessity of cover dominates the dynamics of the organization. The group becomes clandestine, and members enter a hidden world. The Central Intelligence Agency (CIA) may be a clandestine service, but only at times and for what the state decides is a legitimate purpose. Some organizations must have cover to achieve their avowed goals while others find it a convenience. The clandestine underground is different: open to the faithful, closed to all others. The gunman lives among his own until victory. Criminal groups also exist covertly, but forever. There is never an end to criminal aspiration, the search for advantage that shapes a special and rewarding life of crime. One cannot, like the revolutionary or member of a cult, emerge with legitimate interests. A criminal may have friends, may appear socially, but is not in transition to a legitimate life. The criminal is not an aspirant to a different existence like the rebel. Instead the criminal is always seeking illegal advantage, easy money, and the respect offered to power. Criminals may have legitimate associates but only very rarely can they achieve legitimacy except at a distance, often in the form of contributions given or favors offered. Nevertheless, some criminals have not been dissuaded from seeking legitimate avenues of action. *La Cosa Nostra* in New York produced a "civil rights" group to protect the image of Italian-Americans.[2] Criminal organizations in Italy and Russia have been involved in politics, run candidates for office, or made arrangements with patrons in government. Even these arrangements must be hidden despite being obvious.

Thus, all criminal organizations require cover for everything, all the time. When cover is broken out of arrogance—Mafia hits or gangsters on the streets—the organization is endangered and may face confrontation with authority. Denial has been risked because of the necessity for respect among fellow criminals. The criminal integrates secrecy into a special life that may have a patina of normality but is almost as impenetrable as that led by terrorists or the cult out to kill. It is this life of respect and awe that appeals to the criminal as much as the reality of easy money. This life relies on trust in the family and faction, the others within the life. So, again the great fear is betrayal rather than penetration; in Sicily, everyone knows who is the Mafia and who is not, and all is silence—*Omertà*.

Groups defined as illicit by the system, the state, the society, and often by their friends and their own proclamations, must make concealment an overriding concern, not simply a matter of tactics or of practice. Recourse to denial becomes a determining factor in the organization and in the perception of those involved. For such groups to operate, denial must be structured as a central policy: no denial, no operations. Just as there is a spectrum of legitimacy, the emphasis placed on covertness varies among those engaged in illicit activities.

Among illicit groups, a special alternative closed world of the chosen arises that hides as much as necessary and shows as little as possible. Cover is fashioned not simply by techniques and tradecraft but by the transformation of perception so that a hidden sanctuary is masked from penetration. What such strategic denial makes possible is an alternative real world. The gunman has no home but the underground; all that matters is not only hidden but also illegal. For the Mafioso his family is the real world, while the everyday world is to be exploited. This hidden world of perception offers the criminal a life style and the radical or the zealot the revealed truth. It offers all havens to pursue advantage, but most of all it offers a covert parallel life. This transforms denial—cover—into a strategic reality.

Analytical Perception

Covert, illicit organizations, especially revolutionaries and criminals operating often beyond reach of any state, have a romantic appeal. To outsiders, secrecy is imagined to be something that is easily acquired and wonderfully useful. They assume that those who deal in secret operations send out spies or special operators, and that cover is a technical matter cunningly practiced by rebels or hijackers or subversives. The enormous costs of denial, particularly the imperatives that perception imposes on the faithful within the hidden world, are not recognized. The assassin and the Mafioso do not have free will; they cannot operate beyond the accepted norms of their society and their faith.

The public is apt to believe there is not only secrecy but also unfettered capacity and great advantage in the clandestine life. In fact, governments often want to claim the seeming advantages of the unconventional without actually recognizing the cost. Some governments want to operate secretly, create state assassins and special units, and use denial for legitimacy's sake. Others have seen the advantage of co-opting those already hidden, to sponsor crime or terror at one remove. To operate on events at a distance, with the advantages of plausible denial, some governments have made use of gunmen, guerrillas, or terrorists. States can deploy active agents, or find terrorists for hire. For most states, the effort to co-opt criminals is usually less appealing than attempts to seek revolutionary friends. Typically, however, a government reaches out to a congenial movement or even fosters its own movement, as the CIA did with the Contras.

What evolves is a special category of state-sponsored operations based on an assumed mutuality of interests or a simple deal to purchase services: do this to them secretly and we will reward you secretly as well. Officials often dispatch arms and funds and, if possible, advice to those who pursue similar goals. The more independent the recipient, the less state control over the covert operation. The nature of control moves along a spectrum from fully controlled state operations to funds and arms dispatched without any real control of the end result, as was the case with the Libyan donations and arms shipments to the Irish Republican Army. The degree of state control or state sponsorship largely determines the dynamics of operations and the degree of cover necessary. If denial is a technical matter, then an alternative reality seldom exists: there is no faith or commitment to energize the movement. The Contras had to be paid to fight while the IRA could not be paid to stop. The IRA volunteer existed within a revolutionary underground, while the Contras existed as the end product of American policy. States mostly become involved with illicit activities because of the advantages of plausible denial, perceived low costs and high returns—especially ideological—and the assumption that control underground is easier than imagined. The illicit take what they can get.

Nothing is very exact underground, but what is clear is that throughout history, states and politicians, establishments and recognized parties have sought to use the illicit and the illicit have used those who offered aid. The clandestine world is harsh. It is maintained by faith in the case of revolutionaries, and by fear and advantage in the case of the criminal. The general assumption is that denial is effective—the bombs are always a surprise and the drug trade enormously profitable—and that the illicit are in a position to deceive on a grander scale. Some analysts fear that revolutionaries and criminals may be involved in great and complex operations, even involved with the preparation of weapons of mass destruction. There is seemingly money to be made with access to anthrax or plutonium and power to be achieved by the zealous. Russian criminals have stolen radioactive material and the *Aum Shinrikyo* cult planned biological warfare. Even to informed outsiders, the clandestine world is perceived as malevolent, powerful and proficient.

Those underground rarely feel powerful and often are not proficient. What is not readily understood is that secrecy and the awe of outsiders are achieved not by techniques and skills but by perceptions that once achieved penalize the beneficiaries. In return for persistence, the movement must pay in competency. The gunman worries about tomorrow's ambush and the criminal worries about the arrival of the next shipment of contraband.[3] This does not mean that operations have not been shaped to be both spectacular and lethal. If for generations terrorists sought prominence and power, this is no longer exactly the case. During the last decade many Islamic fundamentalists have aspired to punish the system by bringing down the World Trade Center or destroying a dozen American jumbo jets. Not only do the new terrorists operate transnationally, but they also seek to cause serious harm. Given the vulnerabilities of global society, it is not necessary to employ a nuclear device with all its costs or even anthrax to cause destruction. In any case, those who would do so have more often than not hidden their intentions, their preparations and the dynamics of their movement.

Denial and Deception

Denial is the one great triumph that deceives the orthodox into imagining capacity that rarely is to be found in clandestine organizations. The criminal and the radical use denial to obtain advantage because violence can pay disproportionate dividends. Denial allows the illicit from time to time to deploy effective violence, to pursue the campaign or criminal profit, but rarely to exploit novel means, long-range planning, and so strategic deception. What comes first in strategic denial is not deceit but conviction, the faith that drives the revolutionary and conviction that arises from membership in the family, the faction, or the construct of the commitment. Those so empowered live in another world, one that can be penetrated by the clever or the powerful by force, but only rarely by mimicry. The hidden world allows central command to operate, to project false information, and at times to deploy deception to hide behind. With limited resources, much of such deception is technical and tactical, related to specific operations rather than grand strategy. For most armed struggles, the great strategic decisions have already been made: to begin, to persevere, or to rely on the power of the revealed truth and to triumph over the tangible assets of the enemy. The agenda of most criminals is obvious to all.

There are ample examples of technical and tactical deception arising from the security provided by denial. Gunmen must use deceit and denial to operate. Any protracted guerrilla campaign is replete with tactical ruses. Some revolutionaries have the assets to organize major deception operations as did Al-Fatah, the dominant military force in the PLO. Soon after Jordan expelled the fedayeen in September 1970, the secret Black September was created to pursue an operational strategy of terror. Al-Fatah wanted to be both legitimate, moderate, and recognized, while preserving a capability to act on events. This desire of Al-Fatah to be perceived as moderate in the West and militant in the Arab world is apparent in the language of press releases that are mild in English or French, bellicose in Arabic. The deployment of terror by Black September, however, remained secret.[4]

Sometimes cults operate like revolutionary organizations, offering the truth as revelation, a career of service, and a secret, alternative society. Sometimes revealed truth is used to justify recourse to violence. In Japan, *Aum Shinrikyo* prepared to attack the evil world system, stockpiled arms and did release sarin gas in the subways of Tokyo. The leaders simply hid their real agenda, which no one in any case sought to determine. Until a threat is transformed by action, few are apt to notice. Authorities know that criminals are hidden and at work and that revolutionaries may be. Yet only the most authoritarian governments are apt to discover a threat beforehand. In open societies, radical groups are tolerated and religious freedom offered to sects. Thus, cults, lone assassins, secret splinter groups and obscure factions are secure because they are unsought and unseen. Coercion, surveillance and authority cannot prevent their first act. Only the strictures of civil society and the morality of suspicious neighbors can sometimes stop clandestine groups from launching the first attack.

To achieve strategic deception, illicit organizations must deploy denial as a base to fashion a variety of tactical ruses that can lull the authorities into assuming compromise is possible or that the movement possesses hidden assets. Such deceptions are rare for those with limited assets and limited time, or those who are hampered by the restrictions and costs imposed by the secrecy of the clandestine world. Because operations are a surprise—for example, an unexpected armed robbery or the unforeseen murder of the premier—outsiders often assume that more serious deception planning is a clandestine convention. To deploy deception, there must be time to plan, organize, or attempt the novel. However, time is in short supply for many clandestine groups. Some manage to conduct serious deception planning because the times are right or more often the assets are in place. The PLO had havens, time, and planning staffs.

It could afford deception. Most terrorists who are being hunted and are on the run may not have such assets. Strategic denial consumes so much time and resources that revolutionaries often cannot afford the investment in deception planning. They persist in their campaigns by using yesterday's tactics or innovating out of desperation.

Most revolutionary campaigns are composed of congenial, parochial operations within existing capacities. Most planning is hasty and conservative. Revolutionaries tend to do today what was done yesterday. Ambushes, most assassinations, and most operations are tactical matters. They may or may not have strategic results, but often the only deliberate planning that precedes some action is to agree to hide until the deed is done. Strategic intentions are assumed to be visible, found in the party papers, books like *Mein Kampf*, on wall placards, in police records, or the speeches of central command. Strategic planning during a campaign is difficult. In some cases, underground deception—false operations, black propaganda, misleading rumors, and double agents—is a technique of the armed struggle.

Sometimes strategic deception is carried out as a policy option. For instance, General George Grivas on Cyprus deceived his political allies about their prospects to undermine British rule. They regarded a few bombs as assets in negotiation. He saw them as the first step in a classical national liberation campaign. First Grivas sought to impose his agenda on his political allies, and then he sought to deceive his opponents about his assets. Grivas shaped the campaign to have maximum political impact. When the campaign unfolded to the surprise of the British, deceived by Cypriot capacity and the violence of EOKA (Ethnike Organosis Kypriaku Agonos [National Organization of Cypriot Fighters]), Grivas wanted to make less into more. He established guerrilla-groups in the countryside to appear as evidence of a classical armed struggle. These guerrillas seemed to be the main thrust of the campaign when, in fact, they were an elaborate ruse to deceive the Western media and the British. The deception concerned the assets of the campaign as well as its major direction. The EOKA campaign, a few young Greek men operating on a small island, enemies to the Turkish residents, no friend to many Greeks, and targets to the British, could appear to be a classic guerrilla struggle because there were armed bands in the hills. The core of the campaign, however, was assassinations on the streets and the use of sabotage to raise the costs to the British. Thus, Grivas deceived his associates about his intentions, the British about his assets, and everyone about his tactical intentions.[5]

All revolutionaries are apt to use deception to hide from authority. They use deception to make operations possible by deceiving others about their capabilities. The more imposing the underground military, the more legitimate the cause appears. Sometimes deception can be used to define the nature of the struggle itself. The central command regularly uses denial and deception in tactical decisions, although a combination of tactical deceptions may have a strategic impact. In great strategic matters, the revolutionaries are apt to tell the truth about their intentions if not their assets and operational capacities. Criminals, recognized as criminals, have even more difficulty in transforming denial into active deception, while lethal cults have fewer obstacles because until they use violence few pay attention to their actions. For the Sicilian Mafia or the Chinese Triads, denial is a way of life and strategic deception is often beyond their capacity or concern: hiding pays the expected dividends. Cults, by contrast, often find secrecy congenial but seldom have cause to deceive the outside world about their intentions. When individuals or secret movements hide their intentions by concealing a violent reality under a conventional cover, there often is little officials can do until there is gas in the subway or a bomb in Oklahoma City.

Strategic Denial

Cover

Any act of deception that is planned can be strategic, tactical or technical depending on the aspiration of the creator and the nature of reality. Thus, strategic planning may seek to cover the reality of the entire organization, its military or operational capacity, or the very existence of the armed struggle. No cover means no revolution or no criminal enterprise. Any classical armed struggle is a constant effort by the underground to persist against the rising capacity and competence of the regime. In both criminal and revolutionary groups, tactical denial is learned by practice. Techniques are acquired not by training but happenstance. Only at times can extensive deception operations be planned, because of the limitations of time and talent and the paucity of resources.

There are two considerations in shaping cover. The first is the creation of the alternative reality that protects the enterprise by making entry and observation difficult or impossible. The second is the adoption of effective procedures, the tradecraft of clandestine survival. If an armed struggle lasts long enough, there is some common wisdom, some corporate memory, just as there is some advantage for the guerrilla who knows the country and the skills of evasion. The more successful the organization, the more secure the haven, the more likely cover will be lost to the desire for revolutionary legitimacy or by the rise of criminal arrogance. Nothing erodes secrecy like success.

Revolutionary Cover

The revolution seeks any opportunity to leave the underground, which is a transitory existence on the way to power. The hidden desire to be visible and conventional. Al-Fatah wanted to be a real army, not a terrorist organization and so it hid behind Black September. The IRA has titles and ranks. The gunmen and assassins of *Brigate rosse* operate in columns. Conspiracy and tactical operations require secrecy, but legitimacy insists on no cover at all: it is a revolutionary dilemma.

The revolution's persistence assures revelation. Spokesmen emerge and at times the guerrillas pose for the media. The public, however, assumes that denial is first choice and the result of planning, skill and talent. The terrorist is seen as an antihero, technologically adept, cunning, tireless, and ingenious. In reality, most terrorists live in constant anxiety. They are relentlessly pursued and often find themselves alone in strange places without prospect of rescue. They are certain that there is no home for them but the underground. Yet until capture or death, the gunman *appears* free, secure, and dangerous. This is the romance of the Mafioso, often a cruel and coarse peasant empowered only by recourse to the gun. In part, this public perception arises because every underground operation comes as a surprise and because secrecy hides flaws. There is the romance of the clandestine: the terrorist slipping through customs, operating with false documents, disguised, privy to secure communications and safe houses. This is largely, if not entirely, illusion. Yet, the modern terrorist has systemic advantages if no certificate in tradecraft. All operate in an era of weak states, conflicting jurisdiction, and immediate electronic communications. They blend into the constant movement of individuals, making themselves appear as one more tourist or salesman. The global ocean offers easy cover for terror fish.

However congenial the global order, each outlaw still must move at risk, never at ease, never sure the safe house is safe or if the barman is not a police agent. Simply to move, to appear to do nothing, to fill the idle hours, to make a telephone call, present false papers, meet a contact, or speak to a stranger is an exhausting experience. Audacity is punished and so, too, sloth. The feckless do not survive.

Criminal Cover

For the criminal, the secret world largely determines the skills necessary to hide and so survive to profit. What the criminal must avoid is disclosure that leads to arrest and prosecution. One is not a criminal until found guilty in many societies. In a brutal and efficient state, the regime may not wait for disclosure and, as in the case of political dissent, simply arrest the suspected. In many arenas, however, the criminal survives because what matters is to hide the relatively rare act, the discrete violation of the law, not the existence of the organization. The criminal seeks a haven by offering services perceived as inexpensive and convenient in return for impunity from prosecution. The criminal wants the state both as corrupt friend and source of exploitation while the gunman wants the state under proper banners.

From jewel thieves on the Riviera to *La Cosa Nostra* in New York, criminals operate in almost absolute secrecy, speak only to their own, trust—if at all—family and faction, depend—if possible—on the limits of the law, corruption, the toleration of their neighbors and, if need be, on the skills of evasion. Like the revolutionaries, they are apt to be inefficient but persistent, visible enough to be examined but not so rash as to be caught in the act. Power can be achieved only by violence and kept only by intimidation. To succeed, the criminal almost inevitably creates the conditions that assure ultimate failure: arrogance and ferocity beyond the toleration even of friends.

There are criminal organizations that sometimes want to be totally invisible: the Sicilian drug distributors in the United States or the corrupted bankers laundering Russian Mafiya money offshore. The Mafia's code of *Omertà* is simply a Sicilian answer to a universal question: How to deny insight and capacity to the declared enemy and yet achieve public respect? Such respect is one reward of criminality and one means to impose silence. The Mafia in Sicily achieves both cover and recognition. Everyone knows that the old man in a seedy black suit sipping coffee dregs at the café table is capable of ordering death. Everyone knows and no one speaks.

Underground Cover

There are no rules underground but there are imperatives. Governments usually have the tangible assets and the subversives must make do with limited equipment. The authorities may assume a spectacular threat arises from capacity, but this is rarely the case. Few, including analysts, scholars, soldiers and at times the police, realize just how limited in tradecraft a terrorist or a Mafioso may be. Surprise does not mean competence, only effective operational cover. Most operations are aborted and most operatives sooner or later are arrested or killed. The few successes, however, overshadow all else, especially when they produce spectacular results (e.g., murdering a prime minister or destroying a Marine barracks). All the canceled or disrupted operations of the *Brigate rosse* or the IRA were forgotten once Aldo Moro was dead or the center of London was devastated.

The IRA and *Brigate rosse* are not alone in relying on faith over capacity. Even if their skills were inept and their capture swift, a group of Islamic fundamentalists operating in New Jersey and Brooklyn detonated a truck bomb beneath the World Trade Center. No one had noticed the group. No one in authority had imagined that such an attack was looming. In London, in theory, everyone was looking for the IRA. So, too, in Rome the *Brigate rosse* was hunted during the Moro kidnapping. But in New York no one was looking for a truck bomb at the World Trade Center. A little cover until the operational moment can be adequate if the authorities do not even know the threat exists. After an operation, cover must be even better since the authorities have been provoked and made aware of the campaign. In fact, few leaders plan for failure, and many do not focus beyond arriving at the target and completing the operation.

Even the experienced and the shrewd cannot operate undercover indefinitely. In many cases, cover is porous and individual tradecraft is highly limited. For the gunman or guerrilla assets, character, and experience determine cover once the underground haven has been left behind. The clandestine life is part perception and part harsh reality, without a standard operating procedure.

Denial and Deception: A Way of Life

Those living an underground life have different priorities and agendas from outsiders. The zealot goes to the office but is on the way to salvation. An individual is enhanced, lives within special values and speaks in a closed language. Everything, everyone looks the same but they are not the same: conviction has transformed perception. Those in more legitimate concerns such as economic enterprises, religious orders and charitable and humanitarian groups when acting undercover by necessity and often against the wishes of the legitimate, live in secrecy but do not lead secret lives. They use craft but their world is the real world, not the underground.

Strategic Denial and Strategic Deception

The Holy Jihad: New York City 1990-1995

On 26 February 1993, a bomb in a rented truck exploded in a parking garage under the World Trade Center, killing six people and causing hundreds of millions of dollars in damage. The bombing brought transnational terror to America.[7] The operation had been a symbolic strike at the heart of the House of the Great Satan by Islamic fundamentalists engaged in a holy war, a Jihad. Four of the conspirators were arrested, tried and, on 4 March 1994, convicted and given terms that totaled 240 years. They had been untrained and clumsy and were easily caught. They left their fingerprints, went back to get a refund on the rental truck, kept incriminating evidence, and generated a long paper trail. The most effective conspirator, Ramzi Ahmed Yousef, had flown out of New York's JFK airport using a false Iraqi passport before the bomb detonated. Yousef planned to pursue the Jihad against America elsewhere.

On 23 June 1993, five months after the World Trade Center had been bombed, a similar group of twelve militant Islamic fundamentalists were arrested for plotting to bomb targets in New York and assassinate President Hosni Mubarak of Egypt. These conspirators believed that they had learned much from the World Trade Center operation. Their plot was not to be "amateurish" like that of the four in prison but extensive, effective, and dramatic. Instead the zealots and their spiritual leader, Sheikh Omar Abdel Rahman, found themselves in prison, tried and convicted as a result of an informer, the surveillance of the authorities, and a series of blunders.

By contrast, Ramzi Yousef, identified and wanted, remained at large, pursuing the Jihad. After a series of conspiracies, escapes, operations, and incidents in Asia, he would devise a spectacular, multistaged operation out of the Philippines that sought to bomb a dozen U.S. airliners in flight and kill Pope John Paul II for good measure. The plot failed. Ramzi Yousef, too, was captured on 7 February 1995, by American agents in Pakistan after an intensive, worldwide search that deployed computer technology, informers, various intelligence agencies, the Drug Enforcement Agency, standard police procedures and, in the end, luck. Tried and convicted, Ramzi Yousef was imprisoned in Colorado with Timothy McVeigh, convicted of the Oklahoma City bombing, and the Unabomber. The two Americans had relied on simple secrecy, but Yousef had belonged to an underground of the faithful that could only protect him against power and pursuit for so long.

Denial

The fifteen Islamic conspirators involved in the American plots were an almost typical sample of transnational Islamic militants: a dozen men, all but one young, most marginal, emigrants from various countries, one or two with an education. Ramzi Yousef, for instance, had studied engineering in Swansea in Wales. All had moved a long way from their homes in miles but not in terms of attitudes. Two were converts to Islam: one African-American, the other Puerto Rican. Both sought what the others took for granted: the legitimacy of Islam, the assurance of triumph and salvation. The faithful, however, had no home. They could not go back to their village or find a career among their own. Suddenly, they were at home everywhere: one apartment like another, one mosque like the next, one grim job the same as the last. But everywhere they were enhanced by the faith.

The faith surrounds the heretic and the apostate. Neither can enter the new reality any more than can visitors, tourists, agents, scholars, or spies, for they are not saved. What was denied to many of the faithful was not, however, salvation but respect by a world that glittered, a Western high-tech maze of splendid prizes and wondrous benefits beyond reach of the pious. The Sheikh preached that such a world was vile and that people who enjoyed its benefits had to be punished. Each believer heard this message, those who bombed the World Trade Center, those who sought to bomb again in New York, and Ramzi Yousef who would plot a catastrophe. They made operational plans and contemplated targets. Some believers collected arms and set up training camps, acquired manuals and limited skills. All sought justice through the ordained use of violence. No one in authority noticed the zealous sermons in the obscure storefront mosques or imagined that the wars of the Middle East might come to Manhattan. This lack of official concern persisted despite the visibility of militant Islam: the kidnappings and bombs of Beirut, the wars in Algeria and Egypt and the threats of violence directed against the U.S. homeland. Islamic terror appeared on television news but rarely on the agenda of U.S. authorities.

It was the improbability of such an attack on U.S. territory that gave the terrorists cover, demonstrating how effective violence may be in the hands of even the most inept if they deny authorities access to their intentions. Sheikh Omar Abdel Rahman was a blind Egyptian teacher, an orator, and a cleric who fit no American stereotype of a terrorist mastermind. Yet he was the new Jihad personified: a zealot, strange in appearance and vision, who explained but did not apologize, who denied all and yet was credited with all. The American events made him into an international media figure, a world actor instead of simply a voice for the new wave of Islamic fundamentalists. Omar Abdel Rahman was a zealot admired by many as a spokesman who offered Islam as the answer, a prophet with honor but without a home.

Sheikh Omar Abdel Rahman arrived in New York from a small Egyptian village in July 1990. The Sheikh established two mosques in Brooklyn and Jersey City. Short, stocky, his eyes blank and milky, bearded as the prophet required, dressed as he would have been in Cairo, he spoke for Islam with conviction and thunder. Those interested in his religion or his politics found him in Brooklyn and Jersey City. The authorities and a few analysts also knew his whereabouts and his message. His cover was that no American authority could imagine him dangerous. He appeared to be an itinerant emigrant who preached in seedy rented rooms.

At times his language was obtuse. All of his followers, however, knew what he meant. Some knew what they must do: bomb, lend a car, give money, find a place to train, or buy chemicals. Others ignored the entire matter. The crucial cover for the New York operation was the ethos of the faith, the parallel world of the devout that could not be entered except by those assumed to be equally devout. This parallel reality created by the revelation of the truth offered the key answers: What was wrong? Secularism driven by the West. What was needed? Allah. And what was to be done? A Jihad.

Sheikh Rahman's truth imposed obligations and shaped a climate of dedication not easy to penetrate or even to imagine. Elsewhere, young men sharing the same dream had driven to their death in car bombs. The particular reality, the alternative universe, could be found, as Ramzi Yousef did, anyplace. Cover, however, hid the faith but not the faithful. Once the World Trade Center had alerted the American authorities, the cost of secrecy continued to erode capacity but more important the cover of the faith was useless against police and intelligence filters now aware of the potential risks from the fundamentalists. Once the authorities realized the nature of symbolic terror and suspected the reality of an underground, cover was increasingly difficult to maintain. Sheikh Rahman was arrested.

Ramzi Yousef, with a two million dollar price on his head, was wanted worldwide. It might be impossible for the police to attend a meeting without arousing suspicion, but they had no trouble in monitoring the communications, movements, bank accounts, friends and associates of those who did attend. The assets of the state were deployed to track Ramzi Yousef. Born poor in Kuwait to a Palestinian mother and a Pakistani father, educated in Wales, Yousef was a modern nomad once his cover was broken. After he was arrested in Islamabad, he offered no apologies or regrets. He had counted on the parallel Islamic world for aid and comfort. Yet, his operational cover, fashioned by craft, unlike the underground supplied by the faith, was open to penetration by classical means. In time, the power and assets of those determined to pursue terror at considerable cost placed him in an American courtroom. He made no attempt to hide his aspirations to punish the Great Satan and was convicted. Ramzi Yousef was a typical transnational terrorist dedicated to spectacular assaults on global order just as the Sheikh was a traditional zealot eager to find in Allah and the Jihad the answer to the present. The

Sheikh relied almost entirely on his parallel world and the ambiguities of his language as cover; but Ramzi Yousef had to move among others and so had to acquire the techniques of denial. They were two examples of the nature of denial: the strategic and the technical.

Deception

Other than the ambiguities of the Arab language and the Sheikh's words, the conspirators never attempted to hide their analysis, their aspirations or their means. Anyone interested knew that the new wave of Islamic fundamentalism was a fruitful medium for terrorists eager to attack Western targets. What deceived the Western authorities and many Western analysts was the improbability of such attacks, since even a spectacular terrorist attack could not weaken the global system and would only generate outrage and retaliation. The concept of "punishing" the Great Satan was alien to most Western officials. Thus, the appeal of a strategic campaign of terror focused on symbolic targets intended to impress an audience of the faithful rather than only to damage the Western system set off no alarms. New York was not perceived as vulnerable to the forces that killed Anwar Sadat in Egypt or the Marines in Beirut.

Self-deception—the idea that something cannot happen here or to us—is rarely the result of deception planning. Ignorance and innocence made the American operations of a few badly trained zealots possible. This innocence, especially in America, was largely due to the previous lack of exposure to terrorism. The battlefields were supposed to be overseas and the lectures of a blind cleric were beyond understanding. The cover provided by the mosque and the novelty of the sermon as revolutionary agenda combined to bemuse those charged with New York's security. What the New York experience revealed was that with limited tactical cover, very little planning, and considerable audacity, amateurs could shape a strategy of terror that produced symbolic returns even for failed operations. A little violence protected by invisibility goes a long, long way in compensating for lack of resources, training, capacity, and the costs of the underground. Once revealed, however, denial is not as easily reclaimed and by then, deception planning may be too costly or too complex for those who are being hunted.

Terrorist organizations most likely to pursue deception in operational matters beyond denial are those engaged in protracted campaigns that allow experience to be acquired, opportunities noted, and time invested. What Ramzi Yousef needed was tactical cover, which he lost by prudently testing his bombs and so revealing his existence. He had strategic cover. He did not need to plan diversions or mask his intentions or dazzle the opposition with a multitude of messages. All he needed was to maintain the illusion that he was not where he was—for wherever he was the Americans knew his intentions. He could run if lucky. He could hide in the underground. What he could not do easily was pursue his operational goals with impunity. Grand strategy depended on tactical cover. This is not a fatal problem. Luck, cunning, compensating errors, flaws in the system often allow access and so success. The IRA bombed Downing Street, killed Mountbatten, and nearly murdered Prime Minister Margaret Thatcher; they were lucky sometimes even in forewarned, open societies. Ramzi Yousef was unlucky and without operational cover. He had no safe haven that was any use. The Sheikh, on the other hand, knew his words were easily understood by the faithful and unheeded by the infidel. All he needed was to be left alone while the zealots organized operations. No one involved felt compelled to be clever or duplicitous except in matters of denial. Because of this their cover was broken in traditional ways by those alert to the threat.

In a sense, those involved overestimated the protection of the faith and the comfort of the underground. They also underestimated the obstacles to operations. The frailty of denial and the failings of craft meant that the opportunity to pursue symbolic terror on a strategic level had been lost when the authorities were no longer denied insight into the mission of the faithful.

The Provisional Irish Republican Army, 1970

In the autumn of 1969, the Irish republican movement emerged once again from obscurity as a result of the decay of order in the six counties of Northern Ireland. The core of the movement, the Irish Republican Army, inherited a rich variety of experience over two centuries of operations. The Irish Republican Brotherhood—the Fenians—was founded in 1858 and its members were the ancestors of the IRA that emerged in the Easter Rising of 1916 to seek to establish the Irish Republic. After 1916, the movement failed repeatedly no matter what strategy or tactics were adopted: guerrilla war, assassination, conspiracies, bombing campaigns in Northern

Ireland and in England, and rural terror. Partial victory had come with the Tan War of 1918-1921, but the zealous wanted no less than the Irish Republic and so persisted in their campaign. Ireland partitioned was not yet free, not yet one, and not purely Gaelic. Eventually, after the failure of the IRA border campaign in 1962, there were few left who supported a program of violence. The province of Northern Ireland remained British, a Protestant state for a Protestant people administered by the Stormont parliament in Belfast and immune to the tiny IRA. It was the assault on the inequities imposed by the Northern Ireland provincial government that generated new and unexpected conditions.

Until the autumn of 1969, the campaign for civil rights had been a matter of protests, demonstrations and marches. The Catholic-nationalist grievances against unfair housing, voting restrictions, and pervasive sectarian imposition were substantial. The militant unionists were often bigoted and determined to maintain their British Ulster against Papist conspirators and Irish Republican ambitions represented by the civil rights marchers. The provincial government and the largely Protestant paramilitary police, the Royal Ulster Constabulary (RUC), were not sympathetic to Catholics or their grievances. The loyalists used intimidation and then violence to disrupt the marchers. There were disturbances in Derry after a Protestant Masonic march on 15 August. The trouble quickly spread to Belfast where the loyalists attacked and burned Catholic housing, in an act that today might be called ethnic cleansing. Order collapsed and rioting spread throughout the province.

Northern Catholics assumed that they could rely on the IRA to protect them. The secret army, however, was a myth. There were only a few dozen IRA men in Belfast with an arsenal of old, mismatched firearms. And the Irish Republic had neither the resources nor the will to intervene on behalf of the threatened nationalists. Amid the fires, explosions, and petrol bombs, the provincial government was besieged. Belfast was burning and Dublin was in a panic.

In London, the Labor cabinet believed it had no other choice but to send in the army to restore order and protect the Catholics. Shrewd politicians recognized that the army could not easily be withdrawn without local political accommodation. Such an accommodation was unlikely since both sides in the dispute assumed politics was a zero-sum game. What was at stake was the existence of either a united, largely Catholic, Ireland or a Protestant Ulster within the United Kingdom. Security would now depend on the British army.

Strategic Denial

The Northern Catholic nationalists had, despite all evidence to the contrary, assumed that the IRA would protect them. Although a large pool of Republicans might be on the island, few were active within the IRA. The governments or Protestant mobs implied such an IRA threat to legitimize their actions, but neighbors should have known better. Embittered, they scrawled the walls with *"IRA - I Ran Away."* Still, there were many Republicans who saw advantages in the events unfolding in Northern Ireland. To many it seemed there might be a new role for a secret army.

Those who had kept the Republican faith were scattered over the island. They belonged to a secret world, to which entry was through conviction. There were Republican families and Republican towns. Republicans appeared at commemorations. There were enough to split the movement between those who sought to pursue political options and those who saw an emerging military role. All kept their ideals to themselves and were often assumed by others to be cranks or eccentrics. Most were working class without access to power or resources. Much of the Republican underground, however, was waiting for an opportunity to use physical force to achieve its goals. The history of the IRA had almost always been composed of lean years, waiting to strike at the moment that the Irish people would tolerate violence. The traditional Republicans kept their faith in physical force and denied the legitimacy of the British presence in Ireland and the legitimacy of the parliaments North and South. By the end of 1969, they had broken with the official IRA.

The IRA in the 1960s was nearly entirely made up of working class individuals without the skills or experience useful to a contemporary secret army. Some were attracted to radical ideas, but many were not. The Republican movement, a secular cult, was shaped by the conviction that the truth has been revealed. The Irish volunteer knew the answers to the three great questions: What is wrong? The British. What is the goal? The Irish Republic. What must be done? The armed struggle. There was no need for compromise or politics.

The revelation of perceived truth transformed the lives of Republicans. It offered responsibilities, duties and obligations and very few rewards. For the Irish, shaped by a Catholic society, entry into the underground was much like a secular vocation. Ireland is a small island, everyone knows everyone else and nearly everyone knew most of those sympathetic to militant republicanism. The faithful were no different in accent and religion, in habits and character from the everyday Irish: largely poor, largely Catholic, and often still rural. Yet, to reach those in the movement one had to have an entry visa into their world. What was unique was that the very structure of this conspiratorial underground was so old. Dreams of liberation fronts, conspiracies, revolutionary anarchists come and then go, but the Irish dream persisted. The IRA was founded on two centuries of conspiracy illuminated by the same convictions and shaped by the same assumptions.

There was, thus, a national conspiracy legitimized by the goal of a free and united Ireland. It was a conspiracy open to rapid expansion with a role to offer every volunteer. The government in Dublin, proclaiming legitimacy and recognition, denied the pretensions of the republicans. The Northern unionists who saw the IRA as the weapon of a Catholic conspiracy to unite Ireland assumed that the Dublin government's posture was duplicitous. Until 1969, the republicans appeared to be irrelevant, without power or prospect. In any case, the movement was split. During the quarrels in the autumn of 1969, the traditionalist Republicans wanted to be sure that a military capacity existed, that recognition of the illegal states in Dublin or Belfast did not occur for political advantage, and that the movement focused as in the past on achieving the Republic. To do so, they organized a real IRA.

In theory the IRA was a non-sectarian organization. In practice, only Catholics were IRA volunteers and nationalists. All Republicans had been disheartened by the inability of the IRA to protect nationalists in the North. After August 1969, all Republicans believed that what nationalists needed was protection that the British army and security forces could not really supply. The British were the problem, not a solution.

In January 1970, the Provisional IRA Army Council met for the first time. Seven men who had known each other for a lifetime sat down in a cold room in a small house near the border to change history. The Provisionals' analysis of reality was predictable. They drew from Irish history, patriot lore, and personal experience. The result was that the Provisional strategic view varied little from that of their immediate ideological ancestors; but the reality of Ireland had changed dramatically after 1969. Conditions now seemed to favor a concerted campaign to drive the British out of Northern Ireland.

The Provisionals saw immediately that they had a role to play that was unrelated to shaping a theoretical revolution proposed by the official IRA or even the specific needs of the Northern Catholic community. Protest and civil disobedience were now obsolete given the current standoff. The Dublin leadership would do nothing because their strategy to end partition was to wait out the opposition. The Stormont parliament was discredited and so, too, the unionists and loyalists who would only react to provocation. The British were entangled in a situation that could not be finessed or ignored, and so were vulnerable. For once, history favored the traditionalists; their grasp of reality proved a useful guide to what became the Irish Troubles. The British army would soon find that its role defending order would put it at odds with the Catholic search for justice. The British army, no matter what the British Labor government did, would not long remain a Catholic defender. The IRA could use the myth of a secret army to create a militia in Northern Ireland with support from the Irish Republic and the Irish diaspora.

Defending Catholics offered a mission that assured recognition, acceptance and a new role in events. This, however, is not what the IRA wanted. The IRA Army Council wanted an armed campaign to engender nationalist support that would make the province ungovernable, thereby forcing the British to withdraw. They did not want simply to defend Catholics, although the Catholics who wanted a defense were eager to volunteer for combat. The Provisional IRA began to recruit, train, and arm units throughout Ireland. Most observers assumed this was the only role of the IRA. This was not the case. The IRA's mission was to make Ireland a nation once again: free, united, and Gaelic. To do this, they were willing to play the role of defender of local Catholics.

The January 1970 IRA Army Council meeting was one of the movement's few strategic sessions. The seven participants accepted a strategy that would eventually merge role and mission. A revolutionary underground's focus on whether or not to initiate the armed struggle determines most of their first strategic decisions. In Ireland, however, the republicans had long since made that decision and so could focus on timing and assessing their prospects for success. In January 1970, the Army set out its future, which included a strategic deception plan that would disguise the role and mission of the IRA even from many volunteers and most supporters. Defend, provoke, and attack was to be the staging of the new strategy. They would become defenders as a first step, mobilize nationalist support and opinion, grow, and flourish on fear and anxiety while indoctrinating new volunteers. Step two was the provocation of the British by the new volunteers converted to Republican convictions. This second step would lead to a real campaign.

Provocation was easy since the British army soon discovered that the establishment was very British and the unionists exceptionally loyal. They flew British flags, loved the queen, and cheered their army. The Catholic nationalists were Irish, had no queen, and had different names, holidays, aspirations, and attitudes. The British army found the nationalists troublesome: they wanted change, reforms, abhorred the loyalists and their flags, and caused trouble. To make trouble was the policy of the IRA Army, and their provocation succeeded. As the new IRA volunteers became Republican, their operations grew more violent, and the British response became harsher and less discriminating.

In the third stage, provocation merged with a real armed struggle based on a risen people, tangible support from all nationalist Irish, and the sympathy of much of the international community. As the IRA shifted from defensive to guerrilla operations, the British attempted to preempt protest with a more aggressive response. They interned suspects without trial and treated Catholics as subversives. The murder of fourteen innocent people on Bloody Sunday in Derry in January 1972 by British paratroops guaranteed that the insurgency would escalate. The IRA now had a new mission and a new role in an armed struggle. All that need be denied was that this had been planned all along. After Bloody Sunday there was no further need of strategic deception. IRA leaders had deceived their friends and enemies and even for a time their recruits to help transform turmoil into an insurrection.

The three-stage deception plan engendered almost no discussion within the movement. There was nothing resembling deception planning, only an agreement that defense would engender support that would allow provocation, which eventually would lead to an armed struggle that the British could not win. The only strategic error was to assume that the British would concede because of the costs of maintaining their presence in Northern Ireland.

Over the next thirty years, the Irish Troubles often revealed clever technical and tactical use of deception by all involved but never again a single, shining moment when a great deception strategy was selected as a means to change history. Over the last ten years, many traditional IRA supporters would suspect that they had been deceived for years about the intentions of their leaders to enter the peace process by ending the armed struggle. Traditional unionists, by contrast, suspected the same IRA leaders of using the peace process as a facade to maintain the gun in politics. It was the 1970 Army Council meeting, a meeting made safe by the strategic denial provided by the clandestine movement, however, that demonstrated strategic deception planning at its most elegant.

The Sicilian Mafia, 1957-1958

In Sicily during the nineteenth century, rural factions were co-opted by the establishment to protect the great estates in return for control of the villages. These factions extorted money, pursued criminal enterprises and disciplined their own. The families of the western part of the island and the factions of Palermo institutionalized criminal activity within a clandestine structure, a secret world entered by oaths and ceremonies. Membership offered advantages: money on an island without prospects, power to the denied, and most of all respect. The Mafiosi had the privileges to violate the law at the risk only of occasional prosecution. In return for tolerating Mafia crime, the Sicilian establishment and the state in Rome were assured of social peace and at election time political support. The nexus of criminal and political interests persisted in Sicily generation after generation.

Isolated on a marginal island that was always badly administered, the Mafia became institutionalized. Protected, feared, at times respected as local phenomena, and misunderstood on the mainland, few in public chose to note the reality of the Mafia. Sicilian officials—the bishops, landlords, members of parliament, and bankers—denied that there was a Mafia. The everyday people were silent according to the code of *Omertà* so that the organization had the best cover of all: invisibility no matter how arrogant and public the crimes. No one saw anything. No one knew anything. Yet, everyone knew that the Mafia was integrated into Sicilian life.

The clandestine life, the institutionalization of denial, gave every Mafioso—no matter how limited in talent or education—a life enhanced by respect. Some Mafioso might come into Palermo in a sleek white suit, attend dances and charity balls, put on a *bella figura.* Others like the farm boy with a shotgun standing by a crossroad at night could hardly imagine Palermo, but had the respect of the everyday people. The Mafiosi lived a life where all was permitted, law was no obstacle, and even the gentry could not deny them. What the organization had was strategic denial shaped not so much by revealed truth as by the enormous advantages of money, power, respect, and the capacity to act on events.

The Sicilian Mafia exploited the Diaspora abroad and the government on the island. The Mafia persisted during the monarchy, the expansion of democracy, and even when Mussolini arrived and sought to crush them. The Duce stopped short of imprisoning the Mafia's friends in the establishment so that the criminal families survived. After the Allied invasion of 1943, the factions and alliances that had survived both Fascism and the war emerged to exploit new opportunities. In the new Republic, the largest party, the Christian Democrats, needed Sicilian votes to deny power to the Communists. The Mafia could supply the votes and maintain civil order. So the Sicilian Mafia had new patrons and the traditional permission to pursue advantage in extortion, exploitation, intimidation, and vice. There were new local opportunities, new state monies from Rome, and always the traditional operations: usury, licenses, and control of water, jobs and building permits. There were favors to be offered and dissents to be punished with exemplary violence.

Then in 1957, a new-model Sicilian Mafia emerged as the island safe haven was used as a base to go international. At the suggestion of Lucky Luciano, a Sicilian-American in Italian exile, a meeting took place at the Hotel des Palmes in Palermo in 1957. The Sicilians wanted to expand their interests off the island by controlling the then limited heroin trade into the United States. The Sicilians would buy the finished product from the Corsicans and ship it across the Atlantic through President Fulgencio Batista's Cuba into American ports, and then distribute the product. The Sicilians wanted no interference and no entanglement with the Italian-American *Cosa Nostra* who already had been involved in Cuba and the importation of heroin. These Americans, some of whom were cousins and all Sicilians, were in disarray, isolated, far from European action or the emerging heroin trade. In the United States they had few friends in power and were besieged by the federal government. They could do little but agree to the Sicilian offer made across the table in Palermo. The island Mafia had power, respect and a new organization. They could not be denied. Complicity with authority assured the Sicilian leadership time for planning, a haven to consider mutual interests, and a way to end rivalries.

There in the baroque dining room of the Hotel des Palmes under the high painted ceilings with the huge windows offering a view of palms and blue skies, the contemporary Sicilian Mafia emerged.[8] The coalition of recognized families was strengthened by a new, revised structure: a central commission, called the *Cupola*—the Dome. The *Capi* were delegated areas and power. There was a chairman, *Capo di Tutti Capi*. Custom regulated the constant clash of ambitious personalities, overlapping interests and shifting opportunities.

The unanimity displayed at the meeting of the *Cupola* at the Hotel des Palmes simply represented the existing stability achieved by a balance of interests and the prospect of new business opportunities. The Sicilians would operate in America controlling the heroin trade. Everything related to their operations would be denied: the reality of the Mafia organization and the control of the drug trade. Everyone but the criminals involved would be deceived. In Sicily and in Rome, in the transit countries and especially in the United States, the authorities would not know that the Sicilians were involved. Cover was maintained, involvement hidden, and profits were assured for a generation. Since everyone knew there *was* a Mafia in Sicily and Italian emigrant organized crime in America, both would deny involvement in drugs. Announcements were made that drugs were dirty and that as good Catholic Italians dedicated to traditional operations, none in the organization could be involved. The Sicilian Mafia would deny itself publicly and deal clandestinely. The American *Cosa Nostra,* cut out of the heroin trade except for retail sales, would simply forbid dealing in drugs. Everyone knew such a ban would be violated. Those Americans who had to be disciplined would be accused of violating the ban and those who did the disciplining would continue to trade.

The cover proved sound. The Sicilians fashioned a huge transnational enterprise that flooded the factions with money. Retaining the traditional island rackets and the vast sums skimmed off the state programs administered by their political friends, the Mafia established a secret international enterprise that was engaged in many new and highly profitable crimes. The invisible Sicilian involvement in America was to run without serious interruption for twenty years. The American *Cosa Nostra* increasingly became a group of neighborhood criminals.

The Sicilian Mafia, organized as an illicit conspiracy with generations of practice, had institutionalized all the techniques and tactics of denial. In addition to the strategic denial that criminal enterprise required, the *Cupola* had hidden the organization's drug venture. The organization stated that there was no Mafia and that it did not do drugs. Many accepted this self-fabricated image. Both as denial and deception, the Mafia strategy persisted a remarkable twenty years before frayed denial and criminal evidence revealed something of the structure of the organization and its involvement in the drug trade.

Conclusion

Deception is integral to illicit organizations. Cover is a strategic necessity that, at a great cost in efficiency, allows illicit organizations the opportunity to achieve their objectives. The revolutionary organization is, in fact, an alternative reality that seeks to be invisible except when it needs to propagate a version of the truth and to bolster the impact of its armed operations. In the case of the truth, remarkably little deception is deployed. The revolutionaries consider their faith to be inviolate and convincing, without need of apology or equivocation. Reality is often visible. Islamic Jihad preached the truth, the IRA hid it for two years and the Sicilian Mafia makes the hidden truth yield public respect. In operational matters, much that takes place underground is focused on maintenance, supply and distribution, command and control, and communication that needs to be hidden but need not otherwise be duplicitous. Secrecy apart, most operations focus on obvious targets. Strategic deception is rare.

An organization about to embark on an armed struggle usually does so after much contemplation. At the beginning, there is time and motive for deception. Most rebels tend to be truthful about their intentions, means and ultimate aspirations. Most criminals have no choice and most cults are benign. Thus, the big strategic questions usually have been narrowed to the date to begin operations. Once committed, the organizations rarely have the resources or time to make strategic deception planning possible. By contrast, deception is readily found in tactical operations. Rebels have threatened what they did not plan to do or used false warnings and fake devices as ruses to pave the way for the real operation. Many groups seek to project greater assets or greater legitimacy, but most deception is apt to be an operational, technical tool. Such tactical deception, over time, can become quite sophisticated. What is most often sought, however, is simple surprise rather than combining a series of ruses in a grand tactical campaign.

The prime reason that deception planning is scanty and strategic deception operations are rare underground is that time and resources are lacking. The operational leadership is often unable to meet. Planning is by rote, the desire for momentum overwhelming the opportunities for novelty. Outsiders assume that the underground is simply a secret version of everyday life. They assume that in the underground planning and freedom to act are institutionalized. This is almost never the case. Nothing is easy underground. Planning can be halting and communications are always faulty. Faith supplies the energy for an armed struggle, but always at the cost of efficiency. Deception is perceived as a luxury while denial becomes second nature as part of the underground reality. Deception in operational matters is deployed to assure secrecy and at times as an integral part of tactics.

Denial makes everything possible, and on occasion tactical deception makes the spectacular possible for the revolutionary. Unexpected violence can have an exaggerated effect on events. The revolutionary often can be assured that the initial attack or operation will be successful.

Illicit organizations and movements must seek cover to operate effectively. Some organizations are thus partly covert while others, particularly criminals and revolutionaries, are entirely covert. For them denial is so vital that it becomes a strategic necessity achieved by the creation of an alternative reality. Denial is achieved not through planning but mutual possession of revealed truth. Tactical deception arises from the cover so provided as well as necessity, habit and custom, experience, and luck. Those operating covertly seldom have the resources, time or opportunity for strategic deception planning, and instead rely on operational deception to achieve surprise. Such tactics are made possible by effective denial that focuses on the opponent's vulnerabilities. Every armed struggle employs technical and tactical deception as well as strategic denial. With time, a safe haven, and sufficient assets, strategic deception planning is more likely. Thus, the more illicit and hidden the group, the more difficult it is for them to organize strategic deception.

Sources

The sources for this text can be found in the published record or conventional studies and the conclusions drawn from three decades of interviews with those in illicit, covert organizations and their enemies and victims, especially but not exclusively in the Middle East, Africa, and Western Europe—Ireland and Italy. Most published works that focus specifically on deceptions tend to focus on intelligence issues or military surprise. Monographs on the IRA or criminals and deception do not exist. There is, however, considerable history and analysis of illicit and covert actors—ten thousand books on terrorism and thousands on the Mafia. For the case studies in this essay, see J. Bowyer Bell, *The Secret Army, The IRA* (New Brunswick, NJ: Transaction Publishers, 1997); and *The IRA, 1968-2000: An Analysis of a Secret Army* (London: Frank Cass, 2000); Tim Pat Coogan, *IRA* (London: Pall Mall, 1969; then New York: Praeger, 1970, and in various editions since with additions); and particularly Patrick Bishop and Eamonn Mallie, *The Provisional IRA* (London: Heinemann, 1987, republished by Corgi, 1993). There is an even larger literature on all facets of the Palestinian movement if little in particular on deception. See Neil C. Livingstone and David Halevy, *Inside the PLO* (New York: William Morrow & Co., 1990); Aryeh Y. Yodfat and Yuval Arnon-Ohanna, *PLO Strategy and Tactics* (New York: St. Martin's Press, 1981); and Julian Becker, *The PLO, The Rise and Fall of the Palestine Liberation Organization* (New York: St., Martin's, 1984). In English there are adequate works on the Sicilian Mafia, especially but not exclusively concerned either with the social conditions that engender it or the violence of the 1980s. For a general, popular account of the recent past, see Claire Sterling, *Octopus. The Long Reach of the International Mafia* (New York: Simon and Schuster, 1990); and a vivid, accurate and analytical account of the anti-Mafia struggle in Alexander Stille's *Excellent Cadavers, The Mafia and the Death of the First Italian Republic* (New York: Pantheon, 1995).

Notes

1. Denial focuses primarily on hiding the real by masking, repackaging or, if all else fails, by dazzling. See J. Barton Bowyer (Pseudo. J. Bowyer Bell and Barton Whaley), *Cheating: Deception in War & Magic, Games & Sports, Sex & Religion, Business & Con Games, Politics & Espionage, Art & Science* (New York: St. Martin's Press, 1980), pp. 49-50.
2. The literature on the American *Cosa Nostra* is extensive, but there is little that focuses on the theory of deception or denial. In law enforcement books such as those on the Pizza Connection or the Gambino family the authors are apt to give in detail the obstacles to penetration—denial as practiced without theory—that indicate ingenuity, innocence, and the application of technical means. See, for example, Ralph Blumenthal, *Last Days of the Sicilians* (New York: New York Times Books, 1988); and Joseph F. O'Brien and Andris Kurins, *Boss of Bosses, The Fall of the Godfather: The FBI and Paul Castellano* (New York: Simon and Schuster, 1991).
3. For a detailed analysis of the dynamics of the revolutionary underground, see J. Bowyer Bell, *The Dynamics of the Armed Struggle* (London: Frank Cass, 1998); for the feel of the underground almost any of the more famous diaries or journals will do. See Ernesto 'Che' Guevara, *Bolivian Diary* (London: Jonathan Cape, 1968); or Menachem Begin, *The Revolt* (Los Angeles, CA: Nash, 1972).
4. Most analysis of the PLO and Al-Fatah note that Black September was "secretly" a part of Al-Fatah, but not as a result of deception planning.
5. Grivas shaped his revolt very much as an army officer and, like many army officers, wrote memoirs and histories adjusted in recollection. But, the deception planning he undertook arose from his reading of the necessities of Cypriot Greek politics. Thus, he presumed that his view into the future was simply more penetrating than that of his political allies or the Greek Cypriots. See General George Grivas, *The Memoirs of General Grivas* (London: Longmans, 1964), a shortened version of his initial Greek edition.
6. There is a library filled with books on how to be a guerrilla and nothing for the would-be gunman. Carlos Marighella wrote a mini-manual, but he was killed during his struggle; and Abraham Guillén's *Philosophy of the Urban Guerrilla* (New York: William Morrow & Co., 1973) is hardly an action manual. Most gunmen learn on the job in any case.
7. There is not yet a book on the intrusion of the Islamic fundamentalist into New York, and so the major sources remain the media. For more about violent Islamic fundamentalism, an excellent early analysis is Gilles Kepel, *Le Prophète et Pharaon: Les Mouvements Islamistes dans l'Egypte Contemporaine* (Paris, FR: Editions La Découverte, 1984).
8. The best account of this meeting can be found in Claire Sterling, *Octopus, The Long Reach of the International Mafia* (New York: Simon and Schuster, 1990).

Commentary

Robert J. Nieves

For the purposes of analyzing denial and deception and the conditions for success and failure by illicit nonstate actors, Colombia during the early 1990s provides an interesting period for review and discussion. The analysis of the battle between the cocaine cartels and the Colombian government allows us to examine a failed example of denial and a successful example of deception.

In 1990, Colombia was engaged in all out war with the Medellin cartel led by Pablo Escobar Gaviria. By this time, Escobar had orchestrated a well-defined plan of terror and mayhem designed to bring the Colombian government to the negotiating table on the issue of extradition and narco-surrender. He and his surrogates had already killed hundreds if not thousands of Colombian security personnel, judges, and citizens and his trafficking empire had suffered as a result. While on the run, through lack of attention, Escobar had forfeited most of the international cocaine business to the Cali cartel.

During this period, the Cali cartel engaged in an extremely successful, well-orchestrated plan of deception. They fooled a significant percentage of the Colombian people, leading them to believe that the Cali organization was the "kinder and gentler" cartel. They contrasted their gentlemanly, business-like behavior with the terrorist actions of Escobar. This, coupled with corruption and intimidation, enabled them to co-opt the government.

While the national and international law enforcement communities were obsessed with watching the Medellin cartel and hunting for Pablo Escobar, the Cali cartel managed to become the world's most powerful transnational criminal organization. Had they been left unchecked, they would have destroyed Colombia's fragile democracy. We will never know whether or not they deliberately planned to keep the nation and the international community occupied in Medellin, while they built a drug empire in Cali, but in the end this is what they achieved.

By contrast, the Medellin cartel took denial to such an extreme that Pablo Escobar would find himself with only one bodyguard at the time of his demise. This denial led to very inefficient behavior; behavior flawed to a point where Escobar trusted no one except family and very close friends. This paranoia ultimately closed the circle around him tighter and tighter until he was located and killed in an armed confrontation with the police.

The Drug Environment in Colombia

To understand the demise of Escobar, we must examine the political conditions and drug environment in Colombia at the time and the methods the cartels employed to survive. The cartels had a global cocaine monopoly, centered in the cities of Cali and Medellin. These transnational mafias were well financed, well equipped, and extremely well organized. While the Cali cartel was engaged in business-like behavior, a state of terror and mayhem existed in Medellin. The government of Colombia, including the Colombian National Police and others, were trying to wage war simultaneously on two fronts in these cities. However, the focus was clearly on apprehending Pablo Escobar, who by that time had become Public Enemy Number One. The Cali cartel was engaged in limited denial. Bound by the constraints of global expansion and the need to ensure the security of their operations, they ran compartmented cell operations abroad. By 1990, they controlled at least 60 percent of the global cocaine market.

The Political Environment

In 1990, the newly elected Gaviria administration took office amid public demands for an end to drug-related violence. To many in the new administration, a negotiated surrender of the cocaine kingpins was an attractive political option. A Constituent Assembly was drafting a new constitution, and reform was at hand. Proposals to make extradition legal were a very contentious and heavily debated political issue. Carefully orchestrated Cali cartel corruption was thriving in key governmental entities, especially in the Legislative and Constituent assemblies. Many observers believed that democracy itself was under threat. These criminal and political factors all helped to create a fertile environment for denial and deception by the drug cartels.

Strategy for Failure: The Medellin Cartel

Denial created a stranglehold on Pablo Escobar, whose leadership of the Medellin cartel was dedicated to a strategy of terror centered in the town of Medellin. Escobar became a fugitive, hunted by the largest task force ever assembled in Latin America. Living constantly under the threat of arrest, he began to suspect treason among his loyal surrogates. He murdered several of his closest associates. Aware that his communications were being monitored, he was forced to change locations frequently, sometimes moving daily in the hopes of evading his pursuers. Escobar came to trust only family and close friends in his efforts to avoid capture by the police. It was his communications with family members, however, that actually led the police, who had been monitoring his cell phone calls, to his hiding place. In the ensuing firefight, Escobar was killed.

Strategy for Success: The Cali Cartel's Deception Strategy

The Cali cartel's goal was to make the Colombian people, the government, and the international community believe that extradition was unconstitutional. Cartel leaders also repeatedly stated that sovereignty was more important to the Colombian people than better relations with the United States. Ultimately, the goal of their deception campaign was to convince the Colombian people that negotiated surrender was a viable option for dealing with the cartel kingpins and ending the drug-related violence.

The first and perhaps most crucial step in this deception campaign was to create a secure command and control environment for the Cali cartel principals within the city of Cali. Then they established an intelligence collection capability to gather and analyze first-rate intelligence on the opposition, and the U.S. government. Not only did they enhance their personal security, they also created a security protocol for all trusted members of their command structure. Safe houses with elaborate escape mechanisms and state-of-the-art concealment were established. To evade detection, the leadership of the cartel used carefully orchestrated movements and simultaneously deployed decoys whenever they changed locations. They monitored police and intelligence communications, and with the assistance of corrupt employees of the phone company wiretapped phones, including those of the U.S. Drug Enforcement Administration at the U.S. Embassy in Bogotá. They collected surveillance intelligence via hotel agents, travel agents, realtors and other special security teams. They also used sophisticated software to analyze long distance calling data, license plate records, surveillance reports, and U.S. law enforcement documents (obtained through legal discovery from cases in the U.S.).

Once these intelligence efforts began to produce results, acts of carefully orchestrated deception followed. Cartel operatives corrupted or intimidated key elected and career government officials. They cleverly marketed the negotiated surrender option to the people via the media while disseminating the option to the government via their high-priced attorneys and corrupt politicians. Cali leaders successfully sold the public on the notion that they were the "kinder and gentler" cartel.

The Cali cartel succeeded in compromising the government. They also succeeded in influencing the Constituent Assembly and in changing the extradition provisions in the constitution. They influenced legislation with more favorable surrender provisions such as reduced sentences for cooperation, and created options for incarceration at home. Their deception campaign worked. By laying the foundation for legal changes, and controlling their legal environment, the Cali cartel gained the upper hand, and they held on to their ill-gotten gains. Even their prison sentences were significantly reduced.

6

Arms Control: Focus on Denial and Deception

Lynn M. Hansen

Americans treasure openness and truth. But even in this society, denial and deception dwell just below the surface. A woman who commented on my task of presenting a paper at a conference on denial and deception reminded me of this fact when she poignantly asked, "Will either of my ex-husbands present a paper?" While this may not be significant enough to warrant attention here, she, none-theless, made the point that the practice of deception is routine among human beings. It is even more widespread in international relations. In most countries, deception is state policy.

At the official level, we have become too enamored with open-ness. Our citizens want to know what government is doing, and rightly so. Openness and a free press were key ingredients in pro-moting the successful revolution that led to the foundation of this nation. But there are times when this openness is so fundamentally opposed to our basic national security interests that it can reap re-sults every bit as harmful as a well-placed spy. Often, those in gov-ernment are appalled at a media which follows its own judgments and political aims in revealing to the world the context, and, some-times verbatim, the contents of highly classified documents. Some-one is guilty either of a near-treasonous act, or foolish official deci-sions. Often made for political reasons, these unauthorized revela-tions offer antagonists the very secrets that make our intelligence gathering and analytic corps second to none.

In a paradoxical sort of way, our citizens expect the Central Intel-ligence Agency—often believed to be the sole provider of U.S. in-telligence—to be capable of doing everything and knowing everything. This blind faith in the ability of intelligence to know everything to protect our national interest betrays ignorance of the difficulty and complexity that are inherent in the collection and analysis of intelligence. This difficulty is increasing almost daily as budgets decrease, people leave, and we give away secrets that can so easily be exploited by our adversaries to deny us information.

The asymmetry between the American idea of openness and that of both our friends and possible foes is remarkable. Even the Internet is replete with information that might best be kept secret among those who need to know and understand. Try to find such information regarding any other country and frustration will be the result. Restrictions on information are even more severe among those countries that are major competitors and potential adversaries.

It is not an accident that other nations protect their secrets more efficiently than the United States. In many countries, denial and deception are state policy, a part of national strategy that is seldom successfully challenged by the media or well-meaning officials and diplomats. In the Russian language it is called *maskirovka*. In Soviet times it was a fundamental element in the national strategy of the country; today little has changed. The Soviets were much further advanced in this craft than any other country. It seems clear that they have passed on such knowledge to client states like Iraq and Iran, possibly even North Korea and China. Add Libya, India, and Pakistan to these states, and one has a mosaic of those countries where arms control agreements could be useful in creating the basis for agreements that promise greater security and international stability.

The Evolution of Arms Control

Arms control agreements must be outfitted with the most strenuous verification methods if they are to offer long-term benefits. Lately, the U.S. government has moved from negotiating bilateral agreements, for example, the Intermediate Nuclear Forces (INF) treaty, with stringent verification to those of a more multilateral nature such as the Chemical Weapons Convention and the Comprehensive Test Ban Treaty. If one includes the 1972 Biological Weapons Convention, it is plain to see the pattern of agreements that are difficult, or even impossible, to monitor effectively. Simply said, *trust* now outweighs *verify*. This shift toward multilateral treaties is taking place in an era when denial and deception increasingly are being used by those with whom we have made arms control agreements. Here, as in other areas, D&D is a force multiplier.

Arms control agreements are part of U.S. national policy as well as international law. Being a nation based on the rule of law, the nature of the U.S. political system ensures that even unpopular agreements are kept. One need only think of the unratified SALT II agreement that, though never signed into law, was generally honored by the United States. When an agreement has been ratified and signed into law, U.S. compliance with it is seldom an issue. But the compliance of others, particularly those with whom we have the greatest differences (the states that are the likely targets of the arms control process) is always an issue.

What is Not Forbidden is Allowed

One of the fundamental lessons learned by every arms control negotiator is that the verification regime set forth in an agreement or in a treaty also helps the violator to design means to subvert the verification process. Anything not explicitly forbidden is allowed even though it may violate the spirit of the agreements. For example, in 1990 the Soviet military sent thousands of tanks and other Treaty Limited Equipment (TLE) beyond the Ural Mountains into Asia to avoid the provisions of the Conventional Forces in Europe Treaty (CFE), which they knew would soon be signed and ratified. Even precise definitions can be circumvented by a clever violator. Faulty treaty definitions, however, create a verification nightmare.

Even in CFE, when all sides were eager to achieve agreement, deception measures were deployed and were successful to a degree. As the Soviet Union was attempting to get the United States and the North Atlantic Treaty Organization (NATO) to accept its concept of *an object of verification*, the chief of the Soviet General Staff was quoted in the military newspaper *Red Star* as saying there would be some 1,500 objects of verification—a number that more or less corresponded with estimates by the U.S. intelligence community. Based largely on those figures, U.S. officials convinced their allies to accept the Soviet approach. Final data exchanged after the Treaty was signed showed more than a third fewer objects of verification than had been predicted by U.S. analysts or that had been announced by the General Staff. Although relatively insignificant in the final analysis, this example does demonstrate a successful deception effort.

Another useful example of deception is provided in Soviet diplomatic practice. Former Soviet foreign minister Andrei Gromyko declared from the podium at the United Nations that the Soviet Union would not be the first to use nuclear weapons. In the process of the Stockholm Conference on Confidence- and Security-Building Measures, Soviet ambassador Oleg Grinevsky tried to convince then chief of the Soviet General Staff Marshal Ogarkov that since the USSR had a declared no-first-use policy and NATO had none, it would be in Moscow's interest to agree on certain openness measures. Ogarkov smiled to himself and on a map showed Grinevsky the places where preemptive nuclear strikes would be aimed at NATO forces. The military was not going to allow political niceties to put the Soviet Union at risk.

Strategic Arms Reduction Treaty (START)

There is little doubt that the Strategic Arms Reduction Treaty (START) is one of the major achievements of U.S. diplomacy. Properly implemented it significantly enhances U.S. security. Keeping in mind that the nuclear capabilities of the Russian Federation pose the greatest potential threat to U.S. security, arms control verification remains a critical process. In addition to numbers of missiles, a key part of the START Treaty is the prohibition on multiple independently targetable reentry vehicles (MIRVs). Monitoring compliance with this prohibition is challenging, and the potential for using denial and deception to hide the number of warheads actually deployed on missiles is clearly present. Based largely on the acquisition of telemetry data from the Russians, data needed to verify Russian compliance could be denied the U.S. government.

Those who have negotiated with the Russians are sure to have noticed the disdain with which the military regards diplomats and negotiations. Contemporary Russian generals were trained in the military academies of the Soviet Union. They know that the U.S. land-based missile fleet has been de-MIRVed, but also believe it could be re-MIRVed. It is difficult to conceive of the Russians creating a new missile without securing the same capability they believe that the United States has retained. Coupled with a military doctrine that avidly promotes denial and deception, the incentive to cheat on arms control agreements is evident.

One more issue deserves mention in connection with START. The traitor Aldridge Ames passed a number of completed intelligence judgments to the Russians that dealt with the methodology of compliance. A dedicated maskirovka expert could use such information to create means of denying U.S. authorities precisely that information which allows an unambiguous analysis.

The Comprehensive Nuclear Test Ban Treaty (CTBT)

The old Soviet idea of the correlation of forces helps illustrate an important aspect of the Nuclear Test Ban Treaty. "Correlation of forces" is not just an idea; it is an obsession with Russian generals. The CTBT, however, unfortunately, was negotiated against a deadline, which effectively pushed verification experts out of the decision loop. It allows the use of sophisticated computers to simulate nuclear blast results. Such simulation technology, which was not given to them despite hints that it would be, presents a formidable challenge to Russian experts. American possession of simulation technology has led to a strong Russian belief that the nuclear correlation of forces is continually changing to the advantage of the Americans. This provides the incentive and rationale to push the somewhat ambiguous terms of the treaty to their limits. For example, the treaty allows sub-critical tests. These tests can take three forms: one in which a nuclear reaction does not take place; hydro-nuclear tests where the yield is so minuscule that the spirit of the treaty is thought not to be harmed; and real tests, which are definitely illegal. Because it is difficult to distinguish among these tests, the potential to employ denial and deception practices to further exacerbate monitoring difficulties is substantial.

Since most of the monitoring regime is based on seismic signals, two other denial methodologies could be employed. The first is simply to keep the level of an illicit nuclear explosion below observable levels to avoid detection by enough monitoring means so that ambiguity about compliance is preserved. The second is significantly more complex but possible. In this case, efforts are made to decouple the blast from the seismic medium so that the tremors are somehow absorbed or stopped from propagating themselves through the earth. Salt caverns could be used to shield the explosion from monitors, or deep underground facilities constructed to mimic the shielding effect of salt caverns.

As Bill Gertz in a 15 September 1998 article in the *Washington Times* pointed out, China as well as Russia has been actively engaged in pushing the boundaries of the Treaty. The two states that have the nuclear capability to wreak havoc on our nation thus continue to improve that capability through the employment of denial and deception methodologies. Here, China may actually hold the edge.

Biological Weapons Convention (BWC)

When one approaches the question of compliance or non-compliance with the 1972 Biological Weapons Convention, the anthrax episode at the military facility in Sverdlovsk in 1979 comes readily to mind. To Western intelligence, it soon became clear that anthrax spores were being produced in contravention of the BWC, and that some of these had escaped into the air, resulting in numerous casualties. Almost immediately, the old Soviet deception teams went to work. This was not a case of live spores, they argued, but a case of tainted meat. Despite firm evidence obtained by the U.S. intelligence community, the Soviets were quite successful in convincing numerous American scientists that the Soviet cover story was correct and the government was not responsible for the incident. Only much later did the Russians admit this incident corresponded in most significant aspects with the judgments of the U.S. intelligence community.

Thus, we now know the truth. Anthrax, alfatoxins, ricin, and other more widely known poisons were being produced along with such rare things as Ebola pathogens and snake venom. In the business of arms control, it was not critical to keep monitors totally in the dark; it was sufficient to deny them the information that would unambiguously prove that a violation of international agreements was taking place.

The BWC allows research for defensive purposes. So immediately one senses an exploitable loophole in the treaty, unless there are monitoring provisions so intrusive as to deny any possibility for circumvention. Such provisions do not exist and with good reason. Biological pathogens and toxins can be created by any skilled scientist engaged in biotechnology research, even in the most modest of laboratories. Even though a state may reveal the number of laboratories with the facilities needed to contain live organisms and toxins, there is no way to be certain that any particular state has declared all of its facilities. Thus, the monitoring problem is already too large to be able to declare with any conviction that states are complying with the BWC. If the employment of denial and deception practices is added to this basic construct, one quickly recognizes the improbability of effective monitoring. This is only made worse when, for political reasons, the international community attempts to correct an uncorrectable situation. The result engenders false confidence in compliance or provides the violating state with another appeal citing another set of measures.

Chemical Weapons Convention (CWC)

The situation with respect to the Chemical Weapons Convention is not a great deal different from that of the BWC. The global ban applies to a worldwide chemical industry—literally thousands upon thousands of chemical factories and research laboratories. Finding and identifying a violator is pretty much like finding a needle in a haystack. The bottom line is that by employing a modicum of denial and deception measures, a cheating state can easily deflect the sorts of intrusive verification measures that would be required to monitor effectively even a single facility.

While the political aspect of an international verification agency is unquestionable, its effectiveness certainly is. Even within the NATO alliance, other states do not seem to support a policy that is aimed at uncovering possible violations. The U.S. team in CFE, for example, is sometimes regarded as too intrusive, too professional, and too unbending with regard to the provisions of the Protocol on Inspections. Similar problems were encountered by the International Atomic Energy Agency (IAEA) in ascertaining the scope and objective of nuclear programs in North Korea and in Iraq, where denial and deception have been regular and successful practices.

A review of the work of the United Nations Special Commission (UNSCOM) team also reveals multiple cases of denial and deception in the face of an internationally mandated inspection team. Items were moved from place to place ahead of the team. Prevarications of every ilk were given the team leaders. Free access was seldom granted. Practically every move was an uphill walk for the teams. Each new revelation seemed to come from the Iraqis themselves as they felt the pinch or as others, like Kamel Hussein, spilled the beans. Denial and deception was effective. In the end, the problem of eliminating Iraqi weapons of mass destruction was not resolved. Saddam Hussein remains capable of reconstituting all or any part of his program to acquire such weapons.

Not long ago, the U.S. government developed a Web page designed to provide assurance to those who believed that our armed forces were subjected to chemical weapons during the Gulf War. *Gulflink*, as it was called, seemed to have hit the Web with little regard for the exposure of sources and methods involved in intelligence work. Since we do not know what we do not know, we may never be aware of the denial and deception methods employed by the Iraqis against us and the United Nations.

Non-Proliferation

Stemming the proliferation of nuclear, chemical, or biological weapons remains a problem for the international community. When former Secretary of State George Shultz told then German Foreign Minister Hans-Dietrich Genscher that German industry was helping Libya to build a chemical weapons factory at Rabta, relations between the two statesmen soured immediately and never recovered. Economic and internal political issues weighed heavily on the German mind. It took a multipage article in the German periodical *Stern* to unmask fully the German contribution to the Libyan program and force the government to take appropriate steps.

Economic issues sometimes overwhelm promises made and agreements undertaken. The profit motive, perhaps more than the political one, drives firms in a variety of countries to proliferate technologies and technical know-how. With the Russian economy faltering, some will seek hard currency by continuing the sale of items that are critical to the process of developing weapons of mass destruction (WMD). Such sales are accompanied by denials, deceptive practices, and extraordinary security techniques on the part of both seller and recipient. Russian sales to its former client states and to Iran are therefore difficult to detect and even more difficult to prove.

There is little doubt that Russia is assisting Iran in its active and growing programs in the area of weapons of mass destruction. Why do we not know more? The answer is simple: their security practices are impressive and they are well schooled in the art of denial and deception. What we know is sufficient to be sure that such programs exist. What is of concern is that we do not know what we do not know.

If the Russians invented the idea of maskirovka, the Chinese have perfected it. And they have taught it to the Pakistanis, who have been largely dependent on the Chinese for their successes in the development of both nuclear weapons and delivery systems. The press has spoken of the transfer of ring magnets, plutonium expertise, and M-11 missiles, as well as M-11 production. For one reason or another, however, those who have chosen to make such information public also have decided to disclose collection methods they believed were responsible for obtaining such information.

Like the old story of the little Dutch boy who plugged a hole in the dike with his finger, our intelligence targets figuratively try to plug any perceived hole with the intention of stopping the flow of information. It is not an unreasonable action for a state to take, nor is it unexpected. For that reason, intelligence officials used to take significant pains to protect sources and methods. But in the minds of many, this form of secrecy is outmoded, gone with the end of the Cold War, and somehow injurious to the principle of free and open speech.

This trend has two major consequences. First, in a world where information is vital, the information dries up and the potential threat increases. Even our ability to define non-threatening events is reduced, causing worst-case analysis. Second, those against whom we employ our technical and other collection means become more expert in neutralizing those methods, thereby denying us information vital to the protection of U.S. national interests. So, the taxpayer must pay for new and more powerful technologies, often at extravagant cost.

National Security Agency (NSA)

Those authors who claim to speak authoritatively about the National Security Agency and its mission seem to experience some kind of rush. Books have been written, Web sites explain, and pundits of every sort seem drawn to tell what they think they know about this agency. More often than not, truth is mixed with fantasy in almost indistinguishable portions. But occasionally someone comes close to the truth. Everyone has seen movies in which the protagonists try to avoid using telephones for fear that this or that crime could be uncovered. Proliferating states and those receiving illicit assistance employ this and other techniques to deny opponents information vital to identifying proliferation threats.

Perhaps one should be slightly less critical of the media and focus instead on those who fail to understand the instruments handed to the adversary each time reference is made to a specific issue and the specific collection means used to acquire the information being discussed. Often, highly classified information is given to the media to make a political point or to discredit a current administration. Sometimes the source is a congressman, senator, or a member of a congressional staff who understands better than anyone that information is power, but only if it is traced back to an individual. It may be a misguided political appointee who desires to appease the call for greater openness in the intelligence world, believing that secrecy is somehow an anathema to Americans.

It is strange to consider that were an American citizen found guilty of passing this information to a hostile government, he or she would be charged with espionage, while leaking it to the press is okay. It is not okay. The long-term effects undermine the ability of the United States to acquire and process information. Those states that disregard the rule of law and ignore treaty obligations will seek communications technology based on what they know about sources and methods that render our ability to find and exploit information about them impotent and obsolescent.

Reconnaissance Satellites

There was a time when the United States and the Soviet Union were the only states with orbiting satellites outfitted with the capability to photograph objects from space. The operation of these satellites was highly classified and they were prime intelligence platforms. Many times U.S. systems were able to identify events so that appropriate steps could be taken or previous wrong conclusions corrected. The advent of French systems, then Chinese, Israeli, Indian, and Japanese satellite capabilities, means that knowledge of the technology is fairly widespread. Driven by commercial concerns, the United States has approved the creation of at least three firms that will sell overhead imagery for a price, and so the circle of those who understand both the capabilities and limitations of satellite imagery from space is expanded. The Internet is replete with references to satellites, their capabilities, and the orbits they utilize. In fact, so much is offered that one might suppose there is nothing secret left.

The result of this widespread knowledge about satellite reconnaissance is that states allow us to see what we have already seen or what they do not mind us seeing. Because satellites move around the earth at tremendous speed, they are over each target only a few minutes before moving away on their continuous orbits. The resulting gaps of varying lengths in coverage are well known to the maskirovka experts. Those periods when no satellites are overhead can be used to perform illicit activities.

Many believe that the addition of commercial satellites will so flood space with photography platforms that there will be no gaps in coverage. That, of course, remains to be seen. However, when it comes to denial and deception practices, this may not be such a large obstacle as it at first appears. Commercial satellites will optimize their operations so they can take maximum advantage of sunlight hours and cloudless days. The maskirovka expert will see whatever overlapping coverage there may be, do some simple calculations and design activities during periods when the activity is most unlikely to be seen.

Disclosing Capabilities

Historically, U.S. policymakers have decided to show satellite images to a variety of states in which we have an intelligence interest. It is said that Saddam Hussein was shown such imagery during his war with Iran and that later he asked for help from Russian specialists in designing ways to outsmart U.S. reconnaissance satellites. The mere fact that not a single SCUD missile was destroyed during the Gulf War, despite the hundreds of SCUD killer sorties that were launched, would lead to the conclusion that denial and deception worked against the coalition.

U.S. officials also have shown imagery to the North Koreans during negotiations aimed at stemming the development of nuclear weapons. They saw our capabilities, which must have been a huge revelation to them, and they signed an agreement. It became clear to the North Korean leaders that what they were doing was no longer a secret. But no state in the world is better at tunneling into mountainsides and hiding things than North Korea. Tunnels hide virtually all aspects of their military forces, especially artillery and missile systems. Frequently, dummy pieces of equipment are visible to confuse or deceive. This rogue state that threatens South Korea and our armed forces there has one of the better understandings of U.S. overhead intelligence capabilities and is extremely proficient at implementing denial and deception practices.

India also is increasingly proficient when it comes to denial and deception. With four of its own remote sensing satellites in orbit, India understands well the science of operating overhead systems. While the panchromatic resolutions they have achieved are very impressive, it is unlikely that they have or will in the near term match U.S. capabilities. Their understanding of satellite operations, however, undergirds their denial and deception activities vis-à-vis U.S. systems. When it became clear from satellite photography that the Indians were about to conduct an underground test, the U.S. government again asked its ambassador to make a demarche to the Indian government asking them to forego the test. The ambassador evidently questioned the lack of hard evidence in the face of so many Indian denials. He insisted on being able to show imagery. Permission was given with accompanying explanation of how U.S. intelligence agencies knew the test was going to happen. The test was called off, we thought. But over the next year or so, the Indians quietly removed all the telltale signs of a test from their test site, spread camouflage netting in such a way as to deny effective imagery, and generally implemented a set of deception measures, including policy statements. The end result was that the intelligence community was shocked when the first Indian nuclear blast shattered the optimism of those most dedicated to the idea of a comprehensive test ban treaty and those who worked so hard to extend the life of the Non-Proliferation Treaty.

Each of these examples is instructive, but the fundamental point is the same: we seem to have strayed away from the basic principle of protecting sources and means in the vain hope that with the end of the Cold War secrecy is outmoded. Using colloquial language, we have simply shot ourselves in the foot. We will increasingly be hobbled by those who use the knowledge we have provided to deny us information in the future.

Conclusion

Arms control continues to be a key element of U.S. national security policy. Yet, to be a constructive part of our national strategy, stringent arms control verification is required. Of late, the government has moved from agreements incorporating effective monitoring methods to multilateral, feel-good agreements that are very difficult, if not impossible, to monitor. Since the United States is not going to violate agreements, we could be placed at a long-term strategic disadvantage.

Such agreements as the Comprehensive Test Ban Treaty that do not carefully define permitted and prohibited thresholds facilitate the work of the denial and deception experts and make monitoring a very difficult proposition. The culprit state does not need to deny an activity, only to make certain that its practices do not permit the monitoring needed to ascertain compliance or non-compliance. It is now clear that every state in which we have an arms control or intelligence interest practices denial and deception against our national technical means. And each will get better as they learn more about our capabilities.

The proliferation of satellite technology will provide knowledge to denial and deception analysts and enable them to develop better ways of degrading the intelligence from overhead imaging. Despite the large number of satellites that will soon dot space, states seeking to deny information can still do so by a variety of easy-to-implement means or by going underground or into tunnels.

All too often, government officials feed information to the media that can assist the adversary in combating U.S. intelligence capabilities. Under the banner of press freedom, information is printed which, were it to be handed over to a representative of another state by a government employee, would be treasonous. Worse still perhaps are decisions made by government officials to allow others insights into our intelligence capabilities in the naive belief that we can either win friends or cause a change of behavior. The strategic consequences of these activities could be severe.

Finally, the end of the Cold War did not end conflict and did not eradicate threats to the United States. Arms control agreements that are not verified contribute to a prolongation of threat, especially in the area of nuclear and biological weapons. In the future we can expect to be faced with enemies who use asymmetrical forms of attack such as terrorism, information warfare, and proliferation. Information is our best line of defense. Much needed information, however, will be obscured or blurred by the adversary's use of denial and deception practices.

7

Detecting Deception: Practice, Practitioners, and Theory

Bart Whaley and *Jeffrey Busby*

> *"It may well be doubted whether human ingenuity*
> *can construct an enigma of the kind which human*
> *ingenuity may not, by proper application, resolve."*
> –Edgar Allan Poe, "The Gold-Bug"

We are already detectives whether we realize it or not. We do not need a license or certificate or diploma to practice. Detection is an art that each of us uses, usually quite unconsciously, to protect against those who would take unfair advantage of us through deception.

Amateurs lack the systematic procedures, manuals, and theories available to the professional detectives who practice detection as a science. But even amateurs practice it as an art. Faced with a deception, they must operate more or less intuitively, seeking evidence that can winnow out the false to reveal the hidden reality. Along with everyone else, professional detectives began to learn various techniques of detection as children and continued to learn into adulthood as they confronted the deceptions of unscrupulous salespeople, bosses, colleagues, and friends. For most of us it is enough to spot the incongruities that signal the presence of falsehood. As Thoreau wrote in his *Journal* in 1854, "Some circumstantial evidence is very strong, as when you find a trout in the milk."

What, if anything, do ordinary amateur detectives have in common? What methods do they use to detect the cheaters and hoaxers in everyday life? We see our amateurs employing logical thinking, both deductive and inductive, as well as a strong measure of intuition. We'll see that this is also the way of the pros, the only difference being that they use these processes in more systematic fashion.

Deception or Self-Deception? Optimists versus the Pessimists

I am optimistic that deceptions can be detected regardless of the field in which they occur. In theory, deception can always be detected, and in practice often detected, sometimes even easily. Most experts on military and intelligence deception, however, take the opposite view. They are the pessimists. And with good reason, because such a small proportion of military deceptions have been detected in time for the victims to react effectively. These pessimists grumble that, while it is nice *after-the-fact* to show how deception contributed to stunning surprise attacks like Pearl Harbor in 1941 or Yom Kippur in 1973, such historical analyses have little or no predictive value.

That the pessimists hold these negative beliefs should not be surprising. They labor under three major limitations, limitations that apply more to military deception than to any of the scores of deception fields we studied. First, compared to workers in those fields, they have few and infrequent opportunities to learn by personal trial-and-error experience of the subject. They have little and narrowly focused evidence to go on. Second, because military deception has traditionally been an art, deception doctrine largely gets reinvented with each new war, so analysts and officers have little institutional memory to draw from. These two limitations generate a third limitiation: a weak and contentious literature where such fundamental questions as whether detection is even possible continue to be debated.

Even so, the pessimists have good reason to be skeptical. The price for failure to detect a military deception and its consequent surprise attack is measured in body bags and POWs, destroyed or captured weapons, lost ground, and national honor and morale. The weight of responsibility is heavy because leaders expect their intelligence services to protect them from surprises. Even if they can detect four out of five deceptions, heads are apt to roll at the first failure. How handy then for intelligence professionals to be able to cite theories which claim that deception is undetectable and surprise is inevitable. Machiavelli would approve their deploying this argument to save their livelihoods. But he would deplore any who believed that argument.

The weakest point in the pessimists' argument is that they tend to accept an all-or-nothing fallacy. They see either surprise or no surprise, either total or zero. In practice these extreme cases have been the exception rather than the general rule. The usual outcome is partial detection and partial surprise. For example, an examination of sixty-three cases of strategic surprise found at least some surprise in all cases and that 75 percent produced surprise of target or direction of the attack, 73 percent surprise of its time, 60 percent surprise in its strength, and 25 percent of the style of attack.[1]

Deception and Counterdeception Through Time and Across Cultures

Do different cultures produce different styles of deception? That is, does the practice of deception differ between cultures in intensity, frequency, levels of sophistication, or ethical acceptability? It might seem it would. This interesting question has been asked in passing by several scholars, but only two comparative studies have appeared.[2] Both concluded tentatively that each culture produces its own distinctive style of deception. Only Western, Russian, and Chinese cultures were covered in these studies, however, and the evidence was entirely anecdotal. Although it is possible that there are innate differences in cultural styles of deception, such a sweeping conclusion might be misleading. More systematically gathered, cross-cultural evidence seemed to fit this generalization, but not easily. There were curious discrepancies.

Since deception is a psychological process, it should be free of culture except to the degree that any given culture valued deception and encouraged its use or, alternatively, abhorred it and punished its practitioners. Also, since a previous study of military deception in Western culture demonstrated that its practice varied dramatically through history,[3] it seems likely that this variation also had occurred in other cultures, changing along with each culture's perceived needs and ethical and moral beliefs. The reason that other researchers saw deep differences among Western, Russian, and Chinese styles of deception might have been because they had looked only at selected periods in the history of these cultures rather than looking across the entire history of each before making their comparisons. Moreover, they had drawn upon selected individual sources for their examples, sources whose interest was in military or political-military strategy.

In other words, conclusions that might be true of specific periods or individual writers in any one culture might not be typical of that culture as a whole. What if these biases in research method masked a different reality?

To answer this question, I surveyed deception practices and attitudes in eight major cultures across their history. Being careful to include the three previously studied cultures, I examined: the Classical Mediterranean, Byzantine, Western, Russian, Islamic, Chinese, Japanese, and Indian cultures. I examined how each handled crucial wars and battles, how it dealt with political change, and how its leading philosophers and writers viewed the use of deception in general, as graded on a range from ethically repulsive to pragmatically useful. Nearly 300 bits of such data were collected and rated on a five-point scale ranging from no deceptiveness to very high deceptiveness. I then graphed these across the years, decades, and centuries of each culture. The results surprised me. I found that each of these cultures had swings, surprisingly major ups and downs, in their practice of and attitudes toward deception: periods of relatively high deceptiveness alternating with periods of relatively low deceptiveness. In all cases and at all times where either high or low deceptiveness was the predominant style, however, it was never without its challengers within that culture.

But what of cultural differences in *detecting* deception? I have no evidence that points to clear answers. Religion and ethics may be some crucial factors. Many anthropologists have observed that some traditional cultures simply do not make a distinction between supernatural and natural magic.[4] The tricks are invisibly embedded in the ritual and vice versa. Consequently the true believers are unable to detect the trickery of either priests or conjurers. For example, the tent shaking of the North American Saulteau Indians remains mystical to the tribe's members even when the shaman's trick methods are known.[5]

In sum, the effects of culture on deception and counterdeception are found only in specifics. Cultures that do not distinguish between supernatural and natural magic are unable to detect the sleight-of-hand artist—they take him on faith. A Roman Catholic priest's gown is good disguise for a thief or a spy in Italy or Ireland or the Philippines but stupid if one wishes to pass unnoticed in China or Russia or Pakistan. When among nudists, going naked is the best disguise.

The Cost-Effectiveness of Deception and Counterdeception

When the costs of being deceived are high, the benefits of detecting deception are correspondingly high. The costs for both deceivers and detectives can be ethical, psychological, social, or political, as well as simply economic. The economic cost of any deception is best measured by the proportion of the deceiver's resources (money, time, personnel, apparatus) diverted from the main event. In war, for example, this is the proportion of personnel and material diverted from the ordinary hack-and-slash of battle.

By any purely economic accounting, deception can be relatively cheap. In absolute economic terms, the most costly deception of all time was probably "Fortitude," the Allied deception operation to convince Hitler that the Allied invasion of Nazi-occupied Europe would arrive at the Pas de Calais coast and not further west on the beaches of Normandy. It succeeded in keeping nineteen of Hitler's divisions tied down in reserve for fully sixty-six days after the D-Day landings at Normandy. The benefit of this deception was enormous. But at what cost? The total cost of all D-Day deception operations was well under 1 percent of the invasion force. Fortitude required the full-time services for about a year of about eighteen deception planners, the part-time attention of perhaps twenty senior staff planners and intelligence officers, operational commitments of roughly 800 radio technicians (some 500 British and 296 Americans) who were busily simulating the radio traffic of two phantom armies, several camouflage and construction companies (about 2,000 troops drawn from the Royal Engineers and 379 from the U.S. Corps of Engineers) building dummy installations, about 1,000 air force personnel to crew and service the ninety aircraft flying on D-Day spoofing missions, about 200 sailors for the eighteen small launches involved in misleading the German coastal early-warning system, six Special Air Service men parachuted on diversionary missions, the ten members of Twenty ("Double-Cross") Committee directing the disinformation campaign of about eleven of the forty German double-agents then in Britain, perhaps a 100 or so agents and underground members engaged in spreading false rumors on the Continent, and Lieutenant Clifton James, who had been co-opted from the British Army Pay Corps to simulate General Montgomery. In all, there were about 4,500 soldiers, sailors, and airmen, of whom less than a quarter was combat personnel. This represents less than 0.2

percent of the available combat personnel, 0.5 percent of the naval craft, and only 0.6 percent of the aerial sorties flown on D-Day. The total loss among the deception forces was one bomber (its crew safely parachuting), four of the SAS paratroopers taken prisoner (and later murdered), and a few tons of aluminum strip airdropped to deceive German radar.[6]

There is one type of military deception operation that often does prove costly because it commits real combat units to battle. This is the diversionary attack. At its worst it is the most primitive form of deception. It provides evidence of the primitive deceptive thinking of most British, French, and German generals in World War I and the Russians early in World War II. For example, in 1915, the Battle of Scarpe and Vimy Ridge sent twenty-two British and Canadian divisions over the top and cost 18,000 casualties. Both attacks were merely a diversion to cover the forty-six-division French attack that followed elsewhere.[7] More recently, Iran's Khomeini seemed to believe this was the way to fight his 1980-88 war with Iraq. Although common, such profligacy is not only inelegant, it is seldom if ever necessary.

It is harder to judge the relative cost of counterdeception. But it is fair to say that in most cases all but a small portion of the overall costs of detecting deception are prepaid by already existing intelligence capabilities. Otherwise, for the specifics, all we have to go by are scraps of anecdotes.

Case Studies in the Detection of Deception

Data was collected on an opportunity sample of forty-seven different *types* of professional detectives who deal routinely with deception. The purpose was to discover what procedures they use to detect deception. These types of detectives range from military intelligence analysts and image interpreters through police detectives and forensic scientists, examiners of questioned documents and art authenticators, to magicians as detectors of psychic frauds and gambling cheats.

Analysis identified the few special procedures used by all *highly successful* detectors of deception. Conversely, these procedures were found to be never or only infrequently used by middling to poor detectors. Successful detection procedures were found to be largely or entirely intellectual rather than technological in nature, except to the extent that we can characterize as technology such extensions of natural sensors as radar or such computer programs as ones that supply content analyses. Most detection successes were against ongoing deception operations. Consequently, these particular procedures are not, as has been argued by some military pessimists, limited only to after-the-fact historical analyses.

The Detectives Studied

Military and political deception planners and analysts represent only one small part of the larger deception and counterdeception activity. This study examined forty-seven different categories of professional detectives. The first fourteen mainly focus on detecting congruities with only occasional disruption due to incongruities created by deceivers. The other thirty-three types of detectives must directly and regularly confront incongruities created by deliberate efforts to deceive them:

> *Mainly Congruity Testers*
> Scientists: Detecting Patterns in Nature
> Social Psychologists: Deceivers and Deceived
> Censors: Spotting the Forbidden
> Internists: The Physician as Diagnostician
> Medical Lab Technicians: Identifying the Disease
> Epidemiologists: Backtracking the Source of Disease
> Automobile Trouble-Shooters: Malfunction or Sabotage?
> Bank Tellers: It Pays to Be Alert
> Investigative Journalists: Verifying the Five "W"s
> The Spy as Investigative Reporter
> Psychic Readers: Cold Reading and Fishing
> Folklorists: Separating Myth from Fact
> Historians: Sifting Fact from Legend
> Archaeologists: Digging Up the Facts
> Biographers: Revealing the Person behind the Legend

> *Mainly Incongruity Testers:*
> Judges as Detectives
> Police Detectives: Proving the Crime
> Private Eyes: Entrepreneurial Detection
> Skip Tracers: Hiders and Seekers

The Arson Squad: The MO of the Torch
The Mind Analysts: Probing Hidden Motives
Profilers: Mind into Mind
Polygraphers: Machine versus Mind
Pharmacologists: Any Truth in Truth Serums?
Interrogators: Fishing for Truth
Torturers: Truth or Sadism
Security Officers: Finding the Mole
Guards: Spotting Escapees and Enterers
Imagery Interpreters: Evidence in Camera
Intelligence Analysts: Avoiding Surprise
The Codebreakers: Mathematical Detection
Arms Controllers: Verifying Compliance
Airport Security Guards: Spotting the Skyjacker
Customs Inspectors: Spotting the Smuggler
Immigration Officials: Spotting Phony Marriages
Trial Lawyers: Provoking Perjury
Forensic Pathologists: Death by Foul Play?
Auditors: Paper Chasing the Embezzler
Insurance Investigators: Assuming the Worst of Everyone
Machiavelli in the Office: Counterdeception in Office
    Politics
Collectors of Collectibles: Weeding Out the Fakes
Art Experts: Detecting Counterfeits
Questioned Documents: Detecting Forgery
Forensic Editors: Author! Author!
Treasury Agents versus Counterfeit Money
The Gambling Detectives: Spotting the Cheat
The Bunco Squad: Short Cons and the Big Con
Psychic Researchers: Spotting the Charlatan
Magicians: Conjuring for Conjurers

Proto-Theories of Detection and Counterdeception

To date there have been no general theories of how to detect deception. Several insights have emerged, however, from the extensive clinical practices of deception and counterdeception. These have been contributed by various detectives, from amateurs to professionals, in many specialties. As their notions are based entirely on trial-and-error experience and anecdotal evidence, they constitute, at best, rough conjectures or proto-theory, the first steps toward systematic theory.

Deception planners who attempt to put themselves into the minds of their intended dupes confront this problem directly. The few whose thinking has been published give us some valuable pointers toward a theory of detection. Of all those many groups that practice deception, only three have made important contributions to counterdeception theory: magicians, criminologists, and physicists. True, a few military deception planners have contributed to theory, but only ones who were also magicians like Brigadier Dudley Clarke, physicists like Dr. R. V. Jones, or artists like Solomon J. Solomon.

A General Theory of Counterdeception

> "No imitation can be perfect without being the real thing . . ."
> —*R. V. Jones,* Report, 10 January 1942

> "In every field we detect untruth by inconsistency."
> –*Henning Nelms,* Magic and Showmanship

The word "counterdeception" is convenient shorthand for "the detection of deception" and now is a standard jargon among specialists in military deception. William R. Harris coined this useful term in 1968 during an afternoon brainstorming session with me in Cambridge, Massachusetts. We had met through our shared curiosity about the role of deception in war. Harris was then Henry Kissinger's graduate teaching assistant for the latter's course on national security affairs at Harvard's Center for International Affairs. I was working down the road as a research associate in communications at MIT's Center for International Studies. I wanted a single word to express the concept of detecting deception and had been toying with "counter-stratagem" when Harris, agreeing that it was somewhat obscure, suggested "counter-deception." I got it into print the following year,[8] and it soon became such commonly accepted jargon that, to use the language of linguists, it "closed," losing its hyphen.[9]

To detect deception we must first understand what deception is and how it works. When Walter Scott bemoaned the "tangled web" of deceit, the romantic British knight expressed a widely held belief that deception is a convoluted business. And so it is—at the hands and in the tangled minds of convoluted thinkers who insist on making the simple difficult. Even some of my colleagues prefer to pursue inscrutable models of deception. They concede only that it may be possible to develop theories of deception with some after-the-fact explanatory value; they doubt the possibility of any theory that could predict a deception. In other words, they challenge the very possibility of detecting deception in any systematic way. For them detection can occur only by accident. I am reminded of the Wizard of Oz who cloaked his plain self in gorgeous trappings of mystery. Deception is really a simple process, often rich in its details and apparent variety but not in its psychological essence. And, because deceit is basically simple, its detection is, in theory, also simple.

While I was the first to argue explicitly in print that deception is a general phenomenon and therefore susceptible to a general theory[10] the notion is hardly original. Several experts have implied this generalization by asserting analogies among separate fields where deception plays a significant part. Roman statesman-philosopher Seneca (around A.D. 50) saw an analogy between the devious art of rhetoric and magicians' sleights. Both magician Glenn Gravatt (in 1937) and mystery writer Raymond Chandler (in 1948) noted an analogy between inventing magic and plotting a mystery story. Military-political strategist Winston Churchill (1933) saw one between legerdemain and deceptive generalship. Magician-camoufler Major Jasper Maskelyne (1949) saw one between stage illusions and both camouflage in particular and military deception in general. Movie maker-camoufleur Colonel Geoffrey Barkas (1952) made one between military camouflage and "film production on the grand scale." British physicist, practical joker, and military deception planner Dr. R. V. Jones (1957) argued for a common theory linking the scientific method, practical joking, and military deception. British military theorist Captain Sir Basil Liddell Hart (1929) recognized an analogy between military deception and deception in sports and subsequently (1956) added deception in international politics at the level of "grand strategy." But, of course, Machiavelli had long since made the even closer general connection among deception in war, politics, and (implicitly in his one work of fiction) everyday life. Finally, bringing these separate links full circle, both British Field-Marshal

A. P. Wavell (1942) and Major-General Eliahu Zeira (1975), former Director of Israeli Military Intelligence, perceived a psychological identity between military and magical deception.

Toward Theory: Pinocchio's Nose

To build a theory of counterdeception we need sets of categories that theorists call typologies or taxonomies. Happily, we already have some partially tested ones. These include the two Bell and Whaley categories and psychology professor Paul Ekman's checklist to detect deception.

This possibility of detecting deception, any deception, is inherent in the effort to deceive. Every deception operation necessarily leaves at least two clues: incongruities about what is hidden; and incongruities about what is displayed in its stead. The analyst requires only the appropriate sensors and mind-set (cognitive hypotheses) to detect and understand the meaning of these clues. The problem is thus entirely one of the availability of appropriate sensor technology and thought procedures and never one of theory.

Because everything (whether objects or events) can be partly simulated or dissimulated, deception is always possible. Because neither simulation nor dissimulation can ever be done flawlessly, however, their detection also is always possible. In other words, discrepancies (incongruent clues) inevitably suggest alternative patterns (hypotheses) that themselves are incongruent (discrepant, anomalous, paradoxical) at some point with reality. But nature knows no paradoxes, no discrepancies, no incongruities, and no ambiguities. Thus, to detect an incongruity is to detect the false. The lie is as plain as the nose on Pinocchio's face.

The Categories of Detectables

In expanding on "The Categories of Misperception" in *Stratagem* (1969, pp.210-218), I argued that misperception in general and deception in particular apply to only nine types of things. These are the types of information that the deceiver tries to dissimulate or simulate, hide or show. Counterdeception is simply unraveling these categories, which are as relevant to the detective in deconstructing a deception as they are to the deceiver in constructing it in the first place. These nine categories are:

Pattern
Players
Intention
Payoff
Place
Time
Strength
Style
Channel

This is a checklist of all the types of things that the detective need consider in determining whether a deception is occurring or has taken place and, if so, what form it takes.

The Plus-Minus Rule

Each real thing has a large but finite number of identifiable characteristics–"charcs," as J. Bowyer Bell abbreviated them. Its imitation shares at least one and often many of these charcs. But every imitation will lack at least one characteristic that marks the real thing and will usually have additional charcs not present in the original. Even the most perfect clone lacks two characteristics—it is not the first and it has a different history.

If either a plus (added) or a minus (missing) characteristic is detected, the imitation stands revealed.[11] Note that a most important corollary of this rule is that the detective need not discover all the discrepancies or incongruities, a single false characteristic, whether plus (added) or minus (missing), is quite enough to prove fakery. This is why the famous Man Who Never Was ruse was so weak. The body was that of a man who had died of the wrong cause and his personal effects bore another man's fingerprints. This gave the enemy two absolutely discrepant characteristics, either of which, if detected, would have completely blown the hoax. The British deception plan succeeded only because the deceivers had correctly assessed certain weaknesses in German Military Intelligence capabilities and procedures.

Decision Making in Uncertainty

The Plus-Minus Rule and its corollary are all well and good, but they demand 100 percent certainty about the falsity of that one questioned characteristic. While always *possible* in theory, in practice this is seldom *feasible*. Our sensors may fail to catch all the nuances or may distort the data. Or our analytical procedures may be flawed. So, in actual practice, we often find ourselves in the murky realm of probabilities.

If we have reason to believe that the chance of one characteristic being truly discrepant is only, say, fifty-fifty, we may be unwilling to act on such an uncertainty. An unfamiliar shade of lipstick on a husband's collar is a discrepancy to be sure and cause for suspicion, but his excuse ("We both know that Miss Green Eyes is always trying to make you jealous of *her*.") may sound plausible enough to reduce the discrepancy to a fifty-fifty likelihood. If so, more evidence is needed. Learning that the spouse (with attaché case) regularly sees Green Eyes (with a briefcase) immediately after work at the local pub may only raise the discrepancy to a 60-40 likelihood, if some new excuse is even remotely plausible. Finding the two (without office papers) tête-à-tête at a hot-sheet adults-only motel bar should warrant a 90 percent or better likelihood regardless of excuses. Of course, near certainty would have been reached at the beginning, as did Dear Abby in 1986 when advising a concerned wife who had found unfamiliar lipstick on her husband's undershorts.

We seldom enjoy the luxury of having 100 percent or even 80 or 90 percent of the relevant information. Tick-tack-toe, checkers, and chess are among the few games of "perfect information" yet even these are subject to deception. At some point we must decide to make a judgment and take action. Some kind of cost-benefit assessment, whether mathematically precise or just rough-and-ready, can help decide the action point. If the cost of being deceived is very high, obviously one would be wise to assume deception on the basis of rather incomplete information. Conversely, if the cost is low, one may choose to assume innocence and act accordingly while either seeking or keeping alert for additional evidence.

The Congruity-Incongruity Rule

Every real thing is always, necessarily, completely congruent with all its characteristics. Conversely, every false thing will display at least one incongruity.[12] R. V. Jones and a few magicians have come very close to seeing this simple point. Indeed, it may even have been obvious to them; but, if so, they never made it explicit.

Because every deception involves simultaneously showing at least one false thing and hiding a corresponding real thing, the Congruity-Incongruity Rule tells us that the detective has *two* independent opportunities to detect any deception. Thus, a deception will be confirmed if either its simulated or its dissimulated half is detected. Moreover, even this half-disclosure focuses the detective's guesses about what the remaining part could be, thereby greatly simplifying the effort to detect it as well. This one simple fact gives the detective a crucial advantage against the deceiver.

I accidentally stumbled upon this two-directional approach to detection during research on a military case study and first published it in 1973. Part of Hitler's cover story to conceal his firm intention to invade the Soviet Union in 1941 (codenamed Operation "Barbarossa") was his earlier plan to invade Britain (codenamed Operation "Sea Lion"). Having dropped the latter, Hitler maintained it as an illusion to "explain" his real intentions against Russia. "Like the world's intelligence services at the time, historians have *two chances* to solve the mystery of Barbarossa. Because Sea Lion . . . was the main cover story for Barbarossa, the students of Sea Lion could have stumbled upon the reason for Stalin's surprise. However, none of the Sea Lion historians . . . did so."[13]

False Incongruities

Whenever we begin to investigate any suspected deception, we find things that catch our attention, that seem suspicious. Many actions, events, and people may be initially suspect but later prove innocent. The deception analyst must somehow deal with these various false incongruities or pseudo-discrepancies.[14]

A false incongruity looks, at first glance, like a congruity—so much so that it must be treated with equal seriousness. But, because it is extraneous to the suspected underlying deception, it can be identified and discarded during the analytical process in exactly the same ways that true discrepancies are identified. In other words, the detection of false incongruity uses exactly the same technique, as does the detection of an incongruity. Whether this process of elimination occurs sooner or later depends only on the speed, efficiency, and procedures of the individual detective-analyst. As Sherlock Holmes once remarked of one of his preliminary theories, "It *is* impossible as I state it, and therefore I must in some respect have stated it wrong." And asked Dr. Watson, "Can you suggest any fallacy?"[15]

The scientific method is an excellent way to separately identify congruities, incongruities, and false incongruities. The detective has two strategies to choose between: either track the true incongruities or eliminate the false ones. The first course is clearly the more efficient, because according to the Plus-Minus Rule, it requires only a single confirmed incongruity to prove deception. The detective may prefer to begin by eliminating the false incongruities, paring the problem down to its essentials. Then, as Sherlock Holmes also often insisted, "when you have eliminated the impossible, whatever remains, *however improbable*, must be the truth."[16]

False incongruities are a welcome goad to the good detective but the bugaboo of the paranoid ones. As art curator Thomas Hoving cautioned, even the trained professional art historian when "surrounded by a plethora of odd and inexplicable works of art, sometimes get unreasonably paranoid and begin to see forgeries all over the art landscape."[17] A notable example in the art world was James J. Rorimer, during his long stint as Director of the Metropolitan Museum of Art (1955-66).[18] Political-military analysts, with their own "James J.," know this phenomenon as the Angleton Syndrome.

Locard's Exchange Principle

I argue in my ongoing study of criminologists that their greatest single contribution to the theory of detection is Locard's Exchange Principle, first put forward in 1910 by the great French forensic scientist, Dr. Edmond Locard. This is the notion that the perpetrator always leaves some physical "trace evidence" at the crime scene and always takes some away. It is consistent with Incongruity Theory and, indeed, can be melded into the latter by rephrasing to read that the perpetrator always introduces some incongruity into the situation and takes something away that is incongruous with his otherwise normal circumstances.

Although criminologists narrowly limit Locard's Exchange Principle to trace evidence such as hair, fibers, and blood, it applies to all types of physical evidence. Moreover, it also applies to all types of deception, although we must add *psychological* perceptions to Locard's *physical* evidence. Locard's Exchange Principle is one of the two or three most powerful mental tools of counterdeception. It tells us, in effect, that there are no "perfect crimes," only unsolved crimes. And it not only assures us that all deceptions are, in principle, discoverable, it shows us the evidentiary path we must follow to identify the perpetrator.

Verification

When we have a hypothesis that deception is occurring, we can always find a way to verify it. The cost may be prohibitive–psychologically, ethically, economically, or politically—but it can be done. Confirmative data, traps, or provocations are possible approaches to detecting deception.

The Law of Multiple Sensors

What I call the Law of Multiple Sensors was gradually evolved by R. V. Jones as a direct result of his early experimenting with practical jokes, specifically telephone hoaxes. It began in the autumn of 1935 when Jones was at Oxford University, one year out of his doctorate in physics, as a twenty-three-year-old research fellow in the Clarendon Laboratories where he had already distinguished himself as a practical joker.

At this point the Clarendon staff was augmented by a young German physicist, Carl Bosch, Jr., a son of the Nobel Prize-winning president of the huge chemical firm I. G. Farben. Bosch also was a notorious practical joker and the two men quickly joined forces. On the evening they met, their conversation soon turned to a discussion of what tricks one could play with a telephone. Bosch recounted an experiment he had tried two years earlier while he was a research student on the upper floors of a lab that overlooked a block of flats. "His studies revealed that one of the flats was occupied by a newspaper correspondent, and so he telephoned this victim, pretending to be his own professor. The "professor" announced that he had just perfected a television device which could be attached to a telephone, and which would enable the user to see the speaker at the other end. The newspaperman was incredulous, but the "professor" offered to give a demonstration; all the pressman had to do was to strike some attitude, and the voice on the telephone would tell him what he was doing. The telephone was, of course, in direct view of the laboratory, and so all the antics of the pressman were faithfully described. The result was an effusive article in the next day's paper and, subsequently, a bewildered conversation between the true professor and the pressman."[19]

As Jones recalls, "Bosch and I then happily discussed variations on the telephone theme and ultimately I said that it ought to be possible to kid somebody to put a telephone into a bucket of water."[20] Jones proceeded to do just this. Inspired by Bosch's example and his own experiment, Jones reached the important preliminary theoretical conclusion that "Telephone hoaxes were easy to play because one had only to produce a convincing impression in the single communication channel of the telephone: a hoax which had to appear genuine to the victim's eye as well as his ear was much more difficult."[21]

Bosch left Oxford the next year, returning to Nazi Germany. Jones moved on in 1938 to the British Air Ministry where he would refine his theory of practical joking and apply it to the Nazi enemy during World War II. Throughout the war, Jones was occasionally troubled by the thought that Bosch might be his "opposite number" for, as Jones reasoned, "If so, he would know all my weak points; and he was such an expert hoaxer that he might easily have misled us." Fortunately for Jones, the German armed forces in general made no systematic use of scientific intelligence and only tapped Bosch's talents on special problems, only a few of which overlapped Jones' work.[22]

In 1942, Jones had an insight: "No imitation can be perfect without being the real thing."[23] In 1957 he restated this as "no model can be perfect unless it is an exact replica of the original—and even then the perfection is spoilt by the fact that now two exist where there was one before."[24] This seemingly simple insight has enormous practical value for all detectives of deception. The implication of it is important: "The ease of detecting counterfeits is much greater when different channels of examination are used simultaneously. This is why telephonic hoaxes are so easy—there is no accompanying visual appearance to be counterfeited. Metal strips [dropped from one aircraft] were most successful [at simulating an entire fleet] when only radar, and that of one frequency, was employed. Conversely, the most successful naval mines were those that would only detonate when several kinds of signal—magnetic, hydrodynamic and acoustic—were received simultaneously. A decoy that simulates all these signals is becoming very like a ship. From these considerations, incidentally, we can draw a rather important conclusion about the detection of targets in defense and attack: that as many different physical means of detection as possible should be used in parallel. It may therefore be better in some circumstances to develop two or three independent means of detection, instead of putting the same total effort into the development of one alone." [25]

If anything, Jones underestimates the power of his concluding point, which apparently holds true in *most* circumstances. Multiple sensors will almost always prove more effective than a single one, even when each is less precise. The problem is both one of cost-effectiveness and philosophy.

Precision instruments are always more costly than shoddy ones. And generally the cost of improving precision rises geometrically. For instance, high-resolution cameras give that sharper image at much higher prices than low-resolution ones and for each step up in quality the cost increases dramatically.

Cost aside, there is another practical advantage to multiple sensors. A single sensor may break down, leaving us momentarily blind. It may be unreliable, making us doubt its message. The opponent may at any time and without our knowledge develop a countermeasure, as with the history of radar and its successive countermeasures.

Richard Warren has thrown important light on this question. When I first met him at the MIT faculty club in 1961, Dick was working at MIT's Jet Propulsion Laboratory (soon renamed the Draper Laboratory) as its staff philosopher, having recently refused a Harvard doctorate. Much of his time was spent consulting on the Lab's contract with NASA on its space program. NASA confronted a problem without precedent: how to design multimillion dollar sensors that could remain inert for months or even years without any human maintenance or repair and yet still function when they reached the end of their long space journey to Mars or beyond. The conventional engineering solution was a simple extrapolation of earthbound engineering experience: either build the most expensive instruments possible in the hope that they would be more likely to function when needed or put two or more instruments of the same type aboard the spacecraft in the hope that at least one would work. The first solution was too risky, the second, too wasteful of precious weight and storage space, thereby reducing the number of different types of sensors that could be included in any one payload. The price for total failure was not merely a billion dollars a space shot, but a potentially disastrous political embarrassment for NASA with subsequent budget cuts by a displeased Congress.

Warren suggested an alternative solution, indeed a 180-degree opposite approach: build a system of *low*-precision sensors guaranteed to do a lousy job. Each sensor would be designed to continue to function under the worst imaginable conditions, even if at only 10 percent efficiency. Furthermore, certain different types of sensors could be linked so that if one failed completely, another could take over at least part, say 5 percent, of the failed sensor's assignment. For example, if one type of infrared camera failed, another type would automatically reprogram to give partial coverage of the first one's target even at the cost of sacrificing part of its own mission. Sensors to these specifications were developed and used in deep space exploration.

Multiple independent sensors make for a less vulnerable detection system. Even with only two such sensors, it is highly unlikely that both would fail at the same time, any lack of reliability would be apt to cancel both out as to reinforce error, and it is unlikely that the opponent would be lucky enough simultaneously to develop countermeasures to both. This sounds obvious; but the only case I have found where this was done was on D-Day 1944 when the British simultaneously unleashed several new electronic countermeasures to successfully spoof the entire range of German electronic early-warning sensors. [26] And, of course, with three or more such sensors the likelihood of building a reliable and deception-proof system increases.

The detective should remember that Jones' Law of Multiple Sensors is subject to the overriding Plus-Minus Rule. The deceiver need only succeed in simulating one new characteristic to spoof the existing sensors. It is an unending succession of measures and countermeasures. This point was overlooked in 1978 by the then Chairman of the House Armed Services Committee, Les Aspin, when he wrote that: "The multiple and duplicative methods of detection at the disposal of the U.S. are sufficient to reveal any [Soviet] cheating on a scale adequate to threaten this country militarily."[27] Amrom Katz said of Aspin's optimistic statement "Would that this were true!" While the U.S. methods of detection were well known to the USSR, however, U.S. intelligence did not know that it had covered all the Soviet's methods of simulation and dissimulation, leaving the United States vulnerable to certain types of deception.[28]

An exception to the law of multiple sensors could occur only in the rare circumstance where the single sensor is able to measure a characteristic that cannot be either perfectly simulated or dissimulated. For instance, a Geiger counter is triggered by radioactivity and nothing else. Even radioactivity, however, which cannot be simulated, can be dissimulated by screening with lead shields and the like.

Passive and Active Detection

Deception may be detected either by passive or by active analysis.[29] The passive type of detection consists solely of straightforward analysis (deductive or inductive) applied to the evidence in the case. It presupposes that all the essential facts are available to the analyst. Classic examples from detective fiction are in three short stories by Edgar Allan Poe where Chevalier C. Auguste Dupin first inductively solves the "Murders in the Rue Morgue" (1841) and then deductively solves "The Mystery of Marie Rogêt" (1842) and finds "The Purloined Letter" (1845). Incidentally, these three stories are generally credited by historians of the genre to be the first fully developed examples of the detective story.

The bulk of analyses by intelligence analysts, military and political historians, police detectives, forensic scientists, investigative reporters, and auditors are of this passive type. Passive analysis, however, always leads to inconclusive results unless all key facts are available. The recourse in inconclusive cases then, although rare, is to active measures.

The active type of detection is required in those frequent situations where the analyst's working hypothesis cannot be proven because of missing evidence. In all such cases the analyst must actively intervene to collect these missing key facts. Such intervention takes one of two forms, either by defining new "intelligence requirements" or by running a "controlled experiment."

New intelligence requirements are specified by the analyst when the needed facts are believed to exist but have not been laid before her. To add these to the database, the analyst will either research the facts in person (by scanning standard reference works, examining original documentary sources, interviewing participants, or obtaining special clearances) or request such data from appropriate specialists.

Controlled experiments, by contrast, cannot be designed by the analyst for historical circumstances that have ended. These have already produced *all* the evidence that can be produced. Some part of this evidence may have been destroyed, hopelessly lost forever. But whatever remains, however well hidden, can be recovered. It is there somewhere, perhaps in a forgotten memory, a misplaced file, or a private diary. Or perhaps the event has left physical evidence. For example, it took forty-one years to solve the case of the Piltdown Man hoax. The crucial clue was collected at the time of the crime, but it took all those years before an appropriate scientific test (radiocarbon dating) could be developed and used.

Consequently, the controlled experiment is necessarily limited to problems where the deception is ongoing, still underway. Aside from this one limitation, the controlled experiment can be an enormously powerful analytical tool because it is the only way the analyst can provoke or induce the deceiver to produce new evidence. If the analyst remains passive, the deceiver may, of course, inadvertently produce such new evidence as part of the ongoing deception, but not necessarily so. Only by taking the initiative in introducing a controlled experiment into the evolving situation can the analyst provoke the deceiver into creating new evidence.

Traps and Tripwires

It is sometimes possible to trick the deceiver into self-betrayal. This is done by means of psychologically baited traps and invisible tripwires. These require that the detective actively intervene, changing reality to evoke new, key evidence that will disclose the deception. A nice example of a tripwire appears in ancient Hebrew literature. In this legend the detective is personally involved in a power struggle at the highest level of politics and uses a tripwire as his means of detection. This story appears in the Book of Daniel, which, although accepted in the Vulgate version of the Old Testament, is now generally judged apocryphal, despite the fact that it was probably written as early as 130 B.C., only two or three decades after the canonically accepted portions of the Book of Daniel.[30]

The setting is Babylon soon after 539 BC when it was conquered by Persian King Cyrus the Great. There, Cyrus has been converted to the worship of Baal by observing miraculous events in Baal's Temple, presided over by the huge clay and metal statue of that city's mighty god. Hebrew prophet Daniel, suspecting priestly hocus-pocus, is unimpressed and refuses to worship Baal. King Cyrus seeks to convince the delinquent Jew by pointing out the vast quantities of food supernaturally consumed by Baal, but Daniel asks for a test—we would today call it a controlled experiment.

Cyrus agrees to Daniel's test conditions but sets a forfeit. For Daniel, the wager means death if he cannot prove deception and for Baal's seventy priests death will be the consequence if they can be proved to have deceived their king. Both Daniel and the priests accept this life-or-death challenge, each confident of success.

That night, closely and openly watched by Cyrus and Daniel, the priests pile the food and wine upon the sacred altar-table set before the great image of Baal and then leave. Daniel moves through the vast stone hall, apparently satisfying himself that it is indeed empty. Cyrus and Daniel step outside, and the single entrance is closed and the double-doors sealed, marked with the crests of both king and priests. The several parties retire for the night, each with his own thoughts of the morrow.

At dawn, Cyrus and Daniel return to the temple. The great doors are still closed with seals intact. Yet, when the doors are thrown open, all standing outside can see that the altar table has been stripped clean. Cyrus declares that the priests have proven the miraculous powers of Baal. But Daniel invites the king to "Come, see the deceptions of the priests." They enter the empty hall, and Daniel points to the floor. There, with the morning sunlight streaming across it, Cyrus discerns the faint but numerous crisscrossing of bare footprints. On closer inspection, Cyrus sees that these cluster around the altar-table and lead to and from a small area on the floor beneath the table, which is found to be a trap door. During the night, the seventy priests with their wives and children had secretly reentered the temple to consume the feast of Baal and leave their telltale footprints in the fine wood-ash that Daniel had sprinkled over the floor during his earlier "inspection." Outraged, King Cyrus orders the priests, wives, and children slain and gives the temple of Baal to Daniel that he may destroy it.[31]

Another tripwire example is the set of envelopes used in 1943 in *The Man Who Never Was* ruse. The three deceptive letters were sealed in their envelopes in a secret manner that enabled the British deception team to detect, following their return "unopened" by the Spanish Naval Staff, that they had been opened, and presumably copied for transmission to their intended readers in German intelligence. This is exactly what had happened, as the British deceivers learned after the war.[32]

A final example of a counterdeception tripwire is printing banknotes with tiny "flaws." If the counterfeiter overlooks simulating any of these intentional "flaws," the product obviously is a fake. Conversely, the editors of dictionaries, who's-who references, and maps routinely slip in false entries to trap lazy plagiarists. In these cases, the plagiarist must detect and omit the specially coined word, the biography of someone who never lived, or the name of the small town that does not exist. If they overlook these phantoms and publish them, their deception is revealed and they are open to conviction for infringement of copyright. An amusing example of a coined trap-word is "houdinize." It first appeared in the 1920 edition of *Funk & Wagnalls New Standard Dictionary* where it was defined as "To release or extricate oneself from (confinement, bonds, or the like), as by wriggling out." The publishers kept this word in all subsequent editions of their dictionary until 1963, although its only known citations by other books are quotations from Funk & Wagnalls. The real story is that the word was coined by Harry Houdini's able press agent, Arthur B. Chase, specifically for use by F&W's lexicographers.[33]

Other well-known examples of baited traps are King Solomon's ploy that solved the mystery of the two mothers of one child and accountant P. Howard Lyons' ruse of planting false bookkeeping procedures on an embezzler. Police departments across the country nowadays frequently use "sting" operations designed to entrap criminals.[34]

The great Chinese statesman of the Fourth Century B.C., Su Ch'in, was a master of strategy and tactics. The best example was the trap he devised on his deathbed to expose his murderers. Certain political enemies had sent assassins to kill Su Ch'in. Mortally wounded, he told his king to have his body quartered and displayed in the public market under the king's false proclamation that he'd been a traitor. When this was done the killers came forward to claim a reward, proudly admitting their previous patriotic assassination attempt. Convicted by their own testimony, they were executed.[35]

World War II provides another interesting case of counterdeception. The forged documents section of the Abwehr (German military intelligence) prepared the various fake British ID papers and ration books given their secret agents prior to sending them into Britain. These were carefully designed as up-to-date imitations of genuine British documents together with their various appropriate bureaucratic rubber stamps. On arrival in Britain, all these spies and saboteurs were instantly identified as Abwehr agents by British Security (M.I.5) *because* of their papers. The forgers had done their work well enough, but according to specifications given by previous Abwehr agents who were, in fact, British double agents instructed to include a few false telltale details in their descriptions of current British documentation practices.[36]

Pre-Detection, Penetration, and Counterespionage

If Sir John Masterman was right, it is even possible to engage in "pre-detection," a term he coined in 1956 in his last and most remarkable detective novel.[37] In the period between this work of detection fiction and his first published in 1934, Masterman spent World War II as chairman of Twenty Committee, the deception team that coordinated all the German double-agents for the British intelligence and security services. And, while written as fiction, this novel has clear signs of lessons learned from the author's wartime work. Masterman, or rather his detective protagonist, argues that an opponent's specific deception plans can be predicted and thwarted by proper analysis of their deceptive style, capabilities, and goals.

A potent means to ferret out an opponent's most secret and deceptive plans and operations is by secretly penetrating his organization and controlling it from within. In doing so we enter the world of "counter-espionage." Counter-espionage, usually known by its acronym CE, is a widely misunderstood branch of secret operations, particularly in the U.S. intelligence community, which often confuses it with counter-intelligence (CI).[38] CI involves agents and sensors that passively listen in on one's secrets; CE involves agents who penetrate one's Intelligence services in order to influence or sabotage their policies and programs.

The Prepared Mind

> *"He who would distinguish the true from the false*
> *must have an adequate idea of what is true and false."*
> –*Spinoza*, The Ethics

Mannington Mills, Inc., owes much of its current success as a manufacturer of hard-surfaced patterned floor covering to an accident that occurred in the 1920s. Company president Neil Campbell looked in one evening on the print department to see how a new experimental design was coming along. Asking about the test runs, the foreman, gesturing toward a pile of discards, answered, "No good, I threw them away." The CEO picked up one that was lying face down on the blank back of another discard. To his surprise he found not one but two copies of the pattern. It was obvious that the wet discard had "kissed" the blank bottom piece, accidentally transferring the design—smudgy but recognizable. Campbell could have said: "What a mess . . . We've got to do something about getting faster drying paints." Instead he thought to himself: "Two for the price of one." He personally supervised test runs the next day that proved the commercial feasibility of this "kiss process" that made his company a leader in low-cost floor covering.[39]

Sometime in or shortly before 1896, a scientist is reported to have noticed that when a sample of pitchblende (uranium ore) happened to be in the same laboratory drawer with some photographic plates this blackened and ruined the plates. He concluded from this accidental event that photographic plates and pitchblende should not to be kept in the same drawer. As R. V. Jones comments about his fellow scientist, "This was a practical enough decision, but he lacked the scientific curiosity that would have led him to a spectacular discovery."[40] Soon afterwards, in another lab, French physicist Antoine-Henri Becquerel was experimenting with phosphorescence in uranium potassium phosphate salt crystals stimulated by sunlight. The expected result had been duly captured on one photographic plate when Becquerel noticed that clouds were intermittently obscuring the sun. Interrupting the experiment, he placed all the plates together with the salt in a drawer to await a sunnier day. Days passed without sun and the impatient scientist developed the plates anyway. The expected mix of faint or nonexistent images were, instead, all brilliant. Some quick experimenting proved that the salt gave off some hitherto unknown type of "ray" that could pass through black paper in the dark and a few days later he identified uranium as the active constituent. Becquerel had accidentally made the spectacular discovery of radioactivity.

Intuition

> "From long habit the train of thoughts ran so swiftly
> through my mind that I arrived at the conclusion without
> being conscious of intermediate steps. There were such steps, however."
> –Sherlock Holmes in A Study in Scarlet

> "Some ideas may suddenly start to move. Two ideas may
> combine, perhaps because they were meant to combine in the first place."
> –Patricia Highsmith, Plotting and Writing
> Suspense Fiction

Intuition is widely misunderstood. Many, perhaps most, people presume it is a kind of illogical or irrational thought process—even the occult, mystical, or supernatural. And it often seems so to persons who either do not experience it often or consciously reject it as inconvenient. Some, mostly non-intuitive males, even speak dismissively of "women's intuition." But we all have this ability to some degree and the better detectives cultivate and use it.

The last two stories in the previous section showed the stark difference between the inattentive and the "alert mind," as R. V. Jones called it. It is what Louis Pasteur called the "prepared mind." Psychologist Paul Souriau wrote in 1881, "To invent, one must think aside." Einstein called it his "nose." American codebreaker and poker expert, Herbert O. Yardley, called it "cipher brains," a term that some cryptologists continue to use. Magician Dariel Fitzkee called it "the trick brain." German soldiers called it *Fingerspitzengefühl*, literally intuition in the fingertips, a quality widely and correctly attributed to Field-Marshal Rommel. Physicist-psychologist Hermann von Helmholtz, psychotherapist Eric Berne, and Robert Ornstein called it "intuition." Psychologist Jerome Bruner called it "right-handed thinking." Many psychologists and psychotherapists call it "creativity." Dr. Edward De Bono and others following him have called it "lateral thinking." Cosmologist Sir Fred Hoyle calls it "crabwise thinking." I have heard it called "reverse thinking" in cases where the consequence is a solution opposite to the conventional one. By whatever name, it is the same sweet process.

So, what is the process? Edgar Allan Poe waffled around the point in his eccentric book on philosophy that, because it was specifically about intuition, he aptly titled *Eureka* (1848). Poe waffled between describing intuition as a nonrational and a rational process, but seemingly settled for the latter when he did insist that "Intuition . . . is but *the conviction arising from those inductions or deductions of which the processes are so shadowy as to escape our consciousness, elude our reason, or defy our capacity of* expression." Citing the work of cryptanalysts and the astronomer Johannes Kepler, Poe somewhat foreshadowed by twelve decades the work of Thomas Kuhn in claiming that science advanced more by "intuitive *leaps*" than by slow deductive or inductive reasoning.[41] I expect in the near future that experimental psychologists will be able to prove Poe right by showing that intuition is a rational and logical process, albeit on an unconscious or, at most, a semiconscious level of human cognition.

In the mid-1940s Rollo May was a graduate student researching anxiety.[42] His subjects were a group of unmarried and pregnant young women in their late teens and early twenties in a shelter home in New York City. His working hypothesis was one almost universally accepted at the time by psychoanalysts and psychologists, including May's professors and May himself. This notion was "That the predisposition toward anxiety in individuals would be proportionate to the degree to which they had been rejected by their mothers." May's interviews, backed by standard tests like the Rorschach and TAT, showed that while half of the young women fitted the standard hypothesis, the other half did not "carry any unusual degree of anxiety." Moreover this subgroup was made up entirely of women from Harlem and the Lower East Side whose degree of maternal rejection and state of apparent desperation greatly exceeded that of the "anxious" half. As one of these women, from a family of twelve kids whose mother had dumped her on the father who made her pregnant, summed up her group, "We have troubles, but we don't worry." Probing this unexpected subgroup, May found that their lack of anxiety was due to neither of the standard explanations: hardened apathy or psychopathic/sociopathic personality. "How could this be?" May wondered, "I felt myself caught by an insoluble problem."

Then, May recalls:

Late one day, putting aside my books and papers in the little office I used in that shelter house, I walked down the street toward the subway. I was tired. I tried to put the whole troublesome business out of my mind. About fifty feet away from the entrance to the Eighth Street station, it suddenly struck me 'out of the blue,' as the not-unfitting expression goes, that those young women who didn't fit my hypothesis *were all from the proletarian class.* And as quickly as that idea struck me, other ideas poured out. I think I had not taken another step on the sidewalk when a whole new hypothesis broke loose in my mind. I realized my entire theory would have to be changed. I saw at that instant that it is not rejection by the mother that is the original trauma that is the source of anxiety; it is rather *rejection that is lied about.* The proletarian mothers rejected their children, but they never made any bones about it. The children knew they were rejected; they went on the streets and found other companions. There was never any subterfuge about their situation. They knew their world—bad or good—and they could orient themselves to it. But the middle-class young women were always lied to in their families. They were rejected by mothers who pretended they loved them. This was really the source of their anxiety, not the sheer rejection. I saw, in that instantaneous way that characterizes insights from these deeper sources, that anxiety comes from *not being able to know the world you're in, not being able to orient yourself in your own existence.* I was convinced there, on the street—and later thought and experience only convinced me the more—that this is a better, more accurate, and more elegant theory, than my first.

In his posthumous autobiography, nineteenth-century French mathematician and physicist Henri Poincaré describes his first major discovery:

For fifteen days I strove to prove that there could not be any functions like those I have since called Fuchsian functions. I was then very ignorant; every day I seated myself at my worktable, stayed an hour or so, tried a great number of combinations and reached no results. One evening, contrary to my custom, I drank black coffee and could not sleep. Ideas arose in crowds; I felt them collide *until pairs interlocked,* so to speak, making a stable construction. By the next morning I had established the existence of a class of Fuchsian functions . . . I had only to write out the results, which took but a few hours.[43]

At this point, now wondering how his new functions fit into general math, Poincaré was called to military service and set further conscious thought aside. The next day, while mounting the first step of a bus and idly chatting with another soldier, he instantly became aware that the transformations he "had used to define the Fuchsian functions were identical with those of non-Euclidian geometry."

All of us know some things that we do not know that we know. These are perceptions that lurk below the surface of our conscious thought. They are things we observe; but, because they do not seem

salient (that is, of apparent need or relevance), are given only passing notice, brought only momentarily to the outer fringe of conscious attention. There are several techniques for bringing this information back into conscious play.

Indirect Thinking and the Third Option

> *"By indirections find directions out."*
> –Hamlet, *Act II, Scene I*

> *"Circumstantial evidence is a very tricky thing.*
> *It may seem to point very straight to one thing,*
> *but if you shift your own point of view a little,*
> *you may find it pointing in an equally uncompromising*
> *manner to something entirely different."*
> –Sherlock Holmes, *"The Boscombe*
> *Valley Mystery"*

When writing for conjurors, I sometimes use the term "magical
thinking." By this they understand the oblique mental process they
work through when either inventing a new trick or detecting the
method of another magician's trick. But I'll avoid this term here
because general audiences are apt to associate it with the supernatural or the occult. A useful synonym is what I call "indirect thinking,"
a process that usually produces the Third Option.

I call it indirect thinking to honor B. H. Liddell Hart's grand
concept of the "Indirect Approach" in military combat, which he
coined in 1929 to categorize the use of deception to gain surprise
in the attack. Although the specific application to military surprise
was original with Liddell Hart, the general concept was not. Indeed, he explicitly credits Shakespeare's *Hamlet* as his source of
inspiration.

A masterful example of indirect thinking, indeed truly "reverse"
thinking, was supplied by "Dr." Stanley Jaks, a middle-aged magician who had fled Nazi Germany and immigrated in 1946 to
America where he soon switched to the more profitable allied art
of mentalism. Jaks had befriended Ray Hyman, then a young magician and palm reader. Beginning as a skeptic, Hyman had found
his palm readings so well received by clients that he had come to
believe that he must have real psychic power. One day when Hyman
mentioned his belief in palmistry to Jaks, the latter [44]

...tactfully suggested that it would make an interesting experiment if I deliberately gave readings opposite to what the lines indicated. I tried this out with a few clients. To my surprise and horror my readings were just as successful. Ever since then I have been interested in the powerful forces that convince us, reader and client alike, that something is so when it really isn't.

What, I wonder, would be the consequences of randomizing the readings given Tarot cards or I-Ch'ing hexagrams or by setting all astrological readings six months ahead?

Most persons expect to deal with a simple pair of alternatives—either this or that. Consequently, it is an effective and favorite device of deceitful public speakers to present the listener with what rhetoriticians call a False Dilemma, positing a simple dichotomy when other options are possible. Example: "America–Love it or leave it."

It is the magician's talent to confront people with an ever-unexpected and surprising Third Option. It is an odd choice that few others can even fully understand afterwards. Conjurors are masters of options because every magical effect can in theory be achieved by more than one method. Thus, at least three quite different methods each have been used for Sawing a Woman in Half or Catching a Bullet or Levitating a Lady. The fact that any one of several methods can lurk behind any specific effect makes it all the more difficult for the audience (even other magicians) to detect the very natural cause of every seemingly supernatural event.

This is true not just for magic tricks, but also for all deceptions. In his essay on lying, French philosopher Montaigne wrote that[45]

If, like the truth, falsehood had only one face, we should know better where we are, for we should then take the opposite of what a liar said to be the truth. But the opposite of a truth has a hundred thousand shapes and a limitless field . . . There are a thousand ways of missing the bull's eye, only one of hitting it.

Surprisingly, Montaigne didn't take this as cause for despair. On the contrary, he goes on to argue that this very multiplicity of possible departures from any single truth places the deceiver in the awkward position of constantly having to keep his story straight, his memory clear, lest the discrepancies become too obvious in the retelling.

That Other Option

> *"Gentlemen, I notice that there are always three courses*
> *open to the enemy, and that he usually takes the fourth."*
> –Field Marshal Count Helmuth von Moltke

The purpose or goal of indirect thinking is to come up with an indirect answer, the kind of odd option I call the Third Option, although Field Marshal Count Helmuth Von Moltke obviously thought of it as the Fourth Option. Magicians know that if they are to detect the deceptions of other magicians, they must think in terms of this third or other option.

This phenomenon can be illustrated by a simple example. A person sees two apples and two oranges and tells you that you cannot add apples and oranges. You slyly shift the terms of reference and announce that you see four pieces of spherical fruit. Moving up the scale of examples, Amrom Katz once sketched for me the story of his experiences as a leading photo interpreter with the U.S. Air Force. He had started in World War II, rejoined the service during the Korean War, and again in the Vietnam War. Each time he helped refine the techniques of the analysts, but he learned that technical progress was thwarted by the tendency for each new generation of technicians to forget certain key lessons of the past. The Pentagon, increasingly concerned that photo intelligence out of Vietnam was not up to speed, sent Katz to Saigon to inspect and advise analysts. There he learned from interviewing Intelligence and Operational staffs that many ground operations were proving ineffective because of out-of-date aerial photos. This had long been the case for routine priority targets but was increasingly affecting urgent priority ones. No one knew why. Then, while touring the Air Force's photo interpretation center he noticed several large piles of bags scattered under various tables. Puzzled, he pointed to one table and asked:

"What's in that pile of bags?"

"Yesterday's take, sir."

"And that pile?" "Last week's take, sir."

"Why haven't they been filed or thrown out?"

"Because we haven't processed them yet."

"Well, what are you processing right now?" "Sir, the take from two weeks ago."

Soon after Katz returned stateside, orders came down to reprioritize so that the most recent photos, or at least as many as time allowed, would be analyzed first.

What type of person combines the four qualities necessary for first-rate deception and its detection—a prepared mind, a Machiavellian personality, empathy, and the ability to think indirectly?

Edgar Allan Poe had actually performed quite poorly in attempting to apply his own principle of detection, or "ratiocination" as he called it, to real-life mysteries such as the workings of the Automaton Chess Player and the Mary Rogers murder case. But the basic principle that he proclaimed in his fictionalized "The Mystery of Marie Rogêt" (1842) can hardly be improved:[46]

> In the analysis that I now propose, we will discard the *interior* points of this tragedy, and concentrate our attention on its *outskirts*. Not the least usual error, in investigations such as this, is the limiting of the inquiry to the immediate, with total disregard of the collateral or *circumstantial* events. It is the malpractice of the courts to confine evidence and discussion to the bounds of apparent *relevancy*. Yet experience has shown, and a true philosophy will always show, that a vast, perhaps the larger portion of truth arises from the seemingly irrelevant.

Highlighting the relevance of what is apparently irrelevant is a telling point, one that all detectives can put to good use, especially because it is a good starting point for shifting one's thinking from the straightforward toward the indirect.

Busby's Ombudsman: An Intuitive Trigger

> *"There is something about him that I don't quite like."*
> –Eric Ambler, "Spy-Haunts of the World"

> *"I had a gut feeling about the Dutch but it was a bride unwilling to be carried over the threshold of consciousness, and I couldn't pinpoint it . . .*
> *There was something wrong with the Dutch traffic."*
> –Leo Marks, Between Silk and Cyanide

I choose to give Busby's Ombudsman separate treatment to highlight its importance for triggering intuitive analysis when faced with deception. I believe that among all proposed techniques for detecting deception by committee or in a group setting it is the simplest, easiest, least upsetting to individual analysts or bureaucratic power structures, and the most effective.

The ombudsman was originally and still is a Swedish institution. Indeed it is one of the few Swedish loanwords into English, having arrived in 1959 through, of all places, New Zealand, which officially adopted the institution that year. In Swedish it means literally a representative; and in Sweden and New Zealand the ombudsman is a government-paid official whose job is to receive and investigate complaints made by citizens about abuses by other public officials. Some American newspapers, such as the *Washington Post*, more recently (early 1970s) added an ombudsman to their staff as an in-house critic, a readers' advocate. Ombudsman carries a connotation somehow missing from terms such as "devil's advocate"—a clearly argumentative if not openly antagonistic person—or "a consultant" who is too often an uninvited and unwelcome meddler, if not a mere spy for senior management.

Origin of the Busby Method

Jeff Busby created the Ombudsman Method in 1978 in response to an unusual challenge–to teach gambling casino employees to detect cheaters. He taught this course with considerable success in casinos and card rooms in Reno, Tahoe, Emeryville, and South San Francisco. Other magicians, notably the late Mickey MacDougall, the late Audley Walsh, the late John Scarne, Sidney Radner, and Darwin Ortiz also have developed and taught gambling detection courses to casino staff and laymen, thereby earning footnotes in the history of counterdeception. Only small footnotes, I reluctantly admit, because even their best instructions were weak on the how-to-detect side.

Busby's course represents a breakthrough in counterdeception theory as well as practice. As he is the first to admit, it was largely a result of one of those rare and delightfully serendipitous accidents that entitle us to shout "Eureka!" When they hired Busby as a consultant, the Nevada and California casino security directors imposed an unusual but understandably self-serving constraint. He was to teach the floor staff to detect cheating, but he was not to teach them *how* to cheat. To overcome this constraint, he applied Daley's Discrepancy Theory and thereby developed a unique course in counterdeception, the first to teach how to detect deception by looking for the discrepancies rather than recognizing the specific sleights or gadgets. His success proves two important points, both of which run counter to common sense. First, it shows that one need not be a deceiver to detect deception. Second, and even more counterintuitive, Busby did not himself even know the specific rules of the two games that he taught the experts how to detect deception in.

This achievement has two implications beyond the world's gambling tables. Imagine a successful counterdeception course for military-political intelligence analysts who are ignorant (as most indeed are) of the theory and practice of military deception. Imagine further that this course is taught by a deception expert who is not a military-political intelligence expert.[47] Why not apply this technique to every type of deception?

Busby also used this method when teaching conjuring to his students. It was his way of forcing them to analyze each trick, to understand the whys and wherefore of its method, rather than merely learning it by rote. He used this method with me, explaining that, as a professional magician pledged to keep the secrets of the craft, he was not free to answer my "How is it done?" questions with a direct explanation. I, as a layman, would have to figure it out for myself, and he would only confirm or deny each step of my analysis. Of course, I had done my homework in the extensive published literature of magic so I knew all the standard methods and many of the rarer ones. But I was often baffled by a new effect as well as some of the older ones whose methods were still unpublished secrets. Busby would then put me through his "ombudsman method," as he called it.

On Sunday afternoon, 5 February 1984, Busby asked if I would be interested in taking a counterdeception test, explaining that he was curious to see if, by using the ombudsman technique, a non-magician like myself could detect all the discrepancies in a particularly difficult trick, one that no magician beside himself had yet succeeded in detecting. I accepted this challenge, although with much skepticism. It was a pet card trick of its inventor, a world-class American casino house magician and sleight-of-hand man. He had performed it for many years before both magician and lay audiences. Busby had figured it out by acting as his own ombudsman and the inventor had confirmed the solution, requesting only as a matter of professional courtesy that it not be published or given to competitors. Busby then ran a five-minute videotape clip from a national TV show of this performer doing his card trick.

At the end of two hours, the Ombudsman Method had led me to discover all the irrelevancies, all the misdirection, all but one of the discrepancies, and the actual method that made the trick possible. The undetected discrepancy had to exist. It must, I figured, occur in the moment or moments when the magician prepared for his trick.

If, now knowing the whole method, I could not see this "get-ready," I hypothesized that it must have taken place *before* the trick, that is, the "effect," had even begun. I told Busby of my suspicion that the effect I had seen was preceded by at least one other effect and asked whether the videotape recorded it. He said yes, I asked to see that part, and he showed it. And there it was: the "get-ready" needed to work "my" trick had occurred toward the end of the previous trick, a casual gesture having no relevance to that trick. Stretching my hunch a bit, I then asked to see the trick that followed mine. Sure enough, its method also flowed from a get-ready made during my "test" trick. I realized that even most magicians would be fooled. This performer routinely did something that only the most advanced conjurors ever do, namely conceal the entire secret method in the previous trick so that only the *effect* was visible.[48] It was astonishing that I, a semi-informed amateur, could detect an extraordinarily sophisticated magical deception that no professional (including some of the best) had yet penetrated. [49] Busby had convinced me that his method worked. But would it work with anyone? And could it help detect other types of deception?

Development

To test this analytical method outside gambling and magic contexts, we took advantage of an opportunity in 1984 provided by Professor Katherine Herbig of the U.S. Naval Postgraduate School in Monterey, California. At the time, Herbig was teaching a seminar on "Strategic Deception" and invited me to be a guest lecturer for one afternoon session. When I learned that the class comprised a dozen experienced naval and military intelligence analysts, I proposed that I take one of the later class sessions (so they would have a good background on deception) and give mine on counterdeception. I mentioned the recent work with Busby and she agreed that we appear as joint-lecturers and devote one of the two hours to a run-through of the Ombudsman Method. Our appearance was scheduled a few weeks hence and Busby and I quickly worked up lecture notes and a protocol for a test of his method.

As the test subjects were experienced analysts, I was confident they could handle a fairly advanced type of problem in the short time allowed. I suggested the Die Box, and Busby agreed. This trick, also known as the Sucker Sliding Die Box, has several desirable qualities. It is a standard trick of the "sucker gag" type, that is, a double-bluff where the spectators are fed clues (both visual and audible) that point to a logical but false solution of the method of working. The length of performance was about right, running only about five minutes. It was a pure "box trick:" a self-contained single piece of apparatus requiring no sleight-of-hand.

Semi-pro kid-show magician Blake Maxam agreed to be videotaped performing the trick on stage. It would be a single fixed-camera job in one continuous take to avoid any suggestion of film editing or trick photography. To keep all relevant action within the camera frame, Busby blocked out the action and Maxam rehearsed it twice. Then two separate performances were recorded. Tape A ran 5:45 minutes, tape B, 4:45 minutes. On the appointed afternoon Busby and I put on our two-hour "dog-and-pony show." The first hour was given over to lectures by both of us and two mini-tests given by myself. The first was based on their homework that had assigned a counterdeception short story, which they were asked to analyze in class. Those who had read it did fairly well in following the logic. The second mini-test was to read them the Major Thynne-Colonel Clarke story and ask them to guess Clarke's solution. Again they were pretty much on the right track but a bit slow. The second hour ran them through a test of the Ombudsman Method.

The test protocol was carried out as intended. I opened by explaining to the class that they were about to be run through an exercise in counterdeception. They would be shown a videotape of a classic magic trick called the Die Box. Afterwards they would be challenged to try to figure out the method used by the magician. All clues would be on the tape and it was suggested that they should concentrate on detecting the discrepancies. I explained that Busby was there to answer any questions; but as he was a professional magician pledged to not expose trade secrets, he could only verify or deny what they had seen. They were also told that they could request repeats of the entire tape or any portions and were informed of the existence of the second tape. Busby then took over the class.

Tape A was shown, Maxam appearing on stage with a large Die Box and went through the standard sucker routine, which lasted less than six minutes. Then, after a brief discussion in which the group could not agree on what precisely they had seen, they requested a second showing. They then agreed on the sequence of events (correctly, except for certain overlooked details). They then requested and were shown several specific segments of the tape, each time identifying false leads or real discrepancies. At the end of the hour the bell stopped the experiment. The group had succeeded not only in identifying all the pseudo-discrepancies but also in detecting all the real discrepancies. Given the limited time, they had progressed further than expected. We believed that with another round of, say, fifteen minutes of discussion, they would have solved most of the mechanical workings of the box; and, given another quarter-hour, would probably have come up with a working diagram.

Curiously, they had passed up the opportunity to view the second tape. I had presumed professional intelligence analysts would want to see a second set of data. It was as if a photo-interpreter refused to examine the pictures snapped by a photoreconnaissance plane or satellite on a second pass. Perhaps they believed our assurance that all *relevant* clues were present on both tapes was enough. But, if so, they overlooked the possibility that viewing the second performance might have saved them time by showing up the *irrelevant actions*, that is, any verbal or visual "bits of business" that failed to appear in both versions. In cases where such comparisons can be made, it is useful to identify at least some of the irrelevancies so they can be discarded early on.

Application

The Ombudsman Method has at least three applications. It can be used for teaching, training, or analysis of specific deceptions. Moreover, it can be used for on-line analysis of current cases as well as for after-the-fact analysis of past cases. The essence of the Ombudsman Method is to force one to confront straight on that nagging, almost subliminal, sense of unease about a situation or person that somehow does not seem quite right, that does not quite fit as it should those little incongruities that can signal a deception in progress. I have called this phenomenon "Busby's Uneasiness."

NYPD Detective Raymond Pierce gives an example of Busby's Uneasiness. He was asked his advice on the case of a young girl murdered in her home. The crime scene looked as if she had been killed during a break-in robbery. Pierce thought it looked staged and asked the investigating detective, "Can you tell me some more? You know, there's something missing here. There's a big piece of this puzzle missing." So further details emerged. They proved crucial, enabling Pierce to redirect the investigation in a different and quickly successful direction.[50]

American art expert Thomas Hoving gives a particularly fine real-world example of Busby's Uneasiness in operation. In 1965, young Dr. Hoving was in Vienna at dinner with his boss, James J. Rorimer, the prestigious director of New York City's Metropolitan Museum of Art. They were celebrating their handshake acquisition from a private dealer of a magnificent fifteenth-century stone sculpture of *Madonna and Child*:[51]

> We fell silent at dinner's end, each of us thinking rosy thoughts about the truly miraculous acquisition-to-be. Then the strangest thing happened. We both looked up at the same moment and asked each other. "Don't you sense that there's something wrong with this deal?" The mutual paranoid society of James J. Rorimer and Thomas Hoving was called into full session. Something was fishy. The deal was too good, too pat.

The ensuing analytical discussion quickly distilled their vague "anxieties" into four specific questions: (1) Why had neither of them ever heard of this spectacularly important object before? (2) Why had no one published it? (3) Why had it not been featured at the "Year 1400" Vienna art show just a few years earlier? (4) Why had not the Austrian government bought such a choice example of the "Beautiful Style" that was so popular with tourists? These were disturbing questions indeed. A fifth question that they did not discuss but that was probably in their minds was (5) Why was the dealer forcing a quick decision, even using the old I-Have-Another-Drooling-Buyer-in-the-Wings ploy?

The finest example I know of, involving a life-or-death wartime deception-counterdeception game, is the one where British codemaker Leo Marks' "sixth sense" led him to bust the Nazi's cruel "Radio Game" that had captured all the Allied agents in occupied Holland.[52]

Conclusions

Of the forty-six types of detectives studied, all but one used the same general procedures to detect deception. (The exception was the adversarial method used by trial lawyers working in the American judicial system.) All others used standard logical systems (both deductive and inductive) in combination with intuitive methods. The more successful detections seemed to be closely associated with intuitive methods, particularly so-called "indirect thinking."

Effective analytical procedures provide a method that pinpoints the handful of existing procedures for detecting deception that have proved most successful in all forty-six specialties. It also suggests a couple of new procedures that show promise for military-political analysts.

The creative analyst has distilled from the data a preliminary behavioral and psychological profile of the half dozen or so characteristics that distinguish the few highly successful analysts of deception from their less effective colleagues. The evidence strongly suggests that most, possibly all, of these behaviors and mind-sets can be taught to a considerable degree, particularly as part of on-the-job training. The Ombudsman Method seems the most promising of the several suggested approaches.

Authors' Note: The "I" in this chapter refers to the principal author, Bart Whaley. Since it was first written in 1999, Whaley has increased the number of types of detectives studies to over 100, and the number of major works cited to over 500. The most important finding was to reinforce the recommendation that effective detection and deception is crucially dependent on large and accurate data bases based on systematically collected and analyzed case studies.

Notes

1. Barton Whaley, *Stratagem: Deception and Surprise in War* (Cambridge, MA: MIT Press, 1969), pp. 210-223, for section and tables on "The Varieties and Intensities of Surprise and Deception."

2. Pye & Leites, and Scott A. Boorman, *"Deception in Chinese Strategy"* in William W. Whitson, *The Military and Political Power in China in the 1970's* (New York: Praeger Publishers, 1972).

3. Whaley, *Stratagem*, Chapter II ("Deception in National Military Doctrines"), pp. 24-85.

4. Howard Higgins, "An Anthropologist Looks at Magic," *The Linking Ring* (November 1985), pp. 48-50.

5. Roger L. Omanson, "Perceptions in Magic," *The Linking Ring* (August 1987), pp. 38-39; Milbourne Christopher, *The Illustrated History of Magic* (New York: Crowell, 1973) Ch. 5 ("American Indian Conjuring"), pp. 69-81; A. Irving Hallowell, *The Role of Conjuring in Saulteau Society* (Philadelphia, PA: University of Pennsylvania Press, 1942).

6. Figures compiled by Whaley in 1972 from various sources.

7. Whaley, *Stratagem*, pp. A85-A87.

8. Ibid., p. 144.

9.   Unfortunately, some writers muddy this concept, confusing it with pitting one deception against another. That latter concept deserves its own jargon term, which Harris and I agreed in 1969 should, on the principle of waste-not-want-not, be my rejected coinage of "counter-stratagem." However, that term did not catch on, so I would now suggest "triple cross."

10.   J. Barton Bowyer (pseudo. J. Bowyer Bell and Barton Whaley), *Cheating: Deception in War & Magic, Games & Sports, Sex & Religion, Business & Con Games, Politics & Espionage, Art & Science* (New York: St. Martin's Press, 1982) throughout; and Whaley, "Toward a General Theory of Deception," in John Gooch and Amos Perlmutter, eds., *Military Deception and Strategic Surprise* (London: Frank Cass, 1982).

11.   As formulated by the author on 30 December 1986. Years earlier I had recognized the minus-charc side of the detection equation. It was not until drafting this paper that I also saw the plus-charc side.

12.   This notion hit me on 26 January 1987 at the instant I compared the two sections on physicists-chemists and Jones' notion of incongruity. The former, like auto mechanics, are mainly concerned with finding congruity, the latter are mainly concerned with detecting incongruity. But these two processes are merely two sides of the same proverbial coin.

13.   Barton Whaley, *Codeword BARBAROSSA* (Cambridge, MA: MIT Press, 1973), p. 312. This Barbarossa-Sea Lion linkage was later reported, independently of mine, by Charles Cruickshank, *Deception in World War II* (New York: Oxford University Press, 1979), pp. 207-208, based on the postwar debriefing notes of three of the German planners in the U.S. National Archives.

14.   This point was developed in 1984 during discussions with Jeff Busby.

15.   Sir Arthur Conan Doyle, *The Adventure of the Priory School (1904): A Facsimile of the Original Manuscript* (Santa Barbara, CA: Santa Teresa Press, 1985).

16.   Sir Arthur Conan Doyle, *The Sign of the Four* (1890), Ch.6. This was Holmes' (and Doyle's) favorite maxim, being repeated with only slightly different wording a second time in *The Sign of the Four* (1890), Ch.1; and then in Doyle's *The Adventure of the Beryl Coronet* (1892), *The Lost Special* (1898), *The Adventure of the Priory School* (1904), and *The Adventure of the Bruce-Partington Plans* (1908).

17.   Thomas Hoving, *False Impressions: The Hunt for Big-Time Art Fakes* (New York: Simon and Schuster, 1996) p. 209.

18.   Ibid., pp. 115-118.

19.   The background details are in R. V. (Reginald Victor) Jones, *Most Secret War* (London: Hamilton, 1978), p. 26; the quote is from R.V. Jones.

20.   Quoted from Jones, *Most Secret War*, p. 23.

21.   Ibid., p. 26.

22.   Ibid., pp. 28-29, 502-503, 531; and Jones (1957), p. 196.

23.   R. V. Jones in his "D.T." paper of 10 January 1942. See also Jones, *Most Secret War*, p. 288.

24.   Jones (1957), p. 199.

25.   Ibid., p. 199.

26.   Whaley [J. Barton Bowyer]. *Cheating* (1982).

27.   Les Aspin, "The Verification of the SALT II Agreement," *Scientific American*, Vol. 240, No. 2 (February 1978), pp. 38-45, as quoted in Amrom H. Katz, *Verification and Salt :The State of the Art and the Art of the State* (Washington, DC: Heritage Foundation, 1979), p. 21.

28.   Katz, Verification and Salt, p. 21.

29.   I owe this distinction to Jeff Busby.

30.   R. H. Charles (ed.), *The Apocrypha and Pseudoepigrapha of the Old Testament*, Vol. I (Oxford, UK: The Clarendon Press, 1913), pp. 652-657.

31.   Ibid., pp. 658-661. This story is noted by magician Christopher, *The Illustrated History of Magic*, p. 12, in his history of conjuring.

32.   Ewen Montagu *The Man Who Never Was* (London UK: Evans Bros., 1953), pp.114-115, 132-133, 138.

33.   Barton Whaley, *The Encyclopedic Dictionary of Magic* (CD-ROM) (Key West, FL: Black Bart Magic, 2001). See entry under "houdinize."

34.   Case studies are Charles Conconi and Toni House, *The Washington Sting* (New York: Coward, McCann & Geoghegan, Inc., 1979), a joint police-FBI operation in Washington, DC, in 1975-76; Zay N. Smith and Pamela Zekman, *The Mirage* (New York: Random House, 1979), a sting by investigative reporters of the *Chicago Sun-Times* in 1977.

35.   Robert Hans van Gulik, *Murder in Canton: A Chinese Detective Story* (London: Heinemann:, 1966), postscript.

36.   Sir J. C. (John Cecil) Masterman, *The Double-Cross System in the War of 1939 to 1945* (New Haven, CT: Yale University Press, 1972), p. 49. The perceptions of the dupes are in Charles Wighton and Günter Peis, *Hitler's Spies and Saboteurs* (New York: Holt, Rinehart and Winston, 1958), Ch.4.

37.   Sir J. C. Masterman, *The Case of the Four Friends: A Diversion in Pre-Detection* (London: Hodder & Stoughton, 1956).

38.   Christopher Felix, *The Spy and His Masters: A Short Course in the Secret War* (London: Secker & Warburg: 1963), pp. 143-154.

39.   John M. Keil, *The Creative Mystique* (New York: John Wiley & Co., 1985), p. 4.

40.   Jones (1965), p. 539.

41.   See David Ketterer, *The Rationale of Deception in Poe* (Baton Rouge: Louisiana State University Press, 1979), pp.258-261.

42.   Rollo May, *The Courage to Create* (New York: W. W. Norton & Company, 1977), pp. 56-58.

43.   As quoted in Brewster Ghiselin (ed.), *The Creative Process* (Berkeley, CA: University of California Press, 1952), p. 36.

44.   Ray Hyman, *The Elusive Quarry: A Scientific Appraisal of Psychical Research* (Buffalo, NY: Prometheus Books, 1989), p. 409.

45.   Michel de Montaigne, *Essays* (1595, J. M. Cohen translation, London: Penguin Books 1957).

46.   I quote from the original 1842 text and not the version that he edited for the 1845 reprint.

47.   As documented in my circular "Dear Colleague" letter of 18 January 1984, pp. 6-7.

48.   Although the magician who inspired this test has since died, I withhold his name on the grounds that two of his students are still using this particular method.

49.   Nor for the subsequent fifteen years, as Busby updated me on 22 June 1999.

50.   As quoted in Peter A. Micheels, *The Detectives* (New York: St. Martin's Press 1994), p. 150.

51.   Hoving, *False Impressions*, pp. 145-146.

52.   Leo Marks, *Between Silk and Cyanide: A Codemaker's War, 1941-1945* (New York: The Free Press, 1999), throughout.

8

The Denial and Deception Challenge to Intelligence[1]

Paul J. Rossa

Denial and Deception as an Intelligence Community Topic

The Intelligence Community performed much "stocktaking" in the aftermath of the Cold War as overall intelligence activities declined and changed focus. Events of the day shaped perceptions of changing intelligence objectives and of evolving obstacles to effective intelligence. For example, our intelligence capabilities were challenged by Iraq before, during, and after the Persian Gulf War. Further, our metal was tested by the Aldrich Ames espionage case, including revelations of Russian double agentry.

Within this stocktaking, Director of Central Intelligence James Woolsey became concerned that the Community must be vigilant against denial and deception challenges posed by the "snakes in the grass" that had become the primary targets of our intelligence collection and analysis. For example, Iraqi denial and deception (D&D) operations had reduced the effectiveness of some of our intelligence efforts, and continuing Russian D&D was exposed in the aftermath of Ames's career as a spy. There no longer was a single "dragon" conducting D&D operations within a reasonably well-defined strategic struggle. Rather, D&D challenges were popping up in new places on new issues. The age-old subject of foreign D&D was changing faces.

Congressional oversight subcommittees and Directors John Deutch and George Tenet communicated their similar concerns, which they have seen continuously reinforced. In May 1998, for example, India exploded a nuclear weapon and subsequently bragged openly about D&D operations designed to conceal test preparations. Admiral Jeremiah cited Indian D&D as a factor that impeded timely intelligence warning of the event.[2] Later, the Rumsfeld Commission issued a report that challenged the Intelligence Community to overcome foreign D&D operations that seriously threaten our ability to detect acquisition of ballistic missile capabilities and the development of weapons of mass destruction more generally.[3] And even the Cox Committee report generated considerable open discussion by our representatives as well as the media—of possible Chinese deception operations associated with their nuclear weapons espionage activities.[4]

Today, we are reaching out to academics and others outside of the Intelligence Community to address this important topic using their special skills and vantage points. All of us are committed to encouraging government policy and decision making that is effective and free of unwarranted influences. Because foreign D&D challenges to these objectives are and will remain strong, our counter-D&D effort must also be strong.

A Critical Task: Identifying Foreign D&D Operations

That there are secrets to be uncovered has always been a basic principle of intelligence. Uncovering secrets also is key to exposing deceptions. Consequently, counteracting foreign denial efforts is critical to countering foreign denial and deception. Counterdenial efforts require primarily the development and employment of means to obtain information regardless of its degree of protection or security.

Secrets and deceptions, however, are not so easily exposed through counterdenial efforts alone. All information is seldom obtainable as analytic conclusions inevitably rely on limited data (and not all data is equally obtainable). Further, regardless of whether all information on a subject can be obtained, it can be polluted to incorporate misleading data that supports a deception, which may lead to an incorrect conclusion, no useful conclusion, or a highly tentative or partially correct conclusion.

The identification of denial operation actions to conceal information can help direct limited information-gathering resources toward data that will expose a secret and away from neutral or misleading data. Such identification also might raise suspicions of possible associated deception operations and affect interpretations of all data on the subject.

The identification of a deception operation also can affect judgments on what information might be denied, what information to seek, and how to interpret it. By the term "deception operation" I intend to encompass actions designed to provide misleading information to a target, to include "true lies" and "partial truths," and even truths imparted deceptively, as a means to skew the recipient's data to encourage/discourage a conclusion favorable/unfavorable to the deceiver.

How to Detect Foreign D&D, and Then What?

The foregoing simply argues that recognizing foreign D&D is an important means towards overcoming it. Less simple are the actual tasks of recognizing it and using this recognition. Faced with an array of information on a subject, the analyst who is to put the pieces of the puzzle together must first determine which pieces to use and which to discard or reshape on the basis of whether it was obtained despite foreign denial operations, as a result of foreign deception operations, or in the absence of either. Such characterizations of the data are difficult to achieve in practice (and uncertainty levels likely would be associated with each characterization). If such characterizations are accomplished, how to apply them within the puzzle-solving task may not be clear.

Recognizing a foreign D&D operation can require considerable data about the data ("meta data"). The way in which the data was acquired, circumstances surrounding the acquisition, and the content of the information all may contain indications of foreign D&D or its absence. Unfortunately, these indications may be unclear or conflicting. Further, beginning with one piece of information from one source, the assessment likely will have to expand to a matrix of data on more than one subject from more than one source. Sources often provide information on more than one topic and each topic likely has more than one source of information.

Among the most useful types of characterizations of data is information pertaining to the potential perpetrator of a D&D operation. The motives, proclivities, objectives, knowledge (including feedback mechanisms), and D&D tools, for example, of a potential D&D perpetrator may be consistent or inconsistent with manipulation of a specific item of information or source.

Systematic analytic methodologies for organizing and assessing such data to detect foreign D&D are sparse. Systematic analytic methodologies to employ the results of such D&D assessments and reach valid conclusions despite the surrounding D&D also are rare.

Addressing Susceptibilities

Although the identification of foreign D&D is critical, another important counter-D&D method is to reduce susceptibilities to potential foreign D&D. Strategies and methods of collecting information can be more or less vulnerable to receiving misleading data. Similarly, some analytic methodologies are more vulnerable to the manipulation of data than others. And targets of intelligence analysis vary in their talents and capacities to conduct forms of D&D operations against us—and others.

One of the more obvious contributors to D&D susceptibility is target knowledge of our collection, analysis methods, and resulting judgments. If the intelligence target understands what information is being gathered and how it is being processed to reach conclusions, the danger that the data will be cut-off or manipulated is higher than it otherwise might be. Conversely, an unknown source of data or analytic methodology or a target's failure to recognize and understand the value of some types of information given existing analytic methods generally reduces the likelihood of effective D&D. Foreign knowledge of information gathering and analytic methodologies also is more likely to foster D&D if the target understands whether and how the analytic conclusions are employed to reach actionable judgments unfavorable to the target.

The impact of such foreign knowledgeability is variable. Not all known collection and analysis methods are necessarily subject to manipulation. Further, foreign D&D can occur with imperfect or limited knowledge of our intelligence capabilities. The intelligence target may make assumptions about us based on a flawed or limited understanding, and act accordingly perhaps sometimes accepting a low or moderate probability of success. Unknown collection and analysis methods can be affected deliberately or inadvertently through such D&D operations. Although this may lead to some ineffective D&D operations or D&D operations that have unintended consequences, others can be highly successful. Those that affect information in unintended ways also can harm the interests of either or both parties. Additionally, D&D operations can be conducted against one adversary (or friend) and inadvertently affect another in unpredicted ways.

The development of information gathering and processing methods that are unknown (and remain that way) or difficult to manipulate can reduce vulnerabilities to D&D. And these could vary by intelligence target or subject. However, methods for assessing D&D susceptibility and for incorporating such assessments in the development of conclusions are needed.

Looking for Patterns and Tools

The intelligence community would profit by development of conceptual frameworks, indicators, and analytic techniques that hold promise for recognizing and countering foreign D&D as it occurs. The cupboard is not bare, and Cold War experience taught us much about countering a strong D&D practitioner, but the foreign D&D challenge is evolving as issues and technologies change. As a discipline, D&D analysis can similarly develop and evolve.

Qualitative and quantitative analyses of historical D&D cases potentially can help both in the detection of foreign D&D and the reduction of susceptibilities. There is no substitute for empirically grounded analytic devices applicable to ongoing D&D questions. Many of today's D&D practitioners have foreign policy and security objectives that are as familiar as the second-oldest profession itself. Further, age-old D&D methods often are applicable to a wide range of new international actors and issues associated with foreign and security policies and interactions.

In part because new issues confront policymakers and intelligence analysts as we enter the next century, counter-D&D theory and tools may be more important than ever. The D&D practitioner of concern is no longer so likely to be a well-known adversary on a familiar issue against which tremendous information gathering and analysis resources can be committed. More likely the actor and issue are relatively new subjects and analytic resources are limited. Further, rapid changes in information technologies complicate the analytic task. To cope, highly developed counter-D&D theory and analytic aids at-the-ready potentially can be invaluable to effective analytic support to policymakers.

Notes

1.   This article has been reviewed by the Central Intelligence Agency for classified content only. The views presented here are unofficial and those of the author alone, and do not necessarily represent the views of CIA, the National Intelligence Council, or other U.S. intelligence community or government organizations.

2.   On 12 May 1998, DCI Tenet asked Admiral David Jeremiah, USN (Ret), former Vice Chairman of the Joint Chiefs of Staff, to lead an Intelligence Community team to assess the Indian nuclear testing issue and report his findings and recommendations within ten days. The Report is classified. However on 2 June 1998 Admiral Jeremiah held a news conference. Text is available on the worldwide web at http://www.cia.gov/cia/public_affairs/press_release/archives/1998/jeremiah.html.

3.   The Commission to Assess the Ballistic Missile Threat to the United States (The Rumsfeld Commission) was created by the U.S. Congress in 1997. The Commission delivered its classified report to the House and Senate Intelligence Committees on 15 July 1998. The unclassified 27-page Executive Summary is available on the worldwide web at www.brook.edu/fp/projects/nmd/rumsfeld98.html.

4.   The United States House of Representatives Select Committee on U.S. National Security and Military/Commercial Concerns with the People's Republic of China (The Cox Committee), 3 July 1999. An unclassified version of the Report is available on the worldwide web at: http://www.house.gov/coxreport/.

9

The Impact on Foreign Denial and Deception of Increased Availability of Public Information about U.S. Intelligence[1]

James B. Bruce

The intelligence community is concerned with the pursuit of truth. A wonderful quotation from the New Testament is chiseled on the marble wall inside the main entrance of CIA Headquarters in Langley, Virginia: "You shall know the truth, and the truth shall make you free." This inscription was intended to be inspirational. Congress has also passed some laws in recent years dealing with truth—for example, *Truth in Lending* and *Truth in Advertising*. We can wonder why there has not been any Truth in Intelligence legislation.

Suppose Congress were to pass such a law: would the intelligence community be able to certify that the intelligence it disseminates contained the truth, the whole truth, and nothing but the truth? Of course, Congress would not want to do this unless someone could also certify that the effects of foreign denial and deception of U.S. intelligence were fully eliminated from the finished intelligence products provided to policymakers. We can only tell the whole truth to the extent that denial is not effective. Where denial succeeds, we cannot know the whole truth. How can we be sure that deception is not succeeding in the reporting that we use in our analysis? In short, the problem for such hypothetical legislation is our ability to tell the truth, or "speak truth to power." Seen from the perspective of the intelligence customer, our truth-telling ability in intelligence is jeopardized by successful denial and deception conducted by foreign countries about whom we seek truthful information.

Denial, as used here, refers to the actions and programs that foreign countries (or other intelligence targets) undertake to prevent us from succeeding in our most basic mission, namely the collection of secret information by secret means. Denial efforts variously seek to impair, impede, degrade, or otherwise prevent intelligence collection. *Deception* refers to activities and programs that targets undertake to manipulate what we collect, how we collect it, or how we analyze it, that is, efforts to manipulate or influence the intelligence judgments that we provide to customers.

Increasingly, we need to look at the world of intelligence through the optic of denial and deception (D&D). We also need to project our capabilities forward ten or twenty years, and raise the question of the future effectiveness of U.S. intelligence. Let me advance a simple hypothesis: The future effectiveness of U.S. intelligence depends inordinately on our ability to understand and to counter foreign D&D.

Former Chairman of the National Intelligence Council Harry Rowen said at a conference in 1984, "In time, the truth more or less usually comes out. But time is a key parameter, and truth known late may be too late." That is the essence of the problem for us and also for those in strategic warning intelligence. Our ability to tell the truth depends on who the adversary is, how good or bad they are at D&D, and how good or bad we are at countering their D&D. The fundamental dilemma we face is that the higher the collection priority of the target, the better they usually are at D&D. The way we need to think about this issue is to better understand what intelligence is.

Among intelligence professionals, there are two concepts of intelligence: one is related to information, the other to secrets. The analysts' view, generally, is that intelligence is information and knowledge. Former Director of Central Intelligence Stansfield Turner advanced this approach when he renamed CIA's Directorate of Intelligence, its analytical component, the National Foreign Assessment Center (NFAC). Similarly, to further distance analysis from "intelligence," others have proposed an Executive Branch counterpart to the Congressional Research Service, the establishment of an "Executive Research Service" to produce analysis that is pure and uncontaminated by "spying."

The other model of intelligence is clandestinity, which has to do with secrets and secrecy. This concept of intelligence is built around the idea that intelligence is the collection of secret information by secret means. The model of clandestinity is emphasized here because this is fundamentally the value-added that intelligence brings to the policymaking process.

Intelligence obtained by clandestine means is both similar to and different from other information that U.S. policymakers draw upon in their decision-making processes. We know that policymakers get their information from many diverse sources such as newspapers, television, radio, the Internet, and conversations with colleagues and friends. They also read intelligence documents. However, intelligence is never the only source of information for them, and it is rarely the most important source. Intelligence competes with the other sources of information for the policymakers' attention. The issue for the intelligence community and for Congress is: What is the value-added that intelligence brings to the policymaking process? More than anything else, the answer lies in the clandestine aspects.

To the extent that the intelligence community supports policymakers with products based on secret information gathered by secret means, our contribution is unique, and that is the value-added. Without the contribution provided by our clandestine capabilities, we would be little different from the *New York Times*, the academic community, think tanks, or other sources of information not derived from truly secret collection. The four major collection disciplines—HUMINT, SIGINT, IMINT, and MASINT[2]—all contribute in clandestine ways, and together provide the fundamental basis for our ability to contribute unique value-added information to the policymakers' burgeoning inbox.

If we take the idea that clandestinity is chiefly what intelligence is all about, then our ability to counter foreign D&D is the key to doing our job well or not. Thus, we should be concerned with the principal threats to secret intelligence collection. Those threats to the integrity of U.S. intelligence have to do with the "secret" world of intelligence. Unhappily for both the producer and customer of intelligence, much of our collection world today is less secret than ever before. The migration of information to foreign countries about how we do our business is a problem of growing importance that needs to be examined in the context of denial and deception.

Foreign nations—especially our priority intelligence targets—are acquiring more and more U.S. classified information. They obtain this information from several sources, including espionage conducted against the United States. In addition to the Aldrich Ames case, there are several dozen other spies in prison, as well as dozens of others who are not for various reasons but who probably ought to be. Spy cases are not only of counterintelligence interest. Many such cases supply large amounts of important information that is, in effect, enabling countries that successfully spy on us also to degrade the effectiveness of U.S. intelligence. They reduce the unique value-added of imagery, SIGINT, HUMINT, or MASINT collection, and some of these spy cases are extremely costly.

Another very important concern for us is unauthorized disclosures of U.S. classified information containing information about U.S. sources and methods. A recent book, ironically entitled *Betrayal,*[3] has been mentioned. The book's appendix publishes specific classified U.S. intelligence documents. This puts high-cost and high-value sources and methods at risk that may expose sensitive collection. I believe that legal and constitutional hurdles greatly impair the ability of the U.S. government to deter, prevent, and prosecute this kind of publication. The same is true of holding the author or publisher—and, perhaps most importantly, their government sources that do have authorized access to this classified information—accountable for their actions. Leaks and leakers are a legal issue. They facilitate the open compromise of sources and methods, which might land the compromiser in prison under other circumstances, such as providing exactly the same information to a foreign government. That is espionage.

This situation places us in a serious dilemma. What we used to be able to do in full secrecy, clandestine collection, is increasingly jeopardized by unauthorized publicity. The journalist whose book I have cited is also the subject of high praise by admirers, precisely for his well-known practice of exposing U.S. intelligence materials to serve some political ends, in the course of which sensitive collection is often put at risk. According to one observer, he "...has written more stories based on classified government documents than you can shake a stick at, infuriating Clinton Administration officials and making a mockery of official classification policy."[4]

There are now popular Internet websites that also serve as repositories for the exposure of this type of classified information. We often hear of efforts to prevent the posting of pornographic materials on the Internet, or to prevent their downloading. Why don't we expend some effort to do the same for classified information that tends to reveal sources and methods? A good amount of information that we used to think of as sensitive and classified—and it still is—is increasingly available through unauthorized disclosures in open sources. Regrettably for U.S. intelligence and its policymaking customers, the publication of much leaked classified information exposes otherwise protected sources and methods of intelligence collection, and often along with some analytical techniques that exploit what we collect. The result is providing information of significant and practical value to foreign countries that would deny or deceive the United States. Unauthorized disclosures of sensitive sources and methods of U.S. intelligence collection help them, and that is the core of the issue.

I agree with the observation that in documents published in the appendix to *Betrayal*, some collection sources and methods are dealt with in sufficient detail that it is safe to assume countermeasures will be taken against U.S. collection programs that rely on that kind of classified collection.

However, this behavior is not without cost to U.S. taxpayers and citizens. At the peak of the M-11 missile controversy in the mid-1990s, a reading of the Washington press would have revealed a story like this: The State Department asked U.S. intelligence, "Are there Chinese M-11 missiles in Pakistan?" U.S. intelligence replied, "Yes, the missiles are there." And the State Department, which clearly understood how such intelligence could have serious diplomatic and political ramifications if acted upon, then asked how we knew that. In detail that cannot be elaborated here, it was explained that the information had been provided by reliably collected intelligence. For this key intelligence customer, the issue was straightforward: "Is this intelligence convincing, or not?" Based on numerous leaks, articles in both the *Washington Times* and *Washington Post* said that the intelligence was not convincing because the "spy satellites" were unable to "confirm" the presence of such missiles. This indicated that the standards of evidence being imposed on intelligence by customers such as the Department of State are so high that the U.S. intelligence community cannot meet them. The message, as played out in the Washington press was that because the standard is so high, any nation such as Pakistan, and other signatories to the Missile Technology Control Regime who may wish to circumvent its terms, could keep U.S. intelligence from meeting that standard by simply keeping their missiles appropriately shielded from satellite observation.

These articles provided feedback to the intelligence targets that their denial measures were apparently succeeding. They also specified what measures these targets could take to prevent intelligence from meeting needed evidential standards. The newspaper articles referred to are only two of dozens on this subject that appeared during this period when the issue was of extraordinarily high interest to the U.S. policy community because of possible U.S. sanctions. What is going on more generally is a significant effort by some journalists. They traffic in classified information that exposes sources and methods of secret collection. The net effect of all this is to place increasingly serious impediments on our ability to conduct business.

Are these unauthorized disclosures, as we call them, illegal? There is, indeed, legislation that provides some constraints on the publication of classified information and thus a basis to prevent or prosecute these disclosures. But lawyers argue over how effective, or how enforceable, such legislation is. There is only one case that resulted in prosecution. In 1984, Samuel Loring Morison, who was a government employee, not a journalist, deliberately disclosed, without authorization, classified information. He provided a satellite photograph for the cover of *Jane's Defense Weekly*. He was convicted under the espionage statutes and sent to prison. To my knowledge, there has not been a single case since where the U.S. Government has attempted to prosecute an unauthorized disclosure case, despite the fact that there have been literally thousands of instances.

One might ask, why not? Why haven't there been any other prosecutions of unauthorized disclosures? To date, the U.S. Government has not made it a sufficiently important priority to say, "This must stop." Moreover, there is very little pressure from other parts of U.S. society for the government to do so. As a society, we have not taken a stand that unauthorized disclosure of classified information is wrong. However, this practice is jeopardizing and even losing some U.S. intelligence collection capabilities, and that will continue as long as these leaks do.

The final point I want to make about the D&D threats to intelligence concerns the growth of openness. Anyone who has an interest in denial and deception, or in other key issues of intelligence policy, should view the Moynihan Commission Report[5] as required reading. Then-Senator Daniel Patrick Moynihan, who chaired the Commission, makes the central point that we have too much secrecy in government. There is simply excessive secrecy, Moynihan argues, and we need much less than we now have. The argument is a very good one. It is basically that secrecy confounds accountability in government. Genuine accountability, the Commission report argues, means having fewer secrets. I think that's true, in principle.

However, we have to learn how to make a better distinction between secrecy that prevails in intelligence, and secrecy in other parts of the government. That is a key issue for us. There is a fundamental dilemma here—let us call it *the democratic dilemma*—which characterizes the relationship between secrecy and democracy. Unquestionably, democracies do require openness to establish and sustain accountability. Those seriously interested in government accountability must understand the risks inherent in secrecy. Yet, the greater openness required to support U.S. democracy also serves its foreign adversaries. This is a difficult issue, namely, the extent to which any nation feels obliged to supply its citizens with sensitive information that may also empower its adversaries to apply that information to subvert its own national security objectives.

The new twist is not simply the migration of U.S. classified information about intelligence to foreign countries at a growing rate; it is the use that foreign countries are making of this information, particularly the development of countermeasures to U.S. collection. To a large degree, this linkage has not been made systematically. An exception is the convincing case made by David Kay in his work on Iraqi avoidance of U.N. inspections.[6] Informed observers agree that the Iraqis could not have succeeded in evading an elaborate, multilateral inspection regime without having a fundamental understanding of how U.S. intelligence works and knowing the steps they could take to defeat it. That is the bottom line.

What correctives are possible? Let me illustrate. During testimony at a closed hearing in Congress, a Member asked a simple question: "I get the impression," he said, "that we risk losing effectiveness in some of our expensive collection capabilities." He was discussing the relationship between the growth of foreign knowledge of U.S. intelligence and expanding D&D practices in key countries abroad. "How much money does the U.S. taxpayer have to spend to reconstitute the capabilities that we are giving away?" That is a tough but rhetorical question, and one not easily answered. But, also rhetorically, my reply would be, "Mr. Congressman, there is no amount of money the taxpayer can spend to reconstitute the loss of these capabilities." The reason for my fiscal pessimism is that some of our collection capabilities are fragile, and some of these are perishable. Regrettably for the policymaker and for the taxpayer, once lost these sources are lost forever. This is a fundamental dilemma confronting U.S. Intelligence.

We are now faced with the possible loss of some specific capabilities against some specific targets that we may not be able to reconstitute easily or cheaply. Fortunately, in some cases we are protected by what I would term collection resiliency. Occasionally, a technical source can be lost but then possibly a similar collection approach against that target can be reconstituted, although it is rarely as good as the one lost. In most cases that is not possible, and this is a growing problem for us. Once a collection source and method is put at risk it may be compromised through foreign espionage, through press leaks based on unauthorized disclosure of classified information, through intelligence shared with a liaison service of a friendly, cooperative, or even hostile nation, through sensitive intelligence provided in support of a demarche; or through routine declassification processes. The more likely scenario is that a collection source and method might be compromised through the cumulative impact of some or all of these. When that happens, we are likely to experience a diminished collection capability against the same priority targets that are the subject of the compromises.

How can we develop promising correctives for this situation? First, there are internal correctives for the U.S. intelligence community, which is a separate discussion. What I want to focus on here is a second category of things that all of us ought to be alert to. For intelligence effectiveness, we need to deal with the D&D issue head on and recognize that we need to go back to basics. The "basics," the essentials of intelligence, have to do with clandestinity. Clandestine collection (and parts of analysis as well), and the customary secrecy that accompanies the intelligence production process, are fundamental to the business of effective intelligence. Foreign D&D thrives on the exploitation of weaknesses in our ability to maintain secrecy in the conduct of intelligence. So, I have three recommendations for correctives:

First, accept the challenge of the Moynihan Commission to re-conceptualize secrecy in a way that satisfies requirements of openness and also protects essential secrets. This vital job is not for the U.S. intelligence community alone. Society and government must share in this endeavor. If this is not done in the next few years, we will not be able to recover from the threats to secret intelligence that face us now. We cannot escape the openness debate and its consequences for intelligence effectiveness. In short, the current secrecy regime is failing us, and our ability to protect vital information seems increasingly in doubt. Discussions on openness must also address new strategies for secrecy, and new approaches for protecting vital information about how we conduct intelligence against foreign targets.

Second, the enormous value of effective intelligence as a public good must be underlined. Thus, we need to provide a more explicit focus on establishing a causal relationship between unauthorized disclosures and the loss of collection and analytical capabilities. Unhappily, because continuing source protection remains an issue in nearly all D&D cases, little of this work can be carried on in the open press. The most convincing and often the most sensitive cases cannot be made at all in an unclassified setting. We definitely need a more effective two-track approach to address this issue. This must include exerting more effort to convince government officials both inside and outside the intelligence community, as well as the public—principally journalists, media, and publishing companies—of the importance of the linkage between press leaks and jeopardizing fragile collection capabilities that our policymakers require for better informed policy. We should re-visit the long-standing restraint against making this argument more publicly than it has been made in the past.

Third, it is very important to take a stand. We have to say—more articulately and publicly than we have before—that the open publication of information about U.S. sources and methods is wrong. By assisting the countermeasures foreign countries use in their D&D programs, it ultimately deprives our customers of better intelligence, thereby adding unfair burdens on the U.S. taxpayer. If we say and do nothing about this, then nothing will be done. If we continue to accept this situation with complacency, indifference, or hand wringing, continued erosion of sensitive U.S. collection can almost be guaranteed. We must act to stop the leaks and leakers of sources and methods, and hold those responsible accountable for their actions.

Curtailing leaks about U.S. intelligence sources and methods ought to be a top priority of the U.S. government. We probably need new legislation to do this. However, it is a complex legal and constitutional issue with implications for civil liberties as well as for intelligence support to policymakers. But if we continue our present course of near-inaction to what almost amounts to a hemorrhage of U.S. classified information in the open sources, it is unrealistic for us to believe that problem is tractable.

One existing legal remedy could prove very useful. After the publication of Philip Agee's[7] book that disclosed the identities of many CIA case officers and their agents, U.S. collection activities were undeniably hurt. Then add *Counterspy,*[8] a journal created to serve the mission of exposing the identities of CIA agents and case officers. Many believed that the sanctity of First Amendment freedoms, and the inability to pass laws seen to curtail them meant no legislative remedy could be found to prevent such disclosures. Finally, however, Congress passed the Agent Identities Protection Act in 1982. It is true that nobody has ever been prosecuted under that law, but it has apparently served an extraordinary deterrent value. What we need now is companion legislation, a "Technical Sources Protection Act" that would provide the same kind of legal protection for our costly technical sources such as satellite collection, that is now provided to human sources.

Foreign denial of U.S. intelligence is increasingly recognized by outside observers as a problem of growing seriousness. The 1998 *Rumsfeld Commission Report,*[9] occasioned by the controversial 1995 National Intelligence Estimate on the Foreign Missile Threat to the United States, deals with the issue of denial and deception in a very fundamental way. The Commission explicitly addresses "gaps in intelligence," and their corrosive effects on analysis by examining key questions: what are the effects of missing information on analysis? When missing information is the result of successful denial, and much of it is, the next question is: what are the effects of denial on intelligence analysis? We need a much better understanding of those effects. The Rumsfeld Commission was the first serious attempt to address the issue, even suggesting an alternative analytical model as a first step.

We are at an important crossroads, and the old bromides won't work. We will not find solutions to modern intelligence problems by relying on old ways. The dilemma facing U.S. intelligence today is that the decisions we make now and in the next several years will have more impact on our future effectiveness for the next fifteen or twenty years than at any time in modern U.S. intelligence history. We have reached this crossroads not only because of the demise of the Soviet Union and the end of the Cold War, or the budgetary constraints that face us. Rather, it is because we are at a decision point where a generation of complex collection systems is nearing its twilight, and where many of the things that we do now in the short term will have a long-term and indelible impact on the future effectiveness of U.S. intelligence. Dealing with this problem of foreign denial and deception is the single most important way that we can begin to make smart decisions to ensure that effectiveness.

Gary Larsen, the *Far Side* cartoonist, writes implicitly about D&D in many humorous ways. One classic shows a convention of dinosaurs where a Stegosaurus is at the lectern in a large auditorium addressing his Jurassic colleagues: "Gentlemen," he says, "the picture's pretty bleak. The world's climates are changing, the mammals are taking over, and we all have a brain about the size of a walnut." Fast-forwarding to the present, I don't know if we really have a brain that size. But the dinosaurs' Indications and Warning convention is not a wholly inappropriate metaphor for the future of U.S. intelligence. I believe that if we get smart about our future—by which I mean if we integrate countering D&D into the way we conduct intelligence—we won't have to suffer the fate of the Stegosaurus and the others in the auditorium. Otherwise, all bets are off.

Notes

1. This article has been reviewed by the Central Intelligence Agency for classified content only. The views presented here are unofficial and those of the author alone, and do not necessarily represent the views of CIA, the National Intelligence Council, or other U.S. intelligence community or government organizations.

2. HUMINT—Human Intelligence; SIGINT—Signals Intelligence; IMINT—Imagery Intelligence; MASINT—Measurement and Signature Intelligence.

3. Bill Gertz, *Betrayal: How The Clinton Administration Undermined American Security* (Washington, DC: Regnery Publishing, 1999).

4. Steven Aftergood, in *Secrecy in Government Bulletin*, No. 64, January 1997, p. 1. "We believe in stories that make you say 'holy shit' when you read them, said Bill Gertz of the *Washington Times*, in a flattering profile of him that appeared in the *Weekly Standard*."

5. *Report of the Commission on Protecting and Reducing Government Secrecy* (The Moynihan Commission Report), (Washington DC: Government Printing Office,

1997). Comments by the Commission Vice Chairman, Representative Larry Combest are especially insightful.

6.   David Kay, "Denial and Deception Practices of WMD Proliferators: Iraq and Beyond," *Washington Quarterly*, Winter, 1995.

7.   Philip Agee, *Inside the Company: CIA Diary* (New York: Stonehill, 1975).

8.   *Counterspy*, published by the Committee for Action/Research on the intelligence community, 1973; and by the Organizing Committee for a Fifth Estate, 1974-1984. (No issues published in 1977).

9.   The Commission to Assess the Ballistic Missile Threat to the United States (The Rumsfeld Commission) was created by the U.S. Congress in 1997. The Commission delivered its classified report to the House and Senate Intelligence Committees on 15 July 1998. The unclassified 27-page Executive Summary is available on the worldwide web at www.brook.edu/fp/projects/nmd/rumsfeld98.htm

About the Contributors

J. Bowyer Bell specializes in clandestine warfare and terrorism. He has written more than sixteen books, including *Dragonwars, Armed Struggle and the Conventions of Modern War*, and *The IRA, 1968-2000: Analysis of a Secret Army*. He has served as a consultant to the Departments of State, Energy, Justice, Defense, the CIA, and the Nuclear Regulatory Commission.

James B. Bruce is Deputy National Intelligence Officer for Science & Technology at the National Intelligence Council, CIA. He is responsible for work on foreign denial and deception issues in the intelligence community. He was formerly professor of National Security Policy at the National War College, and is currently an adjunct professor in Georgetown University's School of Foreign Service.

Jeffrey W. Busby is a well-known professional magician and owner of Jeffrey Busby Magic, Inc. He has been a consultant on employee training to detect customer cheating for the California and Nevada gaming industries.

M.R.D. Foot is one of the United Kingdom's leading historians on intelligence. He participated in World War II deception operations and later was a professor of history. He is the author of numerous books on intelligence, and has reviewed books for the *Economist* for many years.

Roy Godson is professor of government at Georgetown University. Currently, his focus is on identifying nontraditional security challenges and developing strategies to combat them. His most recent books are *Dirty Tricks or Trump Cards*, and (with John Bailey) *Organized Crime and Democratic Governability: Mexico and the U.S.-Mexican Borderlands*.

Lynn M. Hansen was formerly vice chair of the National Intelligence Council, and currently advises the Arms Control Intelligence Staff and the Intelligence Community's Non-Proliferation Center. Ambassador Hansen has represented the U.S. at several major arms control meetings and is a former assistant director of the U.S. Arms Control and Disarmament Agency.

Richards J. Heuer, Jr. specializes in research to improve analysis and decision making. Currently with the Defense Personnel Security Research Center, he spent his career in the U.S. intelligence community. He is the author of *The Psychology of Analysis,* and *Quantitative Approaches to Political Intelligence: The CIA Experience.*

Walter Jajko, Brig. Gen (USAF Ret.) specializes in special operations and has also written extensively on intelligence matters. He was formerly assistant to the Secretary of Defense for Intelligence Oversight, and director, Special Advisory Staff, Office of the Under Secretary of Defense for Policy.

Ilana Kass is professor of Military Strategy and Operations at the National War College, National Defense University, and director, Studies of Warning, Surprise and Deception. She has also worked for the Joint Chiefs of Staff. Dr. Kass has written extensively about the Middle East.

Robert J. Nieves is former chief of the Drug Enforcement Administration's Office of International Operations and was closely involved in the development and plans for the "Kingpin" strategy that ultimately dismantled the Medellin and Cali drug cartels. He is the author of *Colombian Cocaine Cartels: Lessons from the Front.* He is currently a partner in Berg Associates.

Paul J. Rossa is a manager and analyst in the Directorate of Intelligence, Central Intelligence Agency assessing foreign Denial and Deception challenges. Prior to working in the CIA, he studied political science and international relations at Northwestern University and the University of Pittsburgh.

Abram Shulsky has been director of Arms Control Policy in the Department of Defense and minority staff director of the Senate Select Committee on Intelligence. He has been a consultant to the President's Foreign Intelligence Advisory Board and is now with the Rand Corporation. He is the author of *Silent Warfare: Understanding the World of Intelligence.*

Nina Stewart is former executive director of the President's Foreign Intelligence Advisory Board, and former Deputy Assistant Secretary of Defense for Counterintelligence and Security Countermeasures. Now in private business, she has been appointed to presidential- and cabinet-level advisory boards to review security policies, practices, and procedures.

Bart Whaley has been associated with the Fletcher School of Law and Diplomacy and the Massachusetts Institute of Technology. He is the author of many books, monographs, and articles on deception, including *Codeword BARBAROSSA*, and with J. Bowyer Bell *Cheating.*

James J. Wirtz is professor and chairman of the Department of National Security Affairs, Naval Postgraduate School, Monterey, CA. He is currently exploring the domestic and regional impact of changing the ABM Treaty and U.S. deployment of National Missile Defense. Among other works, he is co-editor with Jeffrey Larsen of *Rockets' Red Glare: Missile Defense and the Future of World Politic.*

Index

CPSIA information can be obtained at www.ICGtesting.com
Printed in the USA
BVOW07s1046241213

339907BV00002B/5/P